W9-ASM-480

Date: 8/5/21

808.1 ROS
Rosenthal, Norman E.,
Poetry RX : how fifty
inspiring poems can heal and

POETRY

Rx

POETRY

Rx

50

HOW FIFTY INSPIRING POEMS CAN HEAL

and BRING JOY TO YOUR LIFE

NORMAN E. ROSENTHAL, M.D.

MEDIA

NOTE: Although the names and identifying details of patients and clients have been changed, the essence of their stories is true.

MEDIA

Published 2021 by Gildan Media LLC
aka G&D Media
www.GandDmedia.com

First Edition: 2021

Front cover design by Tom McKeveny

Interior design by Meghan Day Healey of Story Horse, LLC.

Library of Congress Cataloging-in-Publication Data is available upon request

ISBN: 978-1-7225-0506-6

10   9   8   7   6   5   4   3   2   1

CONTENTS

PART TWO
That Inward Eye

PART THREE
The Human Experience

Chapter Thirty
The Importance of Self-Actualization

On His Blindness *by John Milton*

Chapter Thirty-One
The Power of Faith

Psalm 23 *A Psalm of David*

Chapter Thirty-Two
The Thrill of Discovery

On First Looking into Chapman's Homer *by John Keats*

Chapter Thirty-Three
The Enduring Thrill of the Moment

High Flight *by John Gillespie Magee Jr.*

Chapter Thirty-Four
The Long Reach of Trauma

The Sentence *by Anna Akhmatova* Translated by Judith Hemschemeyer

Chapter Thirty-Five
The Danger of Anger

A Poison Tree *by William Blake*

PART FOUR
A Design for Living and the Search for Meaning

PART FIVE
Into the Night

INTRODUCTION

You may well wonder how I, a psychiatrist with no formal literary credentials, have chosen to write about the power of poetry to heal, inspire, and bring joy to people. It all started with a single phone call that came in late one night.

The caller was my friend David, and I knew immediately by the tone of his voice that something was wrong. He choked up as he told me that he had recently lost someone very dear to him. "How can I go on?" he mused. "How will I manage?"

Clichés and generalities readily come to mind in such situations, but I searched for something specific to say, something that might actually help. Recognizing that David is a person steeped in the arts, I said, "There is an art to losing, and like all art, it can be developed."

He was silent for a while, and when he spoke again, his voice sounded more cheerful, as though he had tapped into some hidden source of hope.

"Do you know the poem 'One Art' by Elizabeth Bishop?" he asked.

I told him no.

"Well, let me read it to you," and he began: "'The art of losing isn't hard to master.'"

As he read on, his voice gathered strength and energy with each stanza. Afterwards his mood was lighter—and strangely, so was mine.

"Can a poem really help a grieving person?" I wondered, "and if so, might other poems also have healing powers?" I marveled also at how David had reached into the depths of his grief and presented me with a gift—a poem that offered me a fresh perspective on how to help someone out of the darkness that can engulf you when you lose someone you love. I shared the poem with patients and friends, many of whom found comfort in its words, and looked for other poems that might have similar effects.

Once I started looking, I found such poems everywhere. One friend, a therapist, had been so moved by a poem about aging by Wendell Berry that she had given copies of it to patients (It's in chapter 46 in this collection). I bolstered my promising findings with Internet reports of comfort and relief in response to particular poems.

The idea of this book is that poetry can not only inspire and delight, but can actually help you feel better, soothe your pain, and heal psychological wounds. In short, as the book's title suggests, poetry can act as a kind of medicine.

Although all literature can console, there is something about great poetry—its rhythms and cadences, its conciseness and brilliance—that has a power and charm all its own. One way in which poetry exerts its effect is that it is easier to remember, recall, and reproduce at will. We can at a moment's notice dip into our memory and conjure up Wordsworth's daffodils or Keats' nightingale.

The Poems

The fifty gemlike poems in this collection have all stood the test of time and appear in published anthologies. They are all relatively short, most fitting on a single page. In their conciseness they deliver their messages in the most efficient, effective, and beautiful way possible.

Friends, patients, and I have all enjoyed and benefited from some or all of these verses. I hope you might find the same healing power and joy from them as we have.

The collection is divided into five sections, each covering an area important for a good and happy life: (1) loving and losing; (2) responses to nature; (3) aspects of the human experience; (4) a design for living and the search for meaning; and (5) the last phase of life.

How to Get the Most out of a Poem

Although reading a poem seems like a very straightforward activity, it can be greatly enriched by a few simple tricks.

Remember to enjoy the poem.

It should be fun, not work!

Actively engage with the poem.

Give it your full attention, and it will reward you.

Read it aloud. That way you can enjoy the music in the words. Also, vocalizing the words involves different sets of nerves and muscles and different parts of the brain compared to reading it silently. Therefore it will create a different experience. But most importantly, reading a poem aloud deepens its therapeutic potential.

Read the poem more than once. One mysterious aspect of a poem is how successive readings reveal new layers of meaning. How strange! After all, the lines are right there on the page. When you read them the first time, they may seem perfectly clear. How, then, can they still yield new insights and rewards when you revisit them? Try it and see for yourself.

Experience the poem with all of your senses. A poem is no more a purely intellectual experience than a song or a painting or a spoonful of ice cream. For an example of a poem that engages all your senses, look at "Sea Fever" (chapter 23).

As the reader, you complete the poem, in the process bringing your past experiences into the collaboration between you and the poet. At the moment of completion, it may feel as if the pieces of a puzzle are falling together. You may delight in the aha! moment as you think, "So that's what the poet meant!" Allow yourself to experience the wonder a poem provides when it opens up new spaces in which your mind can roam.

Listen to others reading the poem. Many of the poems in this collection are read aloud online by talented women and men, and can be found on the Internet. One outstanding example is the sonnet "Pity me not because the light of day" (chapter 3), which is beautifully read by its author, Edna St. Vincent Millay. Neuroscientist Eugen Wassiliwizky and colleagues at the Max Planck Institute in Frankfurt have found that recited poetry can be a powerful stimulus for eliciting peak emotional responses such as chills and goosebumps, by activating the brain's reward circuitry.

Tolerate—and even savor—ambiguity of feeling and thought. Be intrigued by what you don't immediately understand. There is such a thing as creative reading as well as creative writing. Often in poems, circuits are not completed, ideas are left unfinished or equivocal. This is not accidental. The unfinished business may serve as a focus of continued puzzlement, a brain teaser lingering in the mind, begging for a solution. Some experimental data suggest that people remember unfinished or interrupted tasks better than completed ones (the so-called Zeigarnik effect). So it may be that by presenting the reader with unfinished ideas, the poet creates a more memorable and indelible work.

Pay attention to details. Punctuation, the separation of lines, their placement on the page, form, rhythm, and rhyme, as well as the white space that helps give the poem its shape, may all be part of what the poet is trying to communicate.

Remember, when reading a poem, it is *your* interpretation rather than mine or anyone else's that is most important. As Dee Snider from the band Twisted Sister said, "The beauty of literature, poetry, and music is that they leave room for the audience to put its own imagination, experiences, and dreams into the words." So any interpretations I offer are mine alone; I encourage you to differ.

And most of all, have fun engaging with these beautiful and ingenious creations.

PART ONE

Loving and Losing

'Tis better to have loved and lost
than never to have loved at all.

—Alfred Lord Tennyson

Chapter One

IS THERE AN ART TO LOSING?

ONE ART
by Elizabeth Bishop

The art of losing isn't hard to master;
so many things seem filled with the intent
to be lost that their loss is no disaster.

Lose something every day. Accept the fluster
of lost door keys, the hour badly spent.
The art of losing isn't hard to master.

Then practice losing farther, losing faster:
places, and names, and where it was you meant
to travel. None of these will bring disaster.

I lost my mother's watch. And look! my last, or
next-to-last, of three loved houses went.
The art of losing isn't hard to master.

I lost two cities, lovely ones. And, vaster,
some realms I owned, two rivers, a continent.
I miss them, but it wasn't a disaster.

—Even losing you (the joking voice, a gesture
I love) I shan't have lied. It's evident
the art of losing's not too hard to master
though it may look like (*Write* it!) like disaster.

In "One Art," Elizabeth Bishop teaches about loss with examples from her own life. Starting with small everyday losses familiar to all of us, she suggests that loss is a normal part of life. Then she ups the ante as her losses get progressively bigger. Repeatedly she assures us that "the art of losing isn't hard to master." But as her losses mount, we marvel at her stoicism and may even ask whether she is merely putting on a brave face when she writes: "I lost two cities, lovely ones. And, vaster, / some realms I owned, two rivers, a continent."

Add that to "three lost houses," and I can hear someone asking, "Is she for real? That's a lot of stuff to lose! How come it's no disaster?"

At the end of the poem, we find out what she has been holding back through the first five verses. The poem is not only directed to readers, but primarily to a lost loved one, which puts us in the role of an eavesdropper, listening in on an intimate communication to a former lover.

For the first time in the poem, we feel Bishop's pain as she writes, "the joking voice, a gesture I love." When the poet says, "I shan't have lied," she fails to convince, because we realize that although losing may be an art, it can sometimes be a very hard one to master—and it may truly feel like a disaster.

In her grief, Bishop has written a masterpiece that is a gift for anyone seeking solace from the pain of loss. No wonder that it cheered up my friend on that sad day when he called me grief-stricken from the loss of a loved one. And no wonder that the poem has provided comfort to so many people with whom I have shared it.

The Biology of Loss

Bishop's reassurance that we are capable of enduring severe losses is well grounded in the history of our species, which has been biologically programmed to withstand the death of infants, older children, parents, siblings, and friends. As you read through the biographical sketches of the poets in this book, you may be astonished to see how many of them (Bishop included) were orphaned at a young age, lost siblings, or outlived their own children.

Despite our inbuilt survival mechanisms, losses may have serious psychological consequences. Pioneering psychiatrist John Bowlby developed a theory of attachment and loss based on his observations of children in war-torn London in the middle of the last century, particularly those wrenched from parental figures at a young age. Since then, the problems of early loss—notably depression and difficulties with attachment in later life—have been extensively documented and studied.

"One Art" is a type of poem called a villanelle (see sidebar).

The Villanelle

- Nineteen lines.
- Five stanzas of three lines each (tercets), followed by one four-line stanza (quatrain).
- Two key lines that repeat at prescribed intervals.
- An alternating rhyme scheme.
- The meter is typically iambic pentameter: five feet, in which each foot has an unstressed followed by a stressed syllable, as in:

    da-DUM, da-DUM, da-DUM, da-DUM, da-DUM.

This is the most common meter in English poetry, and resembles the sound of the human heartbeat: lub-DUP.

Two other villanelles in this collection are "The Waking" (chapter 39) and "Do Not Go Gentle" (chapter 48).

Takeaways

✘ **There is an art to losing.** Like all skills, the ability to survive loss may improve with experience, a fact that may offer comfort when loss occurs.

✘ **Accept the loss.** Acceptance of suffering is fundamental to dealing with all types of adversity. In general, acceptance of suffering lessens its pain, just as denial of suffering amplifies it. You will see this general principle arise with regard to other poems in this collection, as it does in life. The value of acceptance is perhaps best expressed in the famous Serenity Prayer attributed to theologian Reinhold Niebuhr, which reads in part, "God, give me the grace to accept with serenity the things that cannot be changed."

✘ **Beware of all-or-none thinking.** This type of thinking has been classified as one form of cognitive distortion, which can contribute to depression and other negative mood states. (Confronting and correcting cognitive distortions can help people feel better.) When people engage in all-or-none thinking, they gravitate towards extremes—for example, that something either is or is not a disaster. This may cause emotional problems, such as depression in the former case or denial in the latter. When you encounter adversity, including the loss a loved one, it may be neither a disaster nor easy, but something in between, as the poet finally concludes.

✘ **Write it down.** Bishop's advice to herself to write down her thoughts and feelings is in line with modern science: writing down your deepest thoughts and feelings can be therapeutic and instrumental in recovery from trauma. James Pennebaker, professor of psychology at the University of Texas in Austin, pioneered this line

of work, which has revealed many physical and psychological bene-
fits that can accrue from such writing exercises.

The Poet and the Poem

Elizabeth Bishop (1911–1979) was born in Worcester, Massachusetts,
to Gertrude Bulmer and William Thomas Bishop, owners of the J.W.
Bishop contracting firm. She learned the art of losing early in life.
Her father died when she was only eight months old. Her mother,
who spent the next five years in and out of psychiatric hospitals, was
then permanently committed, and Bishop never saw her again.

After her mother's hospitalization, Bishop was raised at first
by her mother's loving and comforting family in Nova Scotia. Later
she was moved "unconsulted and against my wishes" to stay with
her paternal grandparents. Of her time with them she wrote, "I felt
myself aging, even dying. I was bored and lonely with Grandma, my
silent grandpa, the dinners alone . . . at night I lay blinking my flash-
light off and on, and crying." In 1918 she was rescued by her moth-
er's sister, who lived in a happier home in South Boston. Years later
she confided to her friend and fellow poet Robert Lowell, "When you
write my epitaph, you must say I was the loneliest person who ever
lived."

Bishop was a sickly child, so before age fourteen her education
was limited, but she became an excellent student and was accepted
into Vassar College. She won an important fellowship from the col-
lege and an award from the American Academy of Arts and Letters,
which enabled her to travel to Brazil. There she developed a serious
allergy and, as she recovered, she fell in love with her friend and
nurse Lota de Macedo Soares. She and Lota lived together for fif-
teen years, during which she wrote to Lowell that she was "extremely
happy for the first time in my life." Both women suffered from phys-

ical and psychological distress and were hospitalized in Brazil. On recovery, Bishop left for New York. Soares followed later, but on the day she arrived in New York, she took an overdose of tranquilizers and died.

Bishop returned to the U.S. to teach at Harvard, where she met Alice Methfessel, a much younger woman who was to become a source of strength and love for the rest of her life. "One Art" was addressed to Alice at a time when it seemed that the relationship was over, because Alice was planning to get married. She changed her mind, however, and returned. Bishop suffered from alcoholism, which afflicted her for many years, and drug abuse: she took stimulants during the day and sleeping pills at night, along with Antabuse, a drug used to treat alcoholism, in an attempt to remain sober. Alice stayed with Bishop till the latter's death from a brain aneurysm eighteen months later.

Through all her difficulties, Bishop remained productive. She received multiple honors, including the Pulitzer Prize for Poetry in 1956 and the National Book Award for Poetry in 1970. She is regarded as one of the greatest modern poets. "One Art," which went through seventeen drafts before publication, is her most famous poem.

Chapter Two

CAN LOVE TRANSFORM YOU?

HOW DO I LOVE THEE? LET ME COUNT THE WAYS
by Elizabeth Barrett Browning

How do I love thee? Let me count the ways.
I love thee to the depth and breadth and height
My soul can reach, when feeling out of sight
For the ends of being and ideal grace.
I love thee to the level of every day's
Most quiet need, by sun and candle-light.
I love thee freely, as men strive for right;
I love thee purely, as they turn from praise.
I love thee with the passion put to use
In my old griefs, and with my childhood's faith.
I love thee with a love I seemed to lose
With my lost saints—I love thee with the breath,
Smiles, tears, of all my life!—and, if God choose,
I shall but love thee better after death.

"How do I love thee?" These five small words, clustered together this way, are among the best-known in English literature. The phrase that follows, "Let me count the ways," as famous as the first, has provided titles for songs, books, and TV episodes. What about this poem has led to such immortality, and who was its author?

This poem is a sonnet written in the tradition of the famous fourteenth-century Italian poet Francesco Petrarch. The sonnet form is versatile, used by many poets in this collection.

One of my patients, Rusty, a computer engineer in his mid-forties, reported that his wife complained that he was not expressive enough in telling her he loved her. "I do tell her I love her," he protested. "What else does she expect me to say?"

I referred him to Browning's famous sonnet for inspiration.

In asking, "How do I love thee?" Elizabeth Barrett Browning frames the subject of her love in a novel way. She examines and expresses her *own* feelings towards her beloved. This is an inversion of a common preoccupation of people in love: "Do they love me or not, and if so, how much?" These questions reflect the insecurity and romantic uncertainty of the questioner. In contrast, Barrett Browning examines her own feelings, and in so doing provides a beautiful description of profound love.

The Petrarchan Sonnet

- Named for the great Italian poet Petrarch.
- Fourteen lines (a property shared by all sonnets).
- A miniature story, with a beginning, a middle, and an end.
- Divided into an octet (eight lines) and a sestet (six lines).
- The octet (the beginning) raises a question or problem.
- Then comes the volta (the middle), a shift in topic.
- Finally, the sestet (the end) provides a resolution.
- The meter is typically iambic pentameter.
- Rhyme scheme: octet: ABBACDDC; sestet: EFEFEF (with some variability).

In the first eight lines (octet) of the sonnet, the poet is anchored in the present. She starts her inventory as one might measure some concrete object (its depth, breadth, and height) but soon realizes that her love is so vast as to be out of sight and immeasurable. She then shifts her frame of reference and compares her love to "every day's / Most quiet need, by sun and candle-light."

Her love is not just an entertainment or embellishment to her life. Rather, it is a fundamental need, like other needs that, though crucial, can easily be overlooked because they are "most quiet," such as air, water, and the internal space necessary for contemplation.

In the last two lines of the octet, the poet expresses two qualities she has observed in men she admires: They "strive for right" and "turn from praise." It is with the same free and pure spirit that the poet embraces her love.

To the modern reader, these qualities may seem quaint or out-of-date. I recently asked a graduate student what she was looking for in a partner. She responded with a smile, "Everything, just like everybody else. I want someone who is attractive, fun, adventurous, and sociable. Someone who wants to travel and is good in bed." There was no mention of striving for right or turning from praise. Elements of character were not on the menu. There is much that the modern woman or man can learn from this famous poem.

At the twist (volta), the poet shifts from the present to her less happy past. She refers to "my old griefs," and writes: "I love thee with a love I seemed to lose / With my lost saints." Her relationship has helped her reconnect with those early wellsprings of love, allowing her to experience love with the "breath, smiles, tears, of all my life."

In her final line, the poet may be suggesting that she will continue to love him in the afterlife or that if her husband (the poet Robert Browning, to whom the poem is addressed) dies before she does, her love will continue after he passes away. We will return to this theme of continuing to love people even after they die in "Remember" (chapter 14) and "Do Not Stand at My Grave and Weep" (chapter 50).

Takeaways

✘ Consider words as a "love language." In his book *The Five Love Languages*, author Gary Chapman suggests five different ways in which love can be expressed: (1) quality time; (2) gifts; (3) acts of service; (4) physical touch; and (5) expressions of love. He points out that different people appreciate these forms to different degrees, which is useful for couples to remember if they are to enjoy a loving relationship. For those relationships where words of love are appreciated by one or both parties, Barrett Browning's famous sonnet may offer some helpful insights.

People in relationships often assume that their partners know how they are feeling, or, more commonly, they don't give the matter enough thought. As a result, the other person can feel misunderstood, neglected, or taken for granted.

In my work with couples, as misunderstandings are clarified, I often hear, "Why didn't you tell me? I'm not a mind reader." With the help of therapy or experience, it is possible to move this question into the present tense, as in, "Please tell me what's on your mind, and skip the "mind reader" part, which contains an element of sarcasm.

✘ Put feelings into words. For Rusty, the computer engineer at the start of the chapter, his difficulty in expressing love was just part of his difficulty in understanding his feelings in general and putting them into words—a problem called *alexithymia*.

Often bodily sensations can provide useful clues to emotions. Pioneering psychologist William James brought this idea to general attention in a famous essay entitled "What Is an Emotion?" If you see a bear in the woods, James suggested, you run first, then feel afraid. Your body leads your emotions. Likewise, if you see an attractive person, your heart may flutter before you can find words to express your attraction. Putting emotions into words can advance a relationship. For anybody who has difficulty verbalizing feelings, "How do I love thee?" may be a resource.

With some help, Rusty has now found new ways to let his wife know how he loves her, and the couple is thriving. Even those of us without alexithymia may be able to do better at recognizing and communicating our love and appreciation to those who are important to us. It is so simple to offer words of kindness and appreciation, yet so easy to forget in our busy lives.

✘ **Feel and express gratitude.** Another way to take inspiration from this poem is to regard it as a gratitude checklist. There has been a growing awareness that gratitude is a healthy and enlivening emotion, conducive to happiness. Gratitude is also an antidote to one of the most prevalent maladies of our time—a sense of entitlement. Writing a gratitude checklist regularly can increase your awareness of the good things you have, thereby improving your sense of well-being.

The Poet and the Poem

Elizabeth Barrett, the eldest of twelve children, was born to an affluent English family in 1806. Her life was marked by a curious mixture of suffering, joy, and enormous success.

Barrett was a child prodigy, who read classics such as the works of Shakespeare before her teens and wrote her first book of poetry by age twelve. Despite physical and personal setbacks, she continued to write essays and poems and translated Aeschylus's *Prometheus Unbound*. As a child, she was deeply religious.

Then a series of tragedies occurred. At age fourteen she developed a lung illness, which required morphine for the rest of her life. The following year she sustained a significant back injury. Her mother died in 1828, and financial difficulties required the family to sell their estate and relocate to London. Because of her ill health, she later moved to the seaside to be with her brother. Tragically, he drowned, and Barrett returned to the family home in London. Her father was devoted but notoriously overcontrolling; their relationship became the subject of a play and later a movie called *The Barretts of Wimpole Street*.

Barrett continued to write and gained the attention of the public. Fellow poet Robert Browning wrote to her expressing his admiration for her and her work. Over the next two years, they exchanged hundreds of letters, fell in love, and, because her father disapproved of the relationship, decided to elope. Her father disinherited her and never spoke to her again.

The married couple moved to Italy, where their son was born. Shortly after arriving there, Barrett Browning published *Sonnets from the Portuguese*, a collection of forty-four famous love sonnets. (The title's reference to the Portuguese was deliberately misleading in order to conceal the fact that they had been written to Robert Browning.) Number forty-three, "How do I love thee?", has become her most famous work.

In light of Barrett Browning's history, it is understandable how her relationship with Robert Browning freed her from a background of tragedy and dependency and offered her love, support, a new home in a new country, intellectual passion, and a son. As we read the sonnet, we can feel the all-encompassing nature of her love for her husband. The history of their relationship deepens our understanding of the transformative power of her love.

For reasons that are unclear, Barrett Browning became ill in her midfifties and died peacefully in her husband's arms. According to him, the last word she uttered was, "Beautiful."

Chapter Three

THE HEART VERSUS THE MIND

PITY ME NOT BECAUSE THE LIGHT OF DAY
by Edna St. Vincent Millay

Pity me not because the light of day
At close of day no longer walks the sky;
Pity me not for beauties passed away
From field and thicket as the year goes by;
Pity me not the waning of the moon,
Nor that the ebbing tide goes out to sea,
Nor that a man's desire is hushed so soon,
And you no longer look with love on me.
This have I known always: Love is no more
Than the wide blossom which the wind assails,
Than the great tide that treads the shifting shore,
Strewing fresh wreckage gathered in the gales:
Pity me that the heart is slow to learn
What the swift mind beholds at every turn.

This sonnet came to my attention when a patient of mine, Beth, mentioned that she had found it particularly helpful. A physiotherapist in her mid-thirties, Beth sought treatment for problems with mood swings and romantic relationships, which felt wonderful at first but invariably deteriorated.

Beth found that this sonnet spoke to her. In it, the poet acknowledges that all things pass: the light of day, the beauty of summer, the full moon, and the ebbing tide. Because everyone experiences such losses, she asks for no special pity from the reader, not even when the man she is seeing no longer desires her. She has known these things always and understands that life and love involve risk, like venturing out into a storm.

The key to the poem comes from its last two lines, which Beth found so valuable:

Pity me that the heart is slow to learn
What the swift mind beholds at every turn.

Here the poet is saying that she asks for pity only for a particular problem to which she is specifically vulnerable, not for those issues to which all people are susceptible. For Beth, those two lines illuminated what she needed from therapy. Her mind was swift and recognized the poor choices she tended to make in romantic relationships. Now she needed to bring her heart and mind in line with each other. By viewing her problem as entirely outside her own control, Beth had allowed herself no agency in escaping from the predicament of repeated unhappy relationships. If she could figure out a way to find a sense of agency in her romantic life, Beth realized, perhaps she could turn things around.

In therapy, Beth realized that she had come by her problems honestly. Her mother had often been depressed and unavailable. Her father had been erratic, by turns seductive and rejecting. The times when he had paid her attention stood out as highlights of her childhood but always left her feeling disappointed when he withdrew his interest.

At that point, Beth confessed to me a second set of problems. To comfort herself between romantic relationships, she would go to bars, meet men, and after a few drinks (or maybe more) often ended up in bed with a stranger. She felt ashamed of this pattern, which had taken both an emotional and a physical toll on her. She brought to my attention yet another sonnet by Millay, which once again spoke viscerally to her:

> What lips my lips have kissed, and where, and why,
> I have forgotten, and what arms have lain
> Under my head till morning; but the rain
> Is full of ghosts tonight, that tap and sigh
> Upon the glass and listen for reply,
> And in my heart there stirs a quiet pain
> For unremembered lads that not again
> Will turn to me at midnight with a cry.
> Thus in the winter stands the lonely tree,
> Nor knows what birds have vanished one by one,
> Yet knows its boughs more silent than before:
> I cannot say what loves have come and gone,
> I only know that summer sang in me
> A little while, that in me sings no more.

Beth was determined not to end up like a lonely tree, and I was determined to help in any way I could. Her treatment required more than therapy. She needed medications to stabilize her mood swings and Twelve Step programs to help bring her addiction to alcohol and sex under control. Beth became better at spotting potential problems early on and avoiding them. For example, she became expert at detecting inconsistent men and started to find dependability more appealing.

Beth met a man who treated her kindly, fell in love in a way that felt stable and fulfilling, and married him. The last time I heard from her was in a note announcing the birth of her daughter.

Takeaways

✘ **Recognize and learn to avoid repetitive behaviors.** Many of our problems display repetitive patterns, which is a clue to resolving them. A simple analogy, which I have found surprisingly helpful in my therapy, is that of someone walking along a sidewalk with a hole in it. At first the person doesn't see the hole and falls into it. The next time, the person sees the hole but once again falls into it. The third time, the person sees the hole and steps over it. This analogy reminds us that: (1) it is important not only to recognize a problem, but also your role in it; (2) if a problem recurs, ask yourself whether you may have a role in perpetuating it; (3) it may take several tries before you can correct your error, even after you know what it is; and (4) with recognition of the pattern, a willingness to change your own behavior, and practice, it is often possible to break a cycle of repetition and avoid further injury.

✘ **Use your "wise mind."** The concept of the "wise mind" comes from dialectic behavior therapy (DBT), developed by psychologist Marsha Linehan. The term "dialectic" refers to the juxtaposition of different ways of seeing something. Thus the person entering DBT is taught to recognize the "reasonable mind" and the "emotional mind" and engage them in a debate that produces a synthesis—the "wise mind," which helps the person make a better decision.

✘ **Consider how early experiences may lead even an intelligent person to keep making the same mistake.** This insight-oriented approach may be less directly helpful in curtailing such behaviors than the behavioral approach, but it may provide understanding and a reassuring sense of coherence between your past and your present.

✘ Consider that certain behaviors may be addictive like drugs and alcohol. For this reason, recovery groups patterned after Alcoholics Anonymous (AA) have been established for people with addictive patterns of gambling, spending, eating, sex, and love. As in Beth's case, different addictions may coexist. For those who don't like the Twelve Step model of AA and similar programs, SMART (Self-Management and Recovery Training) recovery is an alternative resource.

Beth realized that seductive men made her feel wonderful (high, in the terminology of addiction). Later, when they put her down or rejected her, she felt as though a drug had been withdrawn, and she would often work hard to recapture their interest or try to find comfort in the company of strangers. For Beth, recovery from this hurtful cycle involved recognizing the pattern and owning her part in it, then finding others who could empathize and support her recovery.

Millay's mastery of the sonnet can be seen in the two sonnets featured here. The former, "Pity me not," is a Shakespearean sonnet (see page 59), and the latter, "What lips my lips have kissed," is a Petrarchan sonnet (see page 16).

In "Pity me not," the revelation that the poem is addressed to a man who has lost interest in the poet (line 8), not just to the reader, resembles the device used by Bishop in "One Art." The final couplet, which so influenced Beth, packs a punch worthy of Shakespeare.

In "What lips my lips have kissed," the volta at the end of the octet marks the shift from the poet's past life of intense sexuality with many partners to her present state of depleted loneliness—like a birdless tree in the winter.

The Poet and the Poem

Edna St. Vincent Millay (1892–1950) was for much of her career one of the most successful and respected poets in the United States, particularly famous for her sonnets. She won the Pulitzer Prize for Poetry for *The Ballad of the Harp Weaver* in 1923. Aside from her professional success (she also wrote plays and a libretto for an opera), she was a famous and popular cultural figure of the Roaring Twenties, embodying the new sexually liberated woman of the period.

Millay was born in Rockland, Maine, to Cora Buzzell Millay and Henry Tollman Millay. Along with her two sisters, Millay was raised by her mother, who divorced her husband for irresponsibility and lack of support. Although the family was poor and moved around frequently, Cora always took along books by great writers. She recognized, nurtured, and unstintingly encouraged Edna's literary talent. Millay (who liked to be called "Vincent") was first recognized for her poem "Renascence," published in 1912. She attracted a benefactor, who enabled her to attend Vassar College, from which she graduated in 1917.

Millay moved to Greenwich Village, where she supported herself by writing poetry and short stories for magazines under the pseudonym Nancy Boyd, while continuing to write serious poetry under her own name.

A woman of intense sexuality, Millay was catnip to both women and men. In a book about her love life, appropriately titled *What Lips My Lips Have Kissed*, Daniel Mark Epstein writes of her serial and simultaneous sexual relationships with women at Vassar. After graduating, she met two prominent men in the literary world: Edmund Wilson and John Bishop. Wilson wrote, "The more we saw of her poetry the more our admiration grew, and we both, before very long, had fallen irretrievably in love with her. . . . One cannot really write about Edna Millay without bringing into the foreground of the picture her intoxicating effect on people, because this so much created the atmosphere in which she lived and composed." Towards the end of his life, with more than thirty years of perspective, Wilson wrote, "Edna ignited for me both my intellectual passion and my unsatisfied desire, which went up together in a blaze of ecstasy that remains for me one of the high points in my life. I do not believe that such experiences can be common for such women are not common."

In 1923 Millay married businessman Eugen Jan Boissevain, having turned down proposals from other suitors. As Edmund Wilson wrote, "She was tired of breaking hearts and spreading havoc." Boissevain supported Millay's career and took care of the logistics of their lives, freeing her up to continue her creative pursuits. They had an open marriage until Boissevain died in 1949. Millay lived alone for the last year of her life at Steepletop, their estate in Austerlitz, New York.

In the last decade of her life, Millay's long-standing addiction to morphine, alcohol, uppers, and downers spiraled out of control. Her husband supported her and took her to rehabilitation centers, to little avail. After his death, her addictions escalated. On the last night of her life, alone at Steepletop, she fell down the stairs to her death. The doctor diagnosed a heart attack as the cause.

Her famous poem "First Fig" may serve as a fitting epitaph:

> My candle burns at both ends;
>   It will not last the night;
> But ah, my foes, and oh, my friends—
>   It gives a lovely light!

🌿 LULLABY
by W. H. Auden

Lay your sleeping head, my love,
Human on my faithless arm;
Time and fevers burn away
Individual beauty from
Thoughtful children, and the grave
Proves the child ephemeral:
But in my arms till break of day
Let the living creature lie,
Mortal, guilty, but to me
The entirely beautiful.

Soul and body have no bounds:
To lovers as they lie upon
Her tolerant enchanted slope
In their ordinary swoon,
Grave the vision Venus sends
Of supernatural sympathy,
Universal love and hope;
While an abstract insight wakes
Among the glaciers and the rocks
The hermit's carnal ecstasy.

(continued)

Certainty, fidelity
On the stroke of midnight pass
Like vibrations of a bell,
And fashionable madmen raise
Their pedantic boring cry:
Every farthing of the cost,
All the dreaded cards foretell,
Shall be paid, but from this night
Not a whisper, not a thought,
Not a kiss nor look be lost.

Beauty, midnight, vision dies;
Let the winds of dawn that blow
Softly round your dreaming head
Such a day of welcome show
Eye and knocking heart may bless,
Find the mortal world enough;
Noons of dryness find you fed
By the involuntary powers,
Nights of insult let you pass
Watched by every human love.

In some ways, "Lullaby" is a curious title for Auden's poem, since a lullaby generally refers to a song sung to children to help them go to sleep. Here, however, the poet addresses an adult lover who is already asleep, his head cradled in the poet's arm. The poem begins with the gentle line, "Lay your sleeping head, my love," which may recall the snug and secure feelings of a child being sung to sleep by a protective adult. In this context, the second line may come as a shock: "Human on my faithless arm."

Right up front we see an extraordinary paradox. How can the poet caress and sing a lullaby to his sleeping lover while acknowledging that he is faithless? Does he mean unfaithful? It seems likely, given what follows. In the same line, the poet recognizes that his lover is human and goes on to speak of the transient nature of beauty, youth, and life itself. He acknowledges a sad truth about life: being human is being mortal. Life is finite. The poet also refers to his lover as guilty. Of what, we are never told. Nevertheless, whatever the nature of the guilt, in that moment of togetherness, his beloved is "entirely beautiful."

In the second stanza, Auden describes aspects of physical love in terms that are at the same time familiar and original. As lovers swoon together on their "tolerant enchanted slope," the boundaries between them disappear. But even in the midst of these idealized feelings of fused identities ("supernatural sympathy"), the poet sounds a cautionary note. Although the vision offered by Venus, the goddess of love, is intoxicating, it would be well for lovers to recognize that her message should also be taken seriously. Just as a hermit living among the glaciers and rocks may feel the thrill of sexual desire and release ("carnal ecstasy"), at the same time he becomes aware that there are vague implications to this experience (perhaps a warning) that require attention.

The theme of warning is sustained in the third stanza, where the poet acknowledges that "Certainty, fidelity / On the stroke of midnight pass."

The poet is pointing out here that there are hazards in the passionate connection between lovers where there is no contract of fidelity nor any certainty about where the relationship is going. That is a common dynamic for people in open or polyamorous relation-ships, where lovers often try to set limits around what is and is not permissible. Yet such passionate connections may be risky and dis-ruptive. As the poet points out, certainty can become as transient as the vibrations of a bell.

The poet goes on to put the harshest warnings in the mouths of "fashionable madmen," who offer "their pedantic boring cry" that it is in the cards that the lovers will have to pay "every farthing of the cost." (A farthing, by the way, was a quarter of a penny, a tiny brass coin whose value was too small for it to survive into our modern inflationary times.) Despite these warnings (which the poet implies may actually be correct), he clearly views his night of loving as worth the price. This speaks to an important theme in poetry, literature, and life. *Carpe diem*. Seize the moment. The power of now. The past is irretrievably gone. The future is uncertain. The present is the only time over which we have dominion. So, the poet says to his sleeping lover (and perhaps himself), set aside the warnings of these fash-ionable madmen, and do not allow a whisper, a thought, or a kiss to be lost from this present moment.

In the first three stanzas the poet has prepared his lover for the last one. He has warned his lover from the very beginning that he cannot promise fidelity and has acknowledged his lover's own frail humanity. Although he has attributed some of the warnings to others—such as the goddess Venus and "fashionable madmen"—the alarm bell has been rung, and the vibrations can be heard loud and clear.

Let us remember that a lullaby is meant to soothe and to induce feelings of protection. In a relationship, part of protecting your partner is to be honest so as to forestall nasty surprises. The poet has fulfilled his deal in the first three stanzas (assuming his lover knows about his infidelity when awake). Now the poet can feel free to pour out his love unqualified by any warnings. And he does that in what is surely one of the most moving and beautiful blessings in literature.

Takeaways

✘ **Romantic love comes in many different forms.** In Barrett Browning's "How do I love thee," we see love that is all-embracing, exclusive, and transformational. It is the kind of love that is held up as an ideal—one in which two people live happily ever after. While such love is undoubtedly a wonderful thing, it is not available to, or desired by, everyone. Nor is it the only valid kind of love. "Lullaby" invites the reader not to judge but to enter into the experience of another person and understand the value of love, even if it is transient and in the context of a complex life.

✘ **There can be a value to peak experiences, though they may come with risks.** In "Lullaby" Auden describes what psychologist Abraham Maslow called a *peak experience*, which he defined as "rare, exciting, oceanic, deeply moving and exhilarating" and may "generate an advanced form of perceiving reality."

A few other poems in this collection also describe and extol such experiences, notably "High Flight" (chapter 33) and "An Irish Airman Foresees His Death" (chapter 43). Some people, when asked what experiences in their lives were most meaningful, will cite such peak experiences, even many years after they have occurred. As Maslow observes, a peak experience is precious in its own right.

In "Lullaby" we encounter a transcendent feeling of love. The experience might have been short-lived, but it appears to have had long-lasting effects for the waking lover, who transformed it into a masterwork, which will endure and continue to give pleasure to readers for years to come.

✘ **Open or polyamorous relationships sometimes work.** I have seen examples where couples live in relationships for years, apparently happily, and remain strongly bonded with each other despite an agreement between the two individuals to permit sexual activity outside the relationship. In such instances, honesty appears to be a prerequisite, and certain rules are generally agreed upon. As you might imagine, issues in polyamorous relationships include jealousy and insecurity. I have also seen examples of people who have experimented with polyamorous relationships for a while but have later chosen monogamy instead.

✘ **In allowing yourself to be swept away by passion, it is important to weigh the risks involved.** These include degradation of quality of your primary relationship, and even the end of it.

I am reminded of one of my clients, a married man who decided to embark on an affair with an old flame. Although his wife apparently did not find out about the relationship, she must have detected that something was amiss, because she disengaged from him in all but the most basic ways. As he put it, "I have a no-perks marriage." After several other affairs, he recognized this loss of "perks" to be a recurrent pattern in their relationship whenever he was involved with another woman and decided that fidelity worked better for him as well as for them as a couple. They remain happily married years later.

✘ **Rapturous experiences are more valued by those who crave novelty and less by those more geared to avoiding harm.** Neurobiologists have identified different brain neurotransmitter systems that mediate novelty seeking and harm avoidant behaviors: dopamine predominantly for the former, serotonin for the latter. With regard to these two divergent behavioral drives, the ancient dictum, "Know thyself," is important to bear in mind when considering risky passion.

The Poet and the Poem

According to Edward Mendelson, the literary executor for Auden's estate, Auden wrote this poem to Michael Yates, a younger man with whom he was in love "at first distantly, later intimately," when Yates was in his late twenties. Auden remained friends with Yates and, after Yates married, with his wife Margaret as well. Auden dedicated his final book of poetry, which was published posthumously in 1974, to the couple. So love turned to friendship, which endured for the better part of four decades.

Auden remained friends with other lovers as well, including the author Christopher Isherwood and, later, the much younger American librettist Chester Kallman. Auden and Kallman had been lovers for two years when Kallman told Auden that he did not want to be in a monogamous relationship with him and had already been unfaithful. Auden chose not to continue their relationship as lovers, but they remained good friends throughout Auden's life. It seems as though the conflicting themes of love and fidelity present in "Lullaby," written years before Auden met Kallman, were destined to play out in the poet's life.

Chapter Five

WHEN LOVE FADES

🌿 FAILING AND FLYING
by Jack Gilbert

Everyone forgets that Icarus also flew.
It's the same when love comes to an end,
or the marriage fails and people say
they knew it was a mistake, that everybody
said it would never work. That she was
old enough to know better. But anything
worth doing is worth doing badly.
Like being there by that summer ocean
on the other side of the island while
love was fading out of her, the stars
burning so extravagantly those nights that
anyone could tell you they would never last.
Every morning she was asleep in my bed
like a visitation, the gentleness in her
like antelope standing in the dawn mist.
Each afternoon I watched her coming back
through the hot stony field after swimming,
the sea light behind her and the huge sky
on the other side of that. Listened to her
while we ate lunch. How can they say
the marriage failed? Like the people who
came back from Provence (when it was Provence)
and said it was pretty but the food was greasy.
I believe Icarus was not failing as he fell,
but just coming to the end of his triumph.

All unhappy relationships that end are destined to unravel differently. Some collapse after escalating anger, repeated fights, and ultimate exhaustion; others, after emotional deprivation, unmet demands, and ultimate withdrawal; yet others come to a surprising and screeching halt. A friend of mine whose marriage had long been troubled came home to find his house stripped of all its furniture, with a Jolly Roger, the pirate's flag, attached to the chimney, flapping spitefully in the breeze.

"Failing and Flying" describes a relationship that ends very differently. Over a summer, against a beautiful Mediterranean landscape, a woman falls out of love with her husband.

In describing the slow descending arc of the relationship, Jack Gilbert draws on the Greek legend of Icarus, which is described more fully in chapter 44 ("Musée des Beaux Arts"). In essence, Icarus, a young boy whose father has fashioned wings out of feathers and wax, is escaping from the island of Crete. He has been warned by his father not to fly too high lest the sun melt the wax on the wings, but giddy with the sheer exuberance of flying, he forgets his father's advice and tragically falls into the sea.

Gilbert begins this poem with the line: "Everyone forgets that Icarus also flew."

He points out that it is easy to devalue the thrill of soaring up into the azure sky towards the sun that will be his demise by focusing exclusively on the value of moderation. The flying, Gilbert argues, has a value of its own, and he urges us not to forget that. This theme resonates with the that of the previous poem, as well as with two other "flying" poems in this collection (chapters 33 and 43).

The risk the poet has taken here is not literal flying but taking a chance on love. Love can be a risky business, which can be mitigated by choosing carefully and proceeding gradually. For some, however, this feels like a boring shopkeeper's approach to love and life. They would rather soar into the blue than take the stepwise approach of the cautious lover.

The loss of love, falling and failing, can be very painful at times, but it seems not to have been too bad for the poet as he describes the summer in which love "came to an end." He was aware even at the time that his wife's love was fading. He recalls the vivid images of this process with the details of memories seared into the mind because of the intensity of the feelings that accompanied them. Scientific evidence suggests that details registered during times of intense emotion are remembered more vividly than those accompanying ordinary events.

The poet shares with us a collage of the luminous mental snapshots of his last summer together with her: "The stars / burning, . . . the gentleness in her / like antelope standing in the dawn mist. . . . the sea light behind her and the huge sky / on the other side of that." Note how the imagery communicates a sense of evanescence. The antelope may run away at any moment, the mist will disappear, and the light will change. Gilbert's description allows us to feel the bittersweet joy of spending summer in such a beautiful place and enjoying the company of a beguiling woman, even as love is ebbing away.

The triumph of the poet's experience is that he is able to hold on to the beauty of his love while realizing that it will be short-lived. He shows no evidence of anger or malice at his wife's impending abandonment. Instead, he remembers moments of quiet intimacy—her sleeping next to him, walking back from an afternoon swim, and talking to him while they eat lunch—each memory captured and savored, perhaps all the more so because recognized as transient.

I have seen many people fall out of love. One couple, Chris and Katie, had been married for about twenty years when they came to me for help with their faltering relationship. We analyzed the roots of their problems from many angles, but in the end it boiled down to a simple conclusion: Katie had just lost interest and wanted to move on. They went through the painful process of separation and divorce with as much civility as possible in the circumstances. Katie left therapy; Chris stayed behind for help in putting together the pieces of his new life. Despite the pain of losing Katie and the resulting turmoil, he was able to hold on to why he had fallen in love with her in the first place and to keep joyful memories of their time together. He remembered her infectious laugh, her charm, and generosity of spirit.

Toward the start of the poem, Gilbert quotes British writer G. K. Chesterton, who parodied the proverb that if a thing's worth doing, it's worth doing well. In Chesterton's version, "If a thing is worth doing, it's worth doing badly." In life we're often unable to do something well, yet we decide it is worth doing anyway. That is what Gilbert seems to be saying about his marriage: "'Tis better to have loved and lost than never to have loved at all."

In the background Gilbert observes how society's gossips are making snide remarks and cluck-clucking about how "they knew it was a mistake, that everybody / said it would never work. That she was / old enough to know better."

Like Auden in "Lullaby," the poet has chosen love that deviates from the bourgeois values of society's gossips, which both poets recognize and ignore. Gilbert's ability to hold on to some happiness in the face of his wife's receding love provides a response to the gossips: if being with his wife gave him so much joy, how can they say the marriage failed?

Beyond their shared disregard for gossip about their romantic choices, Gilbert's "Failing and Flying" and Auden's "Lullaby" have another important theme in common. In each instance the poet recognizes that his love is both precious and fleeting. Many people believe that what matters most about love are the concrete benefits it yields, such as children and grandchildren or a companion in old age. Without detracting from these undoubtedly valuable dividends, to see them as the only fruits of love would be an acquisitive way of viewing this precious emotion. The truth embodied in these two poems is that love can be transformative and should be cherished even when it is as ephemeral as a Mediterranean summer or a night of passion.

Takeaways

✘ **It is not necessary to consider a relationship a failure just because it did not last.** If you hold on to the painful elements in a past relationship, you may become angry and bitter. On the other hand, if you can remember what was enjoyable, fun, funny, or good about it, you will reconnect with how that relationship enriched you.

✘ **Your thoughts and feelings about your relationship are generally more important than those of others.** Obviously it is worth paying attention to what other people say about your relationship when you respect them and their opinions. Gossip, however, is best ignored. Ultimately you are probably the best judge as to whether a relationship is right for you.

✘ **Wherever possible, try to be in the moment even though it may be hard to do.** For example, one evening when my wife and I were visiting Naples with friends. I had a premonition (accurate, as it turned out) that a bad scientific counselor review was awaiting me on my return, and I mentioned that the prospect was interfering with my enjoyment. My friend Tom, who was also awaiting a counselor review, wisely replied, "I always think it's best to be where you are." The Bay of Naples gleamed under a full moon, Mount Vesuvius sparkled in the distance, and a cool breeze blew off the water. I took Tom's advice, and we all had a great evening together.

✘ **Realize that nothing lasts forever.** This seems like a cliché, but often we go about our lives as though they will never end—and there is value to that. But it's also valuable to be aware that life is fleeting and remember to hold on to every precious moment as though it were our last.

The Poet and the Poem

Jack Gilbert (1925–2012) was born and raised in Pittsburgh, Pennsylvania. He attended Peabody High School, then worked as a door-to-door salesman, an exterminator, and a steelworker. He graduated from the University of Pittsburgh, where he developed an interest in writing and poetry with his friend and classmate Gerald Stern. He published his first book, *Views of Jeopardy*, in 1962, which was a success and made him a media darling in the San Francisco poetry scene. He received his master's degree from San Francisco State University in 1963. Gilbert published several award-winning books of poetry, and is a highly esteemed as a poet.

Gilbert retreated from the limelight and traveled through Europe, seeking a quiet, more contemplative lifestyle. According to his obituary in *The New York Times* in 2012, "Famous for eschewing fame, he did not go to writers' conferences or cocktail parties, gave readings sporadically and did not publish a great deal." Yet according to a 2005 *Paris Review* article,

"On the rare occasion when Jack Gilbert gives public readings, . . . it is not unusual for men and women in the audience to tell him how his poems have changed their lives."

After reading "Failing and Flying," I can understand why.

Gilbert had several long-term relationships with women. In Italy he fell in love with Gianna Gelmetti, about whom he wrote many poems. Love for various women appears often in his work. He also wrote two erotic novels under the pseudonym Tor Kung.

Gilbert lived in Japan with Michiko Nogami, a sculptor. After Nogami died of cancer in 1982, he wrote a series of poems expressing his grief at her death. He had a long-standing relationship with fellow poet Linda Gregg in the 1960s, and they remained close until his death.

Chapter Six

GETTING OVER A BREAKUP I: ACCEPTANCE

WHY SO PALE AND WAN FOND LOVER?
by Sir John Suckling

> Why so pale and wan fond lover?
> Prithee why so pale?
> Will, when looking well can't move her,
> Looking ill prevail?
> Prithee why so pale?
>
> Why so dull and mute young sinner?
> Prithee why so mute?
> Will, when speaking well can't win her,
> Saying nothing do't?
> Prithee why so mute?
>
> Quit, quit for shame, this will not move,
> This cannot take her;
> If of herself she will not love,
> Nothing can make her;
> The devil take her.

Henry was a graduate student whom I had seen in therapy for several years. He was intelligent and personable and had a great sense of humor. Although he had a wide and varied circle of friends, he was anxious about the prospect of dating. We talked about this for some time, and finally his eagerness for romance overcame his fear of rejection.

The first young woman he met online fit all his criteria. She was attractive, educated, and well-mannered. They exchanged pictures, and, to his delight, she agreed to go on a date with him. Several dates followed, but though he enjoyed her company, she gave him mixed signals about her interest in him. In conversation she was warm and friendly, but when he made physical overtures towards her, she responded half-heartedly. For example, when he leaned forward to kiss her good night at the end of their second date, she turned her cheek towards him and gave him a discouraging pat on the shoulder.

Undeterred, he redoubled his efforts to engage her attention, and although she stayed in touch with him, it was clear (at least to me) that she had no romantic interest. Henry became disheartened and wondered how he might keep the connection alive. Although not generally inclined to depression, he lost his usual *joie de vivre*, withdrew from friends, and had difficulty focusing on his studies. He mused obsessively about what he might do to win her hand. At that time, I gave him this poem by Sir John Suckling.

When I next saw Henry, he had read Suckling's poem several times, and it became the centerpiece of our session. He recognized that the young lady of his affections had moved on, and that it was not within his control to change that. And why should he, we wondered together, when there were many other women out there who would be happy to date him?

Since Henry had always been fascinated by science and biology, we discussed his experiences in light of Harry Harlow's controversial but groundbreaking studies performed in the 1950s and 60s, in which infant monkeys were separated from their mothers. First they go through a stage of protest, then despair, until finally they reattach themselves to a new love object. Henry smiled as he suggested that maybe in a minor way, he had gone through the first two stages of loss in relation to his girlfriend. In his protest phase, he had redoubled his efforts to recapture her. Then he had withdrawn. Now it was time to reattach to someone else.

In this poem, Sir John Suckling counsels a young man who has been rejected by a woman by reasoning with him. What is the purpose of walking around pale and lovesick? he asks. The young man was unable to win her hand when he was well, so why should he imagine that he would be any more successful when he looks ill? Likewise, Suckling argues, why should silence succeed when eloquence has failed? In the last stanza Suckling sternly directs the young man to stop these behaviors, and makes a profound observation: "If of herself she will not love, / Nothing can make her."

These are wise words that any would-be lover would do well to heed. We read all the time about lovers who are unable to accept that a relationship is over. Sometimes this results in months or years of unrequited longing when, against all reason, it is difficult for the rejected party to relinquish hope. In other instances, the rejected lover becomes enraged and resorts to stalking, occasionally with tragic results.

One aspect of this poem that I find endearing is that it involves an older person taking the time and interest to observe a younger person's distress and counsel him.

As for Henry, he fell in love and is happily married.

Takeaways

✘ **Accept reality.** This is always a good first step in handling adversity, but before you can accept a situation, you have to assess it properly.

✗ **Perceive the facts accurately.** The behavior of the young man in the poem shows that he does not understand that the relationship is over or that his efforts to capture the young woman's interest are doomed to fail. Before he can accept this, the young man has to confront reality. The poet-mentor explains that to him and points out that sulking isn't sexy: that looking pale, ill, and dull will do nothing to advance his cause.

The poet also explains an important aspect of love: that it needs to be freely given for a relationship to succeed. What this mentor is doing here is a type of cognitive behavior therapy (CBT), trying to help the young man align his thinking with reality—the cognitive part of CBT.

✗ **Moving on is sometimes difficult but necessary.** Now comes the behavioral part of CBT: move on. "Quit, quit, for shame," the poet says, and reiterates his central message. As Kenny Rogers famously sings in "The Gambler," "You've got to know when to hold 'em / know when to fold 'em." Coincidentally, as you will see below, Suckling was a famous card player.

✗ **Recognize when someone is just not that into you.** Another client of mine, Fiona, discovered a different spin on Suckling's advice, packaged in a way that is useful and appealing to a modern woman. Fiona was a television producer in her midthirties, highly successful in her career, but less so romantically. She had a problem figuring out when to call it quits when a relationship seemed to be stalling.

She brought to my attention Greg Behrendt's book *He's Just Not That into You: The No-Excuses Truth to Understanding Guys*. The book's central insight is that men often have difficulty being honest with a woman when they are not really interested in her. Instead they may make many and varied excuses about why they don't call or aren't available. In the hope that the relationship can be salvaged, an otherwise intelligent woman may hold on to the hope that these implausible excuses are true, thereby suffering unnecessary heartache and wasting time rather than moving on with her life.

The Poet and the Poem

Sir John Suckling, a contemporary of Shakespeare, tall, good-looking, and highly intelligent, crammed an enormous amount into his short but picturesque life. He inherited his father's estate at age eighteen, studied at Cambridge, and hobnobbed with the intellectuals of the day such as playwright Ben Jonson and fellow poet Richard Lovelace. He loved playing cards and invented the game of cribbage, then made a fortune playing it with other English aristocrats. He assisted King Charles I in his Scottish expedition. It is a wonder that he found time to write poetry. Suckling died an unfortunate death at about age thirty-two, probably by his own hand.

Chapter Seven

GETTING OVER A BREAKUP II: RECLAIMING YOURSELF

LOVE AFTER LOVE
by Derek Walcott

The time will come
when, with elation
you will greet yourself arriving
at your own door, in your own mirror
and each will smile at the other's welcome,

and say, sit here. Eat.
You will love again the stranger who was your self.
Give wine. Give bread. Give back your heart
to itself, to the stranger who has loved you

all your life, whom you ignored
for another, who knows you by heart.
Take down the love letters from the bookshelf,

the photographs, the desperate notes,
peel your own image from the mirror.
Sit. Feast on your life.

This poem advises the reader how to recover from a breakup. By the time we reach a certain age, most of us have had someone break up with us, as in the last two poems. While no two breakups are exactly alike, they resemble one another in various important ways, including how they leave you feeling: Sad. Lonely. Angry. Desolate. Vengeful. Crestfallen. Pessimistic. Pick the adjectives that suit you best, and, if you like, add any others that come to mind.

Walcott's poem "Love after Love" is an antidote to such feelings. Read it a few times, and see if you agree. The poem begins and ends with the image of looking at yourself in the mirror. We do this for many reasons: To groom ourselves: is the tie or hat on straight? Is makeup smudged, shaving cream fully removed? Or for self-evaluation: do we have pimples, dry skin, wrinkles, jowls? But these are not what Walcott is talking about here. He is using the mirror both as an instrument of self-affirmation and as a proxy for our relationship with ourselves.

In the aftermath of a breakup, there are many ways to respond: fill up your time with activities; rush out and find someone else; retreat to your bedroom in sorrow; and eat or drink too much. Walcott is suggesting that a critical part of a healthy response is to renew your relationship with yourself. The mirror is both a method and a metaphor for doing so.

In the early phases of a breakup, you are likely to feel unhappy. Then Walcott's words will begin to help you heal, starting with the first stanza:

> The time will come
> when, with elation
> you will greet yourself arriving
> at your own door, in your own mirror
> and each will smile at the other's welcome.

How strange to think of elation in the context of a breakup! Yet the sure-footedness of Walcott's language assures us that it could be true: someday we may feel elated. What we feel now is not necessarily how we will always feel.

The poet's emphasis on reclaiming your identity is reinforced by his repetition of the word "your:" "your self," "your own door," "your own mirror." With these simple words, the poet raises a crucial point: in the wake of a breakup, you can easily lose your sense of self—or at least your self-esteem. Reclaim yourself, he advises, and that which is yours. And even as he addresses the reader, we get a sense that he may also be addressing himself.

Mirroring is an important aspect of communication in humans and other mammals. If you smile during a conversation, the other person is likely to smile back. The same goes for frowning. If you cross your arms, the person across the room is more likely to do the same. In fact, special cells called mirror neurons in the prefrontal cortex of the brain, the region that orchestrates higher level executive functions, mediate these behaviors.

These mirror neurons are connected through complex neural pathways to the facial muscles, which are important for expression and have probably played a major role in evolution. In fact, Charles Darwin wrote an entire book on the role of facial expressions in animals and humans. Imagine, for example, that a monkey sees a lion approaching the troop. His face registers terror, which is immediately perceived and reflected in the mirror neurons of the other monkeys in the troop, who then experience similar terror. Without a cry having been raised, which might have alerted the lion, the whole troop flees instantaneously, thanks to mirror neurons, the facial muscles of expression, and their connections to the emotional centers of the brain.

The poet suggests that the reader look into the mirror, and "each will smile at the other's welcome." We see here the beginning of the theme of recovery in your relationship with yourself. It starts with a welcoming smile. We know that smiling is contagious and that when we smile, we actually feel better, regardless of whether there is anything to smile about or not. If you smile at yourself in the mirror, your reflection will smile back at you, and the reflexive mood-elevating effects of a smile may be enhanced thanks to your mirror neurons. Conversely, if you frown at yourself, you are likely to feel worse.

Therapists have made much of one's relationship with oneself, and rightly so. We often hear, "How can you love someone else if you don't love yourself?" Even though it has become a cliché, it is often true. The poet is telling us that in the aftermath of a breakup, we would be well advised to befriend ourselves as part of learning to love again.

The poet instructs the reader with words and suggestions that are full of kindness, such as "Sit here. Eat. / ... Give wine. Give bread." The way we talk to ourselves has an important effect on how we feel about ourselves.

Then Walcott makes a more curious suggestion, "Give back your heart to itself." Here he suggests that somehow you have rejected a core part of yourself, just as your former lover rejected you. In a strange way you are siding with that person in concluding that you are not worth loving. You have thrown your heart away. The poet advises you to take it back, implying that it is within your power to do so, and providing you with the strength to act on that suggestion.

He adds that you, the rejected person, have become a stranger to yourself. Sometimes when we fall in love, we lose ourselves in the overwhelming welter of emotions. He reminds us that although we have loved ourselves all our lives, it is easy to forget that fact when we fall in love. We can become dependent on a lover to validate our sense of self and become immersed in the needs and desires of the other person. Retrieve that old self-love, the poet recommends.

The poet continues his advice: remove memories that will only make you unhappy, such as pictures of good times with your ex and "desperate notes," generally written in an attempt to salvage a faltering relationship. Have you noticed how some people dwell upon the details of the lost relationship, making themselves miserable in the process?

Walcott returns to the image from the beginning of the poem of *you* looking into *your* mirror, and in a vivid image of reclaiming yourself, recommends that you peel that image from the mirror as though it is a mask and return it to yourself. This is a physical image of the self-reclamation that he recommends.

The last line is powerful, affirming, and embracing:

"Sit. Feast on your life."

Takeaways

✗ **Be kind to yourself after a breakup.** You may have a lot of negative feelings at that time, such as sadness, loss, anger, self-blame, pessimism, and despair. But recognize that feelings almost always pass and that in future you may actually feel elation.

✗ **It may be helpful to look in the mirror—literally—and smile at yourself.** Just as you smile when you are happy, there is a lot of evidence that smiling makes you happy. In an analogous way, when you frown, it can make you unhappy.

✗ **Use kind and respectful language when you talk to yourself.** If you say things like, "What an idiot I was!" or "How could I have done such a foolish thing!" remember that even if you may have made an unfortunate mistake, you can find kinder language in which to frame it. How you talk to yourself affects how you feel. The

Dalai Lama has famously written, "Be kind whenever possible, and it is always possible." The same applies to dealing with yourself.

✘ Maintain your separate identity even when you are in love.

At first this merging of identities can produce a dizzying high, but you can end up paying a big price if you don't keep your feet on the ground.

So retain your sense of self even when you are in love. As the poet Khalil Gibran writes to would-be lovers in *The Prophet*:

> Fill each other's cup but drink not from one cup. Give one another of your bread but eat not from the same loaf. Sing and dance together and be joyous, but let each one of you be alone, Even as the strings of the lute are alone though they quiver with the same music.

✘ Don't confuse self-love with selfishness.

This is a common error people make these days. Self-love does not mean caring for nobody other than yourself. It means taking care of yourself in ways that are consistent with being a functional member of society. The Jewish sage Rabbi Hillel is often quoted as saying: *"If I am not for myself, who will be for me? If I am not for others, what am I? And if not now, when?"*

This quote distinguishes what a modern therapist might call healthy narcissism (being for oneself) from pathological narcissism (being only for oneself). The former, which refers to proper self-care, is what Walcott is recommending for the rejected lover. Illustrations of the latter are everywhere to be found.

Note some of the techniques Walcott uses to achieve his effects: simple words; a warm, intimate tone; the sustained use of the image in the mirror; the structure of the stanzas; and enjambment—leaving a sentence incomplete at the end of a line or paragraph, which subtly affects the pace of the poem.

The Poet and the Poem

Derek Walcott (1930–2017) has the distinction of being one of only four Nobel Prize winners from the Caribbean. The Nobel Prize committee praised him "for a poetic oeuvre of great luminosity sustained by an historical vision, the outcome of a multicultural commitment." Many other honors and distinctions followed. A prolific writer, he wrote twenty-three books of poetry and twenty-five plays.

Walcott was raised, along with his sister and twin brother, by their mother, a teacher who often recited poetry. Although originally trained as a painter, Walcott later found his calling in poetry. He published his first poem at age fourteen and became established with his collected poems, *In a Green Night*, published in 1962, when he was thirty-two years old. He was embraced by several famous poets and obtained academic appointments in the United States. His epic book *Omeros* (1990) was chosen as one of the best books of the year by the book review section of *The New York Times*.

On a personal level, Walcott appears to have lived fully. He married and divorced three times, so he presumably understood from personal experience the challenge of breakup, recovery, and moving on. Perhaps, like many artists, he took his life experiences and wove them into his art, of which we are all beneficiaries.

✿ SONNET 18:
SHALL I COMPARE THEE TO A SUMMER'S DAY?
by William Shakespeare

> Shall I compare thee to a summer's day?
> Thou art more lovely and more temperate:
> Rough winds do shake the darling buds of May,
> And summer's lease hath all too short a date;
> Sometime too hot the eye of heaven shines,
> And often is his gold complexion dimm'd;
> And every fair from fair sometime declines,
> By chance or nature's changing course untrimm'd;
> But thy eternal summer shall not fade,
> Nor lose possession of that fair thou ow'st;
> Nor shall death brag thou wander'st in his shade,
> When in eternal lines to time thou grow'st:
> > So long as men can breathe or eyes can see,
> > So long lives this, and this gives life to thee.

The first seventeen of Shakespeare's sonnets are a sort of prologue to a love story, which begins with sonnet 18. This is a frank declaration of love, which raises a common question for would-be lovers: how do I take the plunge and express my love for the first time? The sonnets

that follow in this collection (chapters 9 and 10) represent later epi-
sodes in this love story, but for now, let us consider sonnet 18.

I first encountered this famous sonnet in a strange way. In high
school I broke some rule or other (I forget what) and my history teacher,
as punishment, had me memorize sonnet 18. I had never before
encountered Shakespeare's sonnets and knew nothing about them.

When I first read this poem, its novelty was a shock to my system,
like eating ice cream for the first time. I marveled at the tidiness of
its structure. Its words and phrases were like strings of jewels. They
dazzled me then, and they still do.

Consider the startling originality of comparing your loved one
to a summer day. Most people would be flattered by such a compari-
son. But Shakespeare takes the compliment a step further: "Thou art
more lovely and more temperate."

Temperate, a word often applied to good weather, can also mean
not given to extremes—a happy trait in a prospective lover. Consider
how nimbly Shakespeare summarizes the many ways that summer
falls short of his beloved's charms.

Having studied the effects of summer on vulnerable people, I can
attest that many struggle with heat, which can make them depressed,
agitated, and out of sorts. They would no doubt agree that "sometime
too hot the eye of heaven shines." Others struggle on unseasonably
cloudy summer days and become depressed after even a day or two
of bad weather. They might well agree that as far as summer's sun
is concerned, "often is his gold complexion dimm'd." Another prob-
lem that many people have is that summer is over too soon. Its "lease
hath all too short a date."

About two-thirds down the poem comes the volta, or shift,
which introduces a surprising promise: Although summer's beauty
declines, as does everything else in nature, his beloved will be an
exception to the rule:

> But thy eternal summer shall not fade,
> Nor lose possession of that fair thou ow'st;
> Nor shall death brag thou wander'st in his shade,
> When in eternal lines to time thou grow'st.

He follows up with a boast that would seem outrageous hyperbole were it to come from anyone other than Shakespeare:

> So long as men can breathe or eyes can see,
> So long lives this, and this gives life to thee.

Here we are, over four hundred years later, and so far Shakespeare has been proved correct. His words live on.

Flash forward to the present day. Imagine that you have a secret crush on someone but are not sure how to make the next move. Maybe she or he is in your class or a colleague at work, but it could be anywhere. You don't want to stick your neck out. How do you take the plunge?

Think back to Gary Chapman's five love languages, and pick whichever ones suit you. You could give a gift or perform an act of service, for example. But remember, words can sometimes work wonders.

Takeaways

✘ **Be bold**. It is common for people, especially when they first begin to feel the stirrings of love, to wonder if they should act on their feelings and, if so, when and how. Author Anaïs Nin captured this tentativeness with a famous quote: "And the day came when the risk to remain tight in the bud was more painful than the risk it took to blossom." She also observed that "life shrinks or expands according to one's courage." So if you feel your love is worth pursuing, consider making a move (accepting ahead of time the possibility of rejection). If you should be rejected, take comfort in the knowledge that you were bold, that you loved, and chose to express it. And keep your eyes open for other possibilities.

✘ **Use words.** The trickiness of declaring interest in someone you fancy reminds me of two lovely young women in their twenties whose engagement I recently attended, along with a lively crowd of friends and family. The company was chattering away at high volume when all of a sudden there was a hush as the two began to tell the tale of how one first shyly opened up the delicate subject of her interest in the other. They had been hanging out together as part of a group when one, tired of never being in a more intimate setting, gently asked, "Do you think we could ever hang out just the two of us?"

The other replied, "Does that mean you're asking me out on a date?"

"Maybe," said the first one tentatively.

So here they were, many months later after that first gentle exchange of words that led to love, commitment, and a planned future together, celebrating their love with family and friends. In some strange way, they had been in the same dilemma as the poet centuries before, wanting to reach out to each other and waiting for the right moment to do so. People need to choose the approach that suits them best. But if you and the one you fancy both enjoy words, you might think of sonnet 18 and risk opening your heart by saying something.

The Shakespearean Sonnet

- Like all sonnets, it has fourteen lines.
- Three quatrains (stanzas of four lines each).
- A volta, which comes about two-thirds down.
- A final rhyming couplet, like a bow on a gift.
- The meter is, once again, iambic pentameter.
- Rhyme scheme: ABAB CDCD EFEF GG.

In contrast to the Petrarchan sonnet (see page 16), this type of sonnet has a slightly different structure and plays into a particular strength that Shakespeare had for nailing the essence of the sonnet in the last two lines: the rhyming couplet. We saw how Edna St. Vincent Millay used this device to good effect in "Pity me not."

The Poet and the Poem

William Shakespeare (1564–1616) was born in Stratford-upon-Avon, England, the third of eight children to John and Mary Shakespeare (née Arden). John Shakespeare was a glovemaker and held prominent positions in the town until he fell on hard times later in life. Mary Arden came from a minor branch of a prominent family. Will's two elder siblings died in childhood, leaving him as the eldest. He was the only one of the siblings who married.

Will is thought to have attended the excellent local grammar school, but probably received no formal education after age fifteen. At age eighteen, he married Anne Hathaway, who was twenty-six and pregnant with his first child. Their daughter, Susanna, was born six months after the wedding. Later, Anne gave birth to twins, Hamnet and Judith. Hamnet died at age eleven; Judith lived till age seventy-seven, married, and had three children but no grandchildren.

For seven years between 1585, when the twins were born, and 1592 (when Will would have been twenty-eight years old), no records exist that document where he was or what he was doing. They are known as the "lost years."

By 1592, Shakespeare was earning a living as an actor and playwright in London and possibly had several plays produced. By 1597, he had already published fifteen of his thirty-seven plays and was able to purchase the second largest house in Stratford, called "New House," for his family. The journey between Stratford and London took four days by horse. It is believed that he returned home once a year during the forty days of Lent, when theaters were closed. Shakespeare and his business partners prospered, built their own theater called the Globe, and later, in the reign of King James I, became known as the King's Men. Shakespeare seems to have been respected in the dramatic arts, but his genius was not recognized until the nineteenth century.

Shakespeare's Sonnets

Between 1593 and 1594, the London theaters were often closed because of outbursts of the plague. The sonnets were probably written about that time, and the first surviving reference to them refers to the circulation of "Shakespeare's sugared sonnets" among his private friends. The complete Quarto edition of the *Sonnets* came out in 1609, published by Thomas Thorpe, a man whose unscrupulous business practices have raised the suggestion that he might have published them without the author's permission. The sonnets, dedicated to "Mr. W. H.," fall into two suites: the first 126, written to a young man, often called the "fair youth"; and the next twenty-eight addressed to a woman often called "the dark lady." All three sonnets in this book come from the first suite.

Perhaps because the sonnets succeed so well as stand-alone poems, some experts have suggested that they are simply a collection, not a sequence. I, however, agree with Shakespearean scholar David West, who takes a different approach:

> Sonnets 18 to 126 chart the course of the speaker's love for a young man. . . . In sonnets 127 to 152, a black lady is now his mistress, but it soon becomes clear that this is not love but lust, and it ends in loathing. That is the arc of the plot, and the Sonnets of Shakespeare are a drama with three main characters, only one of whom speaks. The first 17 poems, the procreation sonnets, are the prologue to that drama. . . . [The sonnets] form a plot, and therefore cannot be understood unless each one is read in the light of its neighbors.

One tantalizing question is whether the sonnets are autobiographical. The literature is full of arguments for and against this premise. William Wordsworth wrote of the sonnets, "With this key Shakespeare unlocked his heart." If true, this could explain why Shakespeare chose not to publish the poems or delayed publication. When you consider that gay sex was a capital offense in Shakespeare's time (though enforcement was generally honored in the breach), it is understandable that he might have been inclined towards discretion.

To put sonnet 18 in context, West explains that the first seventeen sonnets "use 17 different arguments to persuade the young man to marry and beget children in order to preserve his beauty for posterity." There is a theory that Shakespeare might have been commissioned to write these sonnets, perhaps by the young man's father.

Although the poet is discreet about his feelings towards the young man in the first seventeen sonnets, in the eighteenth he chooses to show his hand. In this one, as well as in the other sonnets presented here (29 and 116), we can see how the poet, while conducting a romantic correspondence, is also able to produce poetry of universal and immortal dimensions.

Much has been written about the identity of the mysterious Mr. W. H., to whom the sonnets were dedicated, and there is no shortage of suspects. Just as a dream tells us more about the dreamer than its subject, however, these love poems may tell us more about their author than their recipient. They may represent a true account of Shakespeare in love.

⟨⟨ SONNET 29:
WHEN, IN DISGRACE WITH FORTUNE AND MEN'S EYES
by William Shakespeare

When, in disgrace with fortune and men's eyes,
I all alone beweep my outcast state,
And trouble deaf heaven with my bootless cries,
And look upon myself and curse my fate,
Wishing me like to one more rich in hope,
Featured like him, like him with friends possessed,
Desiring this man's art and that man's scope,
With what I most enjoy contented least;
Yet in these thoughts myself almost despising,
Haply I think on thee, and then my state,
(Like to the lark at break of day arising)
From sullen earth sings hymns at heaven's gate;
    For thy sweet love remembered such wealth brings
    That then I scorn to change my state with kings.

At the beginning of this sonnet we find the poet in a pitifully dejected state. He feels down on his luck, scorned by others, and alone in his misery. He cries to heaven but gets no answer. He looks at himself and curses his fate.

We often encounter such feelings in people with clinical depression. Reading the early lines of this sonnet made me wonder whether Shakespeare might have been clinically depressed when he wrote it, and prompted me to investigate further.

The previous sonnet in the series suggests that the poet was sleeping poorly, which left him exhausted during the day, as he describes in the first lines of sonnet 28:

> How can I then return in happy plight
> That am debarred from the benefit of rest
> When day's oppression is not eased by night
> But day by night and night by day oppressed.

He ends the sonnet with this pitiful couplet:

> But day doth daily draw my sorrows longer
> And night doth nightly make grief's length seem stronger.

In these lines we see Shakespeare tormented both day and night by the painful symptoms of depression. The day is oppressive, and the night provides no respite or relief. Sleep disruption is a classical symptom of depression. A depressed person may have difficulty falling asleep, staying asleep, or may wake too early in the morning. In addition, whatever sleep such a person does get often seems inadequate and unrefreshing. For the sake of completeness, I should mention that some people experience the opposite type of sleep symptoms when they are depressed—too much sleep. But that is not so here.

In the previous sonnet (27), the poet appears to be under stress as a result of travel, work, or both. His mind turns to thoughts of his beloved, which lifts his spirits. There is a suggestion that he is out of contact with the young man (yet another stress?) and relies on memory for his emotional sustenance.

Let us return now to the focus of our current interest, sonnet 29.

Just as the first four lines document the poet's painful feelings of depression, so the next four lines move on to chronicle the painful feelings of envy:

> Wishing me like to one more rich in hope,
> Featured like him, like him with friends possessed,
> Desiring this man's art and that man's scope,
> With what I most enjoy contented least.

After two quatrains of self-flagellation, what a relief it is to the reader (as it must surely have been to the poet) when the volta comes! And it was worth waiting for:

> Yet in these thoughts myself almost despising,
> Haply I think on thee, and then my state,
> Like to the lark at break of day arising
> From sullen earth, sings hymns at Heaven's gate.

The first line shows a softening of the desolate mood of the first two quatrains. The phrase "almost despising" is less self-denigrating than the earlier lines; it is followed by a switch in mood and the reason for it. The word "haply" can mean "by chance or happenstance" but also brings to mind the word "happily." It may be that a despairing mind casts about for consolation, and in this instance—as is often the case—thinking of one's beloved can provide solace. Shakespeare dramatizes his mood shift by providing a contrast between the grim emotions experienced in the early part of the sonnet and the rapturous image that follows.

Takeaways

✖ **Recognize clinical depression.** It is vitally important to recognize clinical depression when you see it, whether in yourself or someone you care about. By depression, clinicians mean not merely sadness, but also physical changes, which include insomnia, lack of energy, and disturbance of circadian rhythms, all of which we see in this sonnet as well as in those that precede it. Along with these physical changes, depressed people devalue themselves and compare themselves adversely to others, as the poet does here.

According to the World Health Organization, depression is one of the world's most disabling and costly conditions. It is also the leading cause of suicide. Fortunately, the condition is nowadays treatable by lifestyle changes, therapy, and medications. Lifestyle changes include exercise, sufficient sleep, and strengthening circadian rhythms, for example, by exposure to bright environmental light in the morning and darkness at night.

If you see in yourself (or a loved one) the symptoms that Shakespeare so eloquently describes here, you would do well to get (or recommend) professional help.

✖ **Challenge cognitive distortions.** Professionally, I have referred to sonnet 29 several times in treating creative people who blame themselves for producing work they consider inadequate in worth or scope. I point out that artists are often too harsh on themselves. If the greatest writer who ever lived could castigate himself, as Shakespeare does in this sonnet (ironically considered to be one of his greatest), it raises questions about the validity of the self-criticism with which creative people often admonish themselves. So, analyze what you have actually produced, and deal practically with whatever you feel is lacking. Ask a respected friend or colleague for help in evaluating the work and offering you feedback.

Sometimes it's good to take a break from work and do something that clears your mind. You may need to break circular thinking, which can be unproductive and painful. In sonnet 29, reflecting on his love propels the poet out of his whirlpool of despair.

Anyone who has been in love can probably remember a time when just thinking about your love can lift your spirits. I recall for example when, as a junior medical officer in the South African military, I was serving at a mission hospital in the remote countryside. One weekend I was alone on call in the small house allocated to me on a beautiful hillside above the hospital. In other circumstances it would have been an ideal place for hiking and contemplation, but my wife in Johannesburg had just given birth to our son, and I was missing them sorely. Happily (or haply) a friend came to visit and when he saw my dejected spirits, reminded me that I had someone I loved waiting for me back home. That makes a difference, he said, and the thought immediately cheered me up. However, read on.

Do not depend on love alone to lift you out of depression. Although reminding yourself that you love and are loved can certainly lift your spirits, that alone will rarely be sufficient to provide a sustained mood-elevating effect if you are seriously depressed. I have often thought of that in connection with the writer Virginia Woolf, who suffered suicidal depressions. During her final depression, she filled the pockets of her skirt with stones and drowned herself. She left behind a note for her husband in which she assured him how much their love meant to her: "You have given me the greatest possible happiness. You have been in every way all that anyone could be. . . . I don't think two people could have been happier than we have been."

Even though thinking about your love can be a heartwarming exercise, a seriously depressed person should not expect that such thoughts alone can make you feel better. In these situations, it is critical to seek out competent medical help, because depression is a treatable condition.

✖ **Recognize and deal with envy.** Envy is a particularly painful emotion in that it denigrates you and elevates others, thereby compounding feelings of inadequacy. To make matters worse, envy is often accompanied by self-blame for pettiness, for not being glad at a friend's success, and perhaps even wishing him to slip up and fail. What then can you do about such a painful emotion?

An extraordinary supervisor was once brave enough to share with me his past struggles with envy towards more successful colleagues. He tried to assuage these feelings by working night and day "so that my plate would be as full as theirs and I wouldn't have to envy them. But that became a problem in its own right because the pace of work was exhausting and unsustainable."

"So what did you do about it?" I asked.

"I decided it was easier to envy them," he replied with a smile.

As we saw in "One Art" and will see again, it is often easier to accept your feelings, especially the most painful ones, than deny or try to fight them. Accepting (and even welcoming) your feelings is charmingly recommended in "The Guest House" by Rumi (see chapter 26).

I check up from time to time on people who have been meaningful to me in the past. So I looked up my old supervisor on the Internet and found that, sadly but unsurprisingly, he had died (it had been years since we had last spoken). I read his lengthy obituary, which was quite different from those of many other academics I had known. Instead of listing only his academic accomplishments, the obituary described this extraordinary man's many adventures: traveling to faraway places, treating people with leprosy, and observing voodoo rituals, to name just a few. He was a man who embraced life in all its abundance, variety, and strangeness. My eyes moistened as I read it, and I thought, "You had nothing to envy in your colleagues, my friend."

In sonnet 29 we see Shakespeare not only as a great poet but as a great dramatist. The first part of the sonnet plunges the reader into the poet's gloomy mindset. Then at the volta in line 9, his spirits lift, as do the reader's. How amazing it is that in a mere fourteen lines, the writer can induce such a transformation! The poet dramatizes this change by evoking the image of a lark at dawn. As West describes it:

> One of the most joyous sounds in nature is the morning song of the lark, and its joy is all the greater by contrast with the sullen dampness of the earth from which it rises. . . . Larks build their nests on the ground and soar singing at sunrise from the dew-soaked earth.

The Poet and the Poem

When you put together the symptoms that the poet sets forth in sonnet 29 and the previous two sonnets, it is hard to escape the conclusion that the poet knew depression personally. His reports of self-blame, unwarranted feelings of inadequacy, and adverse comparisons with others, combined with severe sleep problems and physical exhaustion, ring true to those of us who have seen depression or experienced it firsthand.

We may wonder where this sonnet falls in the love story between the poet and the young man, eleven poems after his first declaration of love. Things seem to be going well for the two lovers. Although they are separated, perhaps because of other commitments, merely thinking about the young man is enough to cause the poet's mood to soar aloft, singing like a lark at break of day.

Let us move on now to perhaps the most famous of Shakespeare's sonnets.

Chapter Ten

IN PRAISE OF THE
MARRIAGE OF TRUE MINDS

SONNET 116:
LET ME NOT TO THE MARRIAGE OF TRUE MINDS
by William Shakespeare

Let me not to the marriage of true minds
Admit impediments. Love is not love
Which alters when it alteration finds,
Or bends with the remover to remove.
O, no! it is an ever-fixed mark
That looks on tempests and is never shaken;
It is the star to every wand'ring bark,
Whose worth's unknown, although his height be taken.
Love's not Time's fool, though rosy lips and cheeks
Within his bending sickle's compass come;
Love alters not with his brief hours and weeks,
But bears it out even to the edge of doom.
    If this be error and upon me prov'd,
    I never writ, nor no man ever lov'd.

Sonnet 116 has been regarded by many, including Wordsworth, as
Shakespeare's greatest sonnet. It stands as a monument to the idea of
unwavering love. As a young man, stirred by the vision of "the mar-
riage of true minds," I shared it with a friend who was engaged to

be married, and he was impressed enough to read it as part of his wedding ceremony. His rendition of the poem was so powerful that many of the wedding guests must have been as moved as I was.

For those lucky enough to find the marriage of true minds, it serves as a constant and lifelong source of support. Sonnet 116 conveys this concept with unmatched force, set forth in a manner reminiscent of a lawyer's opening statement or the beginning of a priest's sermon. The traditional religious Christian wedding ceremony demands that anyone who knows of any lawful impediment to the marriage should declare it there and then. Likewise the words "let not" recall the line, "Those whom God has joined together let not man put asunder." So in this poem, Shakespeare dons the mantle of high authority.

After his powerful opening declaration, Shakespeare tells us what love is not: something that "alters when it alteration finds, / Or bends with the remover to remove."

In other words, the inevitable changes that life brings should not disrupt true love; true love should not waver even when someone strays ("bends with the remover to remove"). The poet defiantly rejects such impediments with a firm rebuttal:

> O no! it is an ever-fixed mark
> That looks on tempests and is never shaken;
> It is the star to every wand'ring bark,
> Whose worth's unknown, although his height be taken.

Here he is comparing love to something that orients sailors at sea, as a star might do. The star that orients all ships ("every wand'ring bark,") is most likely the polestar: its navigational value was well known to sailors, who measured their course by marking its elevation. Like the star, love can be measured in certain ways, but its true worth is immeasurable.

In the third quatrain Shakespeare addresses a problem that often arises in love: how to handle the ravages of time. His imagery shifts to a classical depiction of Time, sickle in hand, ready to cut off youth's "rosy lips and cheeks" and life itself. We are told that unlike a king's fool or jester, love is not "Time's fool." In other words, love is not subservient to time, but remains constant "even to the edge of doom." Here again we hear echoes of the traditional Christian wedding vow that a couple remain faithful to each other as long as they both shall live.

This sonnet may owe its enduring significance and popularity to its reassurance of the constancy of love (as defined by the marriage of true minds) and its capacity to endure through the course of a lifetime, despite life's inevitable vicissitudes. Others may take comfort in the sonnet's message as a dream and an ideal to which they aspire even if they cannot always hold firm to it. Shakespeare puts all his oratorical powers behind his message, concluding with a flourish that from a majestic author has the authority of a king's seal:

> If this be error and upon me proved
> I never writ, nor no man ever loved.

Takeaways

✗ **For love to succeed over the long term, it is necessary that there be a marriage of the minds.** Although physical attraction often leads the way in choosing a loved one, much more is needed for love to last. One key is whether you agree on important things. It is easy to be fooled by superficial qualities that may attract and mesmerize on first acquaintance but may not wear well over time. In choosing a life partner, consider the advice of the sonnet and ask yourself, "Do we have a marriage of true minds?"

✖ **Can a relationship survive after your partner cheats on you? If so, how?** It is a commonplace observation that infidelity can mark the end of a relationship. Many couples, however, find ways to repair things. Trust can be restored, but if that is to occur, it has to be earned. The couple will do best if they understand the underlying reasons for the infidelity and seek to address them. Some couples actually manage to learn from this crisis and see it as an opportunity to communicate better (sometimes with the help of a professional), thereby improving their marriage.

Time presents challenges to many marriages. Sociologist Helen Fisher found that in various cultures, divorce rates peak around four years after marriage. That seems to be when people are more likely to become bored and inclined to stray.

✖ **Marriages that do not last a lifetime need not be regarded as failures.** Many people set out on a relationship with the best intentions, yet for whatever reason, the marriage doesn't endure, as in the case of my medical school friend who read sonnet 116 at his wedding ceremony. Sadly, some years later, the marriage ended in a bitter divorce. Such are the vagaries of love, where the best intentions are often insufficient to carry two people through "ev'n to the edge of doom." Yet that does not mean that the marriage needs to be regarded as a failure, as Jack Gilbert argues in "Failing and Flying" (chapter 5).

Anthropologist Margaret Mead normalized the concept that a successful marriage does not have to be lifelong. She suggested that people need three marriages: one for love, one for having children, and one for companionship. Some people may find all three marriages in one person. For others, a change of partners may work best.

The Poet and the Poem

You may wonder where this sonnet falls in the romantic tale of the poet and his young love. Its number (116) in a suite of 126 love sonnets provides a clue. So does the contrast in tone between this sonnet and the two earlier ones in this collection. In sonnet 18, the poet first declares his love in the voice of a suitor and promises the gift of immortality. Sonnet 29 finds the poet down and out until thoughts of his beloved boost him into a state of exuberance. In sonnet 116, the poet adopts a tone of authority, defending "the marriage of true minds" against all impediments, including the infidelity of one party.

Another major difference between this poem and the earlier ones is that in sonnet 116 there is a suggestion of a dialogue between the poet and an absent figure (presumably the young man), whose voice is not directly heard but implied. It is as though the reader is listening in on a telephone call where you can hear only one side of the conversation but can only infer what the other is saying.

In this poem, Shakespeare uses the classical devices of rhetoric. He sets up a premise ("Let me not to the marriage of true minds / Admit impediments"), then defends it against challenges. If you think of sonnet 116 as a rebuttal to accusations by someone else, it acquires a new layer of meaning. The sonnets between 109 and 116 revolve around the same themes: confessions of the poet's infidelities, excuses, and flattery of his beloved, whom he begs to forgive his behavior. All of this offers a context for the famous sonnet 116.

An alternative interpretation is that the poet senses that the young man has not been faithful either, in which case the poet is reassuring the young man that he stands fast to the relationship nonetheless. The poet has previously leveled charges of infidelity (in spirit if not in body) against the young man, for example in sonnets 94 and 95.

Whichever interpretation you favor, there have been "imped-iments" in the relationship, and perhaps accusations by the young man, which the poet may be trying to put right by this sonnet.

You may be able to guess what happens to the relationship. The young man moves on. The poet expresses feelings of loss and self-recrimination in the next ten sonnets, but there is no longer any evidence of a dialogue. In sonnet 126 he writes a kind of farewell note to the young man, whom he addresses as "my lovely boy." The sonnet ends sadly with two blank lines, bracketed with parentheses, as though to illustrate the silence that marks the end of the relationship.

Anyone who wants to understand Shakespeare's mind and heart might do well to read his sonnets. Do they really mirror the events in his own life, or are they just one more fictional creation from the mind of a dramatic genius? Nobody knows. Yet there is a persuasive case to be made for Wordsworth's contention that the sonnet was the key with which Shakespeare "unlocked his heart." If so, those of us who have enjoyed Shakespeare's profound understanding of love as expressed in his plays and poems are in the young man's debt for teaching the older one that the course of true love never did run smooth.

Chapter Eleven

LOSS OF A LOVED ONE

STOP ALL THE CLOCKS, CUT OFF THE TELEPHONE (FUNERAL BLUES)
by W. H. Auden

Stop all the clocks, cut off the telephone,
Prevent the dog from barking with a juicy bone,
Silence the pianos and with muffled drum
Bring out the coffin, let the mourners come.

Let aeroplanes circle moaning overhead
Scribbling on the sky the message He Is Dead,
Put crepe bows round the white necks of the public doves,
Let the traffic policemen wear black cotton gloves.

He was my North, my South, my East and West,
My working week and my Sunday rest,
My noon, my midnight, my talk, my song;
I thought that love would last for ever: I was wrong.

The stars are not wanted now: put out every one;
Pack up the moon and dismantle the sun;
Pour away the ocean and sweep up the wood.
For nothing now can ever come to any good.

This poem first came to the attention of the general public when it was recited in the movie *Four Weddings and a Funeral* (1994) by a character (played by actor John Hannah) following the death of his male partner. He apologizes for not having the words to express his grief himself, deferring to this poem by Auden, who was also gay. The reading of the poem was a climactic scene in the movie as the camera moved from one mourner to another, each registering the gravity of the moment and the magnitude of the impact of this loss on the life of the young man reading it.

Although not widely known before the movie appeared, the poem has since become deservedly famous and entered the cultural mainstream. One curious aspect of the poem's history is that the first two stanzas started out as part of a satirical play called *The Ascent of F6*, written by Auden and his friend Christopher Isherwood, where it was put to music. That production was obviously a far cry from the serious work the poem later became.

This poem might have struck such a powerful chord when it appeared in the movie partly because by 1994 we had seen the horrific impact of the AIDS epidemic, which had disproportionately killed gay men. The tide of public opinion was changing. Recognition of the profound love that people of the same sex had for one another, so long suppressed, and the profound grief when that love was cut short, was now becoming widely appreciated. The universality of the poem touched everybody and heightened awareness of the power of love and loss in all who heard and read it.

The poem is deceptively simple. The first stanza reasonably requests quiet: silence the phone, the dog, and the pianos so that the mourners can grieve in peace and the funeral can proceed with dignity. In certain cultures there was a tradition to stop the clocks in a house when a family member had died, which makes sense emotionally. When someone close to us dies, it has a profound impact on our perception of time. Sometimes people divide their life into before and after a loved one's death. Perhaps the poet orders that the clocks be stopped so that this personal fracture in time can be observed and respected. In the stanza's last line, the poet orders the pallbearers to bring out the coffin and let the mourners come. By taking this step, the poet tries to organize all the details of the funeral arrangements in an attempt to exercise some control of a situation over which he has fundamentally no control—the death of his loved one.

In the second stanza, the poet's desire to let the world know about the enormity of his loss extends further: to a plane scribbling in the sky, crepe bows around the necks of doves, and black gloves on the traffic policemen.

There is a profound need among mourners to have their grief acknowledged. I learned this personally and viscerally when my father died. Though not an observant Jew, I went to the synagogue in Johannesburg he had attended and, at the appropriate times in the service, stood up with my fellow mourners to say the ritual Jewish prayer of mourning—the Kaddish. As I stood up to read, other members of the community looked at me, their faces grave and earnest, nodding as they caught my eye as if to say in ways both subtle and powerful, "I know how you are feeling. I am sorry for your loss." The most surprising thing to me about this ritual was the enormous comfort that I derived from others acknowledging my loss, even if just for a moment and in some small way perhaps even feeling it. So why would one not want to have it scribbled all over the sky instead of in small print on some obituary page? Why should the public doves and traffic policemen not show some sign of respect? We all know they won't, but it's part of the imagination of a great poet to ask, "Why not?"

The first three lines of the third stanza describe how much the dead man meant to the mourner in terms of the four directions of the compass, the middle of the day and night, and the talk and song that makes up our daily communications. In these words I hear echoes of Elizabeth Barrett Browning describing her love in terms of its breadth and depth and height "by sun and candle-light," and considering it her "every day's most quiet need." Both poets are describing the quotidian comforts and joys of profound love, as well as the way it stretches out to encompass both space and time.

The last line of the third stanza is especially powerful. I wonder how many people who are deeply in love would feel a sense of disbelief at the loss of a loved one and say: "I thought that love would last forever: I was wrong." When it comes to the death of a loved one, time can easily fool us.

In *Four Weddings and a Funeral*, the person who dies was a vibrant middle-aged man who earlier in the evening had been dancing, making jokes, and having fun. His sudden death was unexpected and shocking. Many of us have become used to the hope that with the help of societal advances and modern medicine we will live long lives. Unexpected disasters such as the destruction of the Twin Towers upend our assurance that our loved ones will live long and healthy lives. It is no surprise that "Funeral Blues" became popular after that tragedy, when the poem was widely circulated over the Internet. I can imagine many people reflecting on their loss and thinking, "I thought that love would last forever: I was wrong." This line and the poem as a whole took on new relevance at the time of the Covid-19 pandemic.

The last stanza describes the devastating impact of a great loss on the life of a loved one. The mourner's instructions, which began so simply in the first stanza when he asked for respectful silence, now tell the entire universe to cease: the stars, the moon, the sun, and the ocean. His world has been stripped of everything, and he wants the universe to acknowledge that and be stripped of everything in sympathy: "For nothing now can ever come to any good."

Takeaways

✘ **It can be comforting to read about someone else's experience of grief.** If you are grieving (or if memories of grief are fresh), there is comfort in knowing that someone else shares those feelings, particularly when they are so creatively conveyed as in this poem. It may seem paradoxical, but observations going all the way back to ancient times indicate that people find emotional release in tragedy. Even people who are not currently going through tragedy in their own lives may find sad tales cathartic.

✘ **There is an emotional value to recognizing the impermanence of life, that death is inevitable.** This realization makes what we have more precious, including loved ones.

✘ **Great relief can come with the statement, "I thought that love would last forever; I was wrong."** Acknowledging death is part of reorienting yourself to the reality of life's transience. Saying "I was wrong" may also be valuable in your personal dealings, for example in reopening a damaged relationship.

The Poet and the Poem

W. H. Auden, poet, author, and playwright, was a leading literary influence in the twentieth century. He was born in York, England, in 1907 and raised by a physician father and a strict Anglican mother. He was admitted to Oxford University, where he began studying science and engineering, but shifted soon to English to pursue his love of poetry.

Auden's work spanned almost half a century from the late 1920s to the early 1970s and encompassed almost every verse form. His literary executor, Edward Mendelson, writes, "Auden's massive output was written with unmatched virtuosity in a vast range of verse forms, and covered an encyclopedic range of experience and emotion."

Auden moved to America in 1939, just before World War II, with his friend Christopher Isherwood, and he lived there most of his life. He befriended or collaborated with many of the most famous cultural icons of the era.

"Funeral Blues" serves as the centerpiece of a special edition of Auden's love poems (*Tell Me the Truth about Love: Ten Love Poems*) published in 1994, after the release of *Four Weddings and a Funeral*.

This small collection achieved great success, sold approximately 300,000 copies in the English-speaking world, and was translated into half a dozen other languages.

Chapter Twelve

WILL I EVER FEEL BETTER?

🌿 TIME DOES NOT BRING RELIEF
by Edna St. Vincent Millay

> Time does not bring relief; you all have lied
> Who told me time would ease me of my pain!
> I miss him in the weeping of the rain;
> I want him at the shrinking of the tide;
> The old snows melt from every mountain-side,
> And last year's leaves are smoke in every lane;
> But last year's bitter loving must remain
> Heaped on my heart, and my old thoughts abide.
> There are a hundred places where I fear
> To go,—so with his memory they brim.
> And entering with relief some quiet place
> Where never fell his foot or shone his face
> I say, "There is no memory of him here!"
> And so stand stricken, so remembering him.

I first encountered this poem in *An Unquiet Mind*, a powerful memoir in which my friend and colleague Kay Redfield Jamison recounts her struggle with manic depression. In a tragic part of the book, the author describes the sudden and shocking death of a man she loved and her long slow journey towards recovery. Some years after his

death, she was asked to speak about it and ended her talk with the
above poem by Edna St. Vincent Millay.

Compare and contrast this sonnet with "Pity me not" (page 22)
and "What lips my lips have kissed" (page 24). All three poems deal
with the loss of love, but the nature of the loss could not be more dif-
ferent. In the previous poems, romantic connections were unsatis-
factory or fleeting. In them, the poet's sense of loss is accompanied
by self-blame, as though she is saying, "What was wrong with me for
exercising such bad judgment in choosing love that left me feeling
so depleted?" By contrast, in the present poem, the poet's feelings
of loss are directed outwards, towards the man she has loved deeply,
and the resulting emptiness in her life.

Everything in the outside world evokes feelings of sadness: the
rain, the tide, the snows of winter, and the autumn leaves. These
memories do nothing to relieve the pain; rather, they compound it,
as the poet writes in the last two lines of the octet:

> But last year's bitter loving must remain
> Heaped on my heart, and my old thoughts abide.

Then comes the volta:

> There are a hundred places where I fear
> To go,—so with his memory they brim.

Even the places they never visited together evoke a sense of loss, so
pervasive is it a part of her being. Her loss is with her everywhere
she goes. So here we have a picture of a profound love for someone
deeply missed in a way that doesn't seem to get better over time.

In the opening lines the poet chastises those who have tried to
comfort her:

Time does not bring relief; you all have lied
Who told me time would ease me of my pain!

So what can be said about whether time can ease the pain of grief? And should you tell someone who is grieving that time heals all wounds? There is of course no one answer. I address this in the takeaways below.

As to my friend whose memoir first led me to this memorable poem, she wrote, "Time finally did bring relief. But it took its own, and not terribly sweet, time in doing so."

Takeaways

✘ **The reality is that for most people, time does bring relief.** They just may not want to hear that in the early phases of grief.

✘ **Holding on to your grief may be a way of holding on to your deceased loved one, keeping him or her ever present in mind.**

✘ **Consider where the person is in the grieving process before trying to offer comfort.** For someone who has just lost a loved one, saying that time will bring relief may be jarring. In the acute phase of grief, that may be unthinkable.

✘ **At a certain point, it might be appropriate and useful to address the time-dependent aspects of grief.** Questions like, "How have you been feeling?" are almost always preferred to statements like, "It's only a matter of time."

Chapter Thirteen

LOVE REMEMBERED

WHEN YOU ARE OLD
by William Butler Yeats

When you are old and grey and full of sleep,
    And nodding by the fire, take down this book,
    And slowly read, and dream of the soft look
Your eyes had once, and of their shadows deep;

How many loved your moments of glad grace,
    And loved your beauty with love false or true,
    But one man loved the pilgrim soul in you,
And loved the sorrows of your changing face;

And bending down beside the glowing bars,
    Murmur, a little sadly, how Love fled
    And paced upon the mountains overhead
And hid his face amid a crowd of stars.

I recall this famous poem from my school days in South Africa over fifty years ago, and it has stayed with me. Often, as I have seen my elderly patients nodding off in a chair or hospital bed, I have thought, "When you are old and grey and full of sleep."

Initially I thought of the poem as a bitter remonstrance by a rejected lover—until a friend told me a story that completely changed my mind about it.

Stephen was a man in his mid-fifties when he fell madly in love with Panchali, a beautiful and exotic woman. Tall and regal, with olive skin and almond eyes, she reminded him of an Asian goddess. They enjoyed an intense relationship for several months, but in the end, for reasons that were never clear, she called it off. Heartsore, he cast about for any source of comfort, and found it in this poem by Yeats. So helpful was it to him that he copied it, stuck it to his refrigerator, and read it often.

As he explained: "After Panchali rejected me, I felt badly about myself and wondered what it was about me that caused her to lose interest. Then I found Yeats' poem, and it spoke to me. There was nothing wrong with me, I concluded. The love I had offered her was pure and profound. It was she who had been unable to recognize that. The poem helped me understand that maybe someday she would realize how much she had lost—someone who could understand her more deeply than most people ever would." Stephen credits the poem with empowering him to feel better about himself and reenter the world of dating with a new sense of his own value. Here, then, is another example of how a poem can give you the right words at the right time to make a significant difference in your life.

I have stayed in touch with Stephen since his relationship with Panchali ended some twenty years ago. Not long afterwards he met a woman who did realize how much he had to offer. He married her, and they have been very happy together. Stephen developed a loving relationship with his wife's children and grandchildren and relished the experience of being part of a large, harmonious family for the first time. The couple lives a rich and adventurous life. Without knowing it, Panchali did Stephen a big favor when she rejected him. By helping Stephen realize that his love was of value, the poem provided him with a critical step in allowing him to move on. To this day, he credits Yeats' poem as having been central to that realization.

In "When You Are Old," the speaker (perhaps Yeats himself) addresses a young woman and invites her to think of some future time when she is old. In a few words he graphically sketches a sad picture of old age that includes being sleepy and slow. In that state, he suggests, she may take down a book containing this poem and reflect on his past love for her, which by then may be a distant memory. His prediction that the book containing his poem will be on her bookshelf many years down the line suggests his confidence in the longevity of his work.

In the second stanza, Yeats invites the woman to reflect on the men who loved her in past years for her beauty and charm, her "moments of glad grace." He contrasts the superficiality of their love for her, some of which might not have even been genuine, with the love shown by himself, the one man who loved "the pilgrim soul in you," and noticed "the sorrows of your changing face." These last two quotes communicate with extraordinary precision the poet's observations of his beloved. The term "pilgrim soul" is unusual and mysterious. Perhaps it refers to a desire on her part to wander afar or to make a pilgrimage to some metaphorical place within herself that she holds as dear as a shrine. Part of the fascination of the poem is that, like all great poetry, it is open to multiple interpretations.

In the last stanza, Yeats extends the image of the old woman leaning before the fire, musing sadly about "how Love fled." Why does he capitalize the word "Love"? Perhaps because he is referring to himself or perhaps because we sometimes capitalize an important abstract idea. Yeats leaves us wondering whether it is he who has fled or whether it is love itself, obscured by distant objects such as mountains or stars. Or maybe the stars are the glitterati who briefly captured her attention, distracting her from the devotion of a young and not yet famous poet, who loved her far more deeply than they ever would.

Takeaways

✘ **Sometimes being rejected is the best thing that can happen to you.** If it's not meant to be, far better to learn that sooner than later.

✘ **Don't give the person who rejects you the power to define how you see yourself.** Reclaim your self-image and self-worth (as recommended in chapter 7).

✘ **If you are capable of loving someone deeply and observing that person closely in a caring way, that is a precious gift, deserving of someone who can appreciate it.**

The Poet and the Poem

"When You Are Old" appeared in print in 1893 and is believed to have been written to the Irish actress and revolutionary Maud Gonne, who was the obsessive focus of Yeats' romantic interest for many years. He first met her in 1889, when he was twenty-three and she was eighteen months younger. He likened falling in love with her to "a sound as of a Burmese gong, an over-powering turmoil that had yet many pleasant secondary notes." He first proposed to her in 1891, but she rejected him then as well as three more times over the next decade. She went on to an unhappy marriage with an Irish revolutionary. After years of hankering for Gonne, at age fifty-one Yeats married Georgie Hyde-Lees, and they had two children together.

Yeats, who died in 1939, is regarded as one of the greatest poets of the twentieth century. He won the Nobel Prize for Literature in 1923 and was hailed by fellow poet John Masefield (see chapter 23, "Sea Fever") as the greatest living poet at that time. Another of his famous poems, "An Irish Airman Foresees His Death" can be found in chapter 43.

Chapter Fourteen

LOVE AFTER DEATH

REMEMBER
by Christina Rossetti

> Remember me when I am gone away,
>   Gone far away into the silent land;
>   When you can no more hold me by the hand,
> Nor I half turn to go yet turning stay.
> Remember me when no more day by day
>   You tell me of our future that you plann'd:
>   Only remember me; you understand
> It will be late to counsel then or pray.
> Yet if you should forget me for a while
>   And afterwards remember, do not grieve:
>   For if the darkness and corruption leave
>   A vestige of the thoughts that once I had,
> Better by far you should forget and smile
>   Than that you should remember and be sad.

What happens to us when we die? I'm not referring to our bodies, of course, but to what some might call the spirit and others might call the soul—the aspect of ourselves that gives us our unique stamp and makes us who we are. Although many people may have specific belief systems involving, for example, angels playing harps or the devil with his furnace ever blasting (and who can say they are wrong?), to the best of my knowledge there are no good data to support any particular theory.

Nevertheless, those who harbor such beliefs may derive comfort from them. The rest of us must find our comfort about the inevitable prospect of our death elsewhere. Christina Rossetti, in her famous poem "Remember," makes no claim to any specific knowledge of life after death, which she refers to as "the silent land." Yet the poem, despite its melancholic theme, is strangely comforting. At least I find it so.

The immediate focus of Rossetti's poem is not the person who dies but the one left behind. How is she or he to deal with the loss of a loved one? One clue comes from the title of the poem, "Remember," and its first line. Rituals of remembering are part of every culture. We commemorate the anniversary of a loved one's death, light candles, say prayers, and share anecdotes. Since such rituals are universal, they must meet some profound human need. In this instance, they are most likely fulfilling a deep desire to retain the connection with those who are departed.

I hadn't realized how the people we love remain alive within us until my mother passed away. Since then, she has been an astonishingly lively presence within me to such a degree that it sometimes feels almost as though she never died. I continue to get a charge from her inveterate optimism. If, for example, a vacation was for the most part dreary, the sun emerging only on the very last day, she would say, "That's good. Now we will remember the whole vacation as being sunny." If, on the other hand, the last day was rainy, she would say, "That's good. Now we don't have to feel bad that the vacation is over and can look forward to going home."

Being mindful of the continued presence of a departed loved one within is a central theme of Rossetti's poem. Stimulated by her words, I conducted an informal poll of those around me and, to my astonishment, found a world I had not realized existed—the dead within us, still alive and kicking. You might legitimately say that for a psychiatrist of forty years or more, such an omnipresent fact should not come as a surprise. Well, it did. I am excited at the prospect of a new world to explore—and if you are not already versed in this line of thinking, I hope you might be as well. For this, I have Christina Rossetti and her poem to thank.

Having the spirits of our loved ones living within us and announcing themselves as unexpectedly as someone barging into a room can be a source of comfort. A wise rabbi I know gave a sermon in which he acknowledged his joy at feeling the continued presence of a close childhood friend, who had died in his teens. His friend returned to the rabbi in dreams as he grew up, studied, and graduated, reporting periodically on his progress.

The friends I surveyed divulged no shortage of loved ones whose welcome presence was a mainstay of their daily thoughts. Often they experienced the deceased as comforting and supportive. One friend, for example, described his father's presence as follows:

> Whenever I'm doing something difficult, he comes to mind. I hear him say, "Steady now, look around, and think of what's best to do." His masterful calm presence is always with me. I felt it on a recent hike down the Grand Canyon and swimming in the tempestuous waters around Provincetown when the wind was blowing, churning up the surf. The sound of his voice and his steady words changed my whole feeling from anxiety to joyful calm. He is always with me, a resonant emotional touchstone.

Another friend, emphasizing the valued presence of a deceased loved one, remarked wryly, "Just because they're dead doesn't mean we have to kill them," and directed me to James Joyce's celebrated short story "The Dead," which accords with our present topic.

Rossetti's Petrarchan sonnet (see sidebar on page 16) offers two gifts to her beloved. In the octet, Rossetti encourages him to retain memories of their love and the experiences they shared. She reminds him that there will be many things they cannot do when she is gone, such as counsel each other, pray together, or carry out plans. But there is one very important thing that her beloved can do: retain the bond they shared as a vital presence within himself.

(At this point I should mention that I am assuming that the beloved is a male to simplify the grammar and flow. As far as I can tell, however, we don't know to whom the sonnet was written, and it is quite possible that it was not written to anyone in particular.)

At the end of the octet, Rosetti asks just one thing of her beloved: "Only remember me."

Then comes the sestet with its shift and a second gift for her loved one. Here she reassures him that she doesn't want her words to restrict or control him. If he should forget her for a while and later return to her in his thoughts, that is natural. He should not feel guilty or sad. Her primary interest is for him to be happy; her wish to have him remember her arises from that source.

One finding that emerged from my informal poll is that not everybody has the experience of the dead as a vital inner presence. One woman, for example, who had lost her twin sister some years before, said that she did not feel her sister as alive inside her—just one huge empty hole in her life which her sister used to occupy.

Can the enlivening spirit of our departed be cultivated and developed within us, and would there be some value in doing so? Rossetti's poem convinces me that it can be done.

On reflection, I realize that it was also what my mother sought to do when she realized that she was declining slowly as a result of progressive heart failure. She decided to crochet afghans for her children, grandchildren, nieces, and nephews, using their favorite colors. I vividly remember our trip to the wool store in a rundown section of Johannesburg, which she explained had the best selection, to pick the colors for my afghan. Its brilliant hues retain a special place in the home, where it serves as a regular reminder of her vibrant personality.

When my mother died, and my sisters and I went to find her will, alongside it was a letter far more precious than any material things she could have left us. She told us in the letter how much she loved us, how proud she was of us, and how confident she was that we could accomplish what we set out to do in life. I keep her letter in my desk drawer as a constant source of comfort and inspiration to be my best self. In thinking of her letter, I am reminded of the words of the famous nineteenth-century British novelist George Eliot, who wrote: "I like not only to be loved, but also to be told that I am loved; the realm of silence is large enough beyond the grave."

What Rossetti is doing in her famous sonnet "Remember" (and what each of us can do in our own way) is to bridge that gap between this world and that silent land, thereby infusing our enlivening spirit in those of us who remain.

Takeaways

✘ **Memories of our loved ones generally stay with us, and can serve as a source of comfort and joy.** Consider cultivating these memories and thereby soften the pain of their loss. This can be done in many ways, including talking about them with people who knew them, writing about them, and making a point of thinking about them.

✘ If you sense that you are approaching the end of your life, consider leaving meaningful keepsakes for your loved ones, including perhaps a note along with your will, to comfort them when they need it the most.

✘ Part of loving someone is giving your loved one permission to move on after you are gone.

The Poet and the Poem

"Remember" invites comparison with "How Do I Love Thee?", featured earlier in this section. They were published almost in the same year (the former in 1849, the latter in 1850). Both are the works of brilliant women who had evidenced their prodigious talent from childhood. Both poems are perfectly crafted Petrarchan sonnets that can be found in many anthologies. But it is also informative to consider their differences.

Although it is hard to believe, Rossetti's poem was published when she was only nineteen years old, while Barrett Browning's was the work of a woman in her mid-forties. Although both poems are about love, Barrett Browning's describes the blissful experience of being deeply in love, while Rossetti's focuses on the loss of love and is tinged with melancholy. Unsurprisingly, Rossetti suffered from bouts of depression from her mid-teens onward. She had three suitors of record, and was engaged to one of them, but ended all three relationships for one reason or another.

If you listen to "Remember" being recited online (as I encourage you to do; it has also been set to music), you will appreciate the power of this poem to heal and inspire. Notwithstanding her bouts of depression, or perhaps because of them, Rossetti cared deeply for others and was especially attuned to those who suffered. Besides writing extensively, she volunteered for over a decade at a London refuge for former prostitutes. She opposed slavery, the exploitation of underage girls, and cruelty to animals. She had a wide circle of friends and associations with fellow writers. In short, she is a poet and a person worth remembering.

PART TWO

That Inward Eye

They flash upon that inward eye
Which is the bliss of solitude.

—William Wordsworth

Chapter Fifteen

TRANSCENDENCE IN NATURE

DAFFODILS
by William Wordsworth

> I wandered lonely as a cloud
> That floats on high o'er vales and hills,
> When all at once I saw a crowd,
> A host, of golden daffodils;
> Beside the lake, beneath the trees,
> Fluttering and dancing in the breeze.
>
> Continuous as the stars that shine
> And twinkle on the Milky Way,
> They stretched in never-ending line
> Along the margin of a bay:
> Ten thousand saw I at a glance,
> Tossing their heads in sprightly dance.
>
> The waves beside them danced, but they
> Out-did the sparkling waves in glee:
> A Poet could not but be gay,
> In such a jocund company:
> I gazed—and gazed—but little thought
> What wealth the show to me had brought:

(continued)

For oft, when on my couch I lie
In vacant or in pensive mood,
They flash upon that inward eye
Which is the bliss of solitude;
And then my heart with pleasure fills,
And dances with the daffodils.

Wordsworth's "Daffodils" is a great favorite for anthologies and in popular culture. In 2004, 150,000 British students read the poem aloud amidst celebrations of the bicentennial anniversary of its publication.

You may ask what is so special about the poem.

To answer this question, read it to yourself with fresh eyes, as though you are seeing it for the first time. Then read it aloud.

What images came to mind as you read it, and how did it make you feel? It is in the answer to these two questions that I believe the fame of the poem resides.

Let's start with the first two lines:

I wandered lonely as a cloud
That floats on high o'er vales and hills.

How does a cloud feel when it floats high up all by itself? How do the lines make *you* feel?

Then consider the next two lines.

When all at once I saw a crowd,
A host, of golden daffodils.

Now how do you feel?

I don't know about you, but somehow for me, even after reading the first two lines many times, the word "lonely," tempered by the word "floats," evokes a peaceful, untroubled state.

The second two lines communicate that flash of pleasure when all at once something of surprising beauty darts into your field of vision.

Then the pace of the poem picks up. In a few words, the poet communicates both the profusion of the daffodils and how alive they seem.

> Ten thousand saw I at a glance,
> Tossing their heads in sprightly dance.

Once again, Wordsworth communicates his own feelings to us in response to this natural marvel:

> A Poet could not but be gay,
> In such a jocund company.

The poet refers to the daffodils here, not as things, but as living beings, "jocund company." The poet takes his time to drink in and store this natural wonder and the emotions it evokes. Even so, as he tells us, little did he realize at the time what wealth this experience had brought to him.

He then shifts the scene to his couch where he lies "in vacant or in pensive mood" and tells us how

> They flash upon that inward eye
> Which is the bliss of solitude.

That in turn energizes him with the dance of the daffodils, and his heart fills with pleasure and once again he dances with them.

Note the distinction between *solitude*, a blissful state of being on one's own, as compared with the painful state of *loneliness*, which I describe elsewhere. Being alone can be either blissful or painful, depending on how you view it.

Consider two alternating emotional states—serenity and vibrancy— as they travel through the poet's description of the daffodils and again as he contemplates them later.

Such variations in consciousness are typical of transcendence, the signature state of consciousness experienced during Transcendental Meditation (TM). Having practiced TM for some years now, I am happily familiar with this highly enjoyable state of consciousness.

In his masterpiece, *The Varieties of Religious Experience*, William James wrote:

> Our normal waking consciousness . . . is but one special type of consciousness, whilst all about it, parted from it by the filmiest of screens, there lie potential forms of consciousness entirely different. We may go through life without suspecting their existence; but apply the requisite stimulus and at a touch they are all there in all their completeness.

The requisite stimulus could be a mantra (a special sound chosen to produce a meditative state) or a great poem, such as this one. Further descriptions of transcendence can be found in Wordsworth's "Lines Composed a Few Miles above Tintern Abbey" (which I present in chapter 17) and in the following excerpt by the ancient Chinese philosopher Lao Tzu in his classic work the *Tao Te Ching*:

> Become totally empty
> Quiet the restlessness of the mind

Only then will you witness everything
    unfolding from emptiness
See all the things flourish and dance
    in endless variation
And once again merge back into perfect emptiness.

What an amazing example of this variegated state of consciousness "Daffodils" offers! To an ordinary person, Wordsworth's walk might have seemed commonplace. Yet thanks to his genius, here we are, over two hundred years later, enjoying the spectacle through his eyes and mind, and resonating with his capacity to experience its effects again and again.

To further examine the therapeutic effects of Wordsworth's poetry, let us consider the curious case of John Stuart Mill, the famous nineteenth-century British philosopher. Mill had fallen into a depression from which he saw no escape until he started reading Wordsworth's poetry. In his autobiography, Mill called it "a medicine for the mind," which cured his depression. He attributed this effect not only to the poet's descriptions of nature's beauty but also to his sensitive responses to nature. They offered Mill a model for how he might also respond to, and derive benefits from, natural beauty. After reading "Daffodils" many times, I agree that Wordsworth's poems have the remarkable ability to soothe and enliven. What do you think?

Takeaways

✗ Poetry inspired by natural settings can evoke feelings in the reader corresponding to those in the poet, which may change the reader's mood or state of consciousness.

✖ In some instances, these changes may be profound enough to lessen anxiety or depression.

✖ Responsiveness to the natural world can be cultivated to good effect, and poetry is one way to do so.

The Poet and the Poem

William Wordsworth (1770–1850) was a prominent British poet whose long life straddled the eighteenth and nineteenth centuries. His early years were marked by a mixture of privilege, love, loss, and access to great natural beauty. His father was an assistant to a British earl, Sir James Lowther, and the family lived in an imposing house.

Wordsworth, the second of five children, was particularly close to his younger sister, Dorothy. His mother died when he was seven, and he and Dorothy were separated and did not see each other again for nine long years. His father died when he was thirteen.

Wordsworth described himself as a child of "stiff, moody, and violent temper," who resented every slight as a reminder of his dependent status. When he spent time at his mother's parents' house, his unpleasant interactions with his grandparents and uncle distressed him to such a degree that he contemplated suicide.

In contrast, Wordsworth's school days were happy. He roamed freely around the Lake District, boating on Windermere Lake and Coniston Water, skating, bird nesting, nutting, walking through the fells, and riding. In later life, he recognized that these experiences had filled his mind with images of the natural world. He railed against the overemphasis on book learning in educating children, describing himself as "one who spent half of his boyhood in running wild among the Mountains." The importance of childhood to later development is captured by Wordsworth's famous line, "The child is father of the man."

After school, Wordsworth graduated from Cambridge University.

He visited France in 1790 in the midst of the French Revolution, and fell in love with Annette Vallon, by whom he had a daughter, Caroline. The declaration of war between Britain and France in 1793 separated the two, but Wordsworth acknowledged his daughter and took financial responsibility for her.

When Wordsworth was twenty-five, he received an inheritance that enabled him to live with Dorothy. In the same year, he met Samuel Taylor Coleridge, a fellow poet with whom he was to establish a lasting friendship of mutual intellectual support. In that same year, he published lyrical ballads and began writing *The Prelude*, an epic autobiographical poem that he would revise throughout his life and would only be published posthumously, in 1850.

In 1802, Wordsworth married his childhood friend Mary Hutchinson, with whom he had five children. Two died in childhood, and a third, Dora, passed away in 1847, which was a particular blow for him. At age seventy-three, he became England's poet laureate and held that position until his death in 1850.

"Daffodils" was inspired by a walk that Wordsworth and Dorothy took in England's Lake District. Dorothy later made a journal entry in which she described coming across "a long belt of them along the shore, about the breadth of a country turnpike road." In her journal, Dorothy described elements that found their way into Wordsworth's poem: the heads of the daffodils that "tossed and reeled and danced and seemed as they verily laughed with the wind." Later Wordsworth's wife, Mary, contributed some key lines to the poem—including the penultimate two lines, which he acknowledged were the finest in the poem:

> They flash upon that inward eye
> Which is the bliss of solitude.

"Daffodils," published in *Poems, in Two Volumes*, was initially harshly reviewed by his peers but subsequently praised. That should give heart to poets whose work is panned at the outset.

Special credit for Wordsworth's poetry should go to the Lake District, a large and glorious region in the north of England. Wordsworth lived there for several years in Dove Cottage, now a tourist site for visitors. I visited Dove Cottage once in autumn many years ago, accompanied by a few friends. All around the trees were ablaze with the red, orange, and green leaves of the season. One of my friends, who has never aspired to be a poet, remarked, "If I lived here surrounded by such beauty, even I could write poetry."

Chapter Sixteen

THE MEMORY OF DAFFODILS

⋘ MIRACLE ON ST. DAVID'S DAY
by Gillian Clarke

All you need to know about this poem is that it is a true story. It happened in the '70s, and it took me years to find a way to write the poem.

"They flash upon that inward eye
which is the bliss of solitude."
(from "The Daffodils" by William Wordsworth)

An afternoon yellow and open-mouthed
with daffodils. The sun treads the path
among cedars and enormous oaks.
It might be a country house, guests strolling,
the rumps of gardeners between nursery shrubs.

I am reading poetry to the insane.
An old woman, interrupting, offers
as many buckets of coal as I need.
A beautiful chestnut-haired boy listens
entirely absorbed. A schizophrenic

on a good day, they tell me later.
In a cage of first March sun a woman
sits not listening, not feeling.
In her neat clothes the woman is absent.
A big, mild man is tenderly led

(continued)

to his chair. He has never spoken.
His labourer's hands on his knees, he rocks
gently to the rhythms of the poems.
I read to their presences, absences,
to the big, dumb labouring man as he rocks.

He is suddenly standing, silently,
huge and mild, but I feel afraid. Like slow
movement of spring water or the first bird
of the year in the breaking darkness,
the labourer's voice recites "The Daffodils."

The nurses are frozen, alert; the patients
seem to listen. He is hoarse but word-perfect.
Outside the daffodils are still as wax,
a thousand, ten thousand, their syllables
unspoken, their creams and yellows still.

Forty years ago, in a Valleys school,
the class recited poetry by rote.
Since the dumbness of misery fell
he has remembered there was a music
of speech and that once he had something to say.

When he's done, before the applause, we observe
the flowers' silence. A thrush sings
and the daffodils are flame.

The staff of a psychiatric hospital has invited Clarke to visit and read
poetry to the patients. It is St. David's Day, March 1, the day to com-
memorate the patron saint of Wales, who famously said, "Do ye the

little things in life." The daffodils are out in bloom, and celebrations of St. David's Day all over Wales are festooned with the traditional daffodils.

Clarke has a good eye for the telling detail. Her descriptions are vivid and full of contrasts. The old woman, who offers her "as many buckets of coal as I need," is confused of mind but generous of spirit. Clarke refers to one woman as sitting in "a cage of first March sun . . . not listening, not feeling." Despite the beauty of the day, she is trapped inside her mind.

I can see part of the difficulty Clarke must have faced in telling the story. Should she use the language of the 1970s, which would now be unacceptable, or current terminology, which is more clinical and considerate? Yet in communicating how the mentally ill were treated back then, the poet's language is accurate, and I recall those inconsiderate terms used freely when I was a junior psychiatrist.

Clarke's attention now shifts to the central focus of the poem, "a big, mild man," who is "tenderly led to his chair." He was a laborer who had not said a word in ten years. Then Clarke starts to read. At first we see the big man, sitting in his chair as "he rocks gently to the rhythm of the poems." Then:

He is suddenly standing, silently,
Huge and mild, but I feel afraid.

I can relate to the fear that this large, silent man might strike in the poet. Instead she describes a "miracle." The laborer recites "The Daffodils." He is hoarse, presumably from not speaking for years, but word-perfect.

Briefly Clarke shifts back to the daffodils outside. Unlike Wordsworth's dancing, vibrant daffodils, the ones outside the mental hospital are "still as wax," reflecting the stillness of the people inside the hospital walls. Like the large man, they are silent, "their syllables unspoken."

Perhaps the poet waited so long to write the poem in part because she needed something to bring all of its elements together. For that, we have the daffodils—in bloom and in poetry—to thank for helping her pull the story together so beautifully.

Perhaps it was those daffodils, in all their different forms, that flashed upon the inward eye (or ear) of the tall, lumbering laborer. In the solitude of his mutism, the poem might have awakened some memory of a time long past when children were taught to learn poems by heart at school, and helped him find his voice.

Takeaways

✖ **There is great value to memorizing poetry.** As a simple exercise, try to memorize your favorite poem or poems. You never know when they might become a resource on which you may wish to draw.

✖ **If anyone you know seems shut in, for example by a stroke or dementia, remember that there may well be a sentient being trapped behind the unresponsive facade, and treat that person accordingly.** Also, try to activate in that person some locked up inner source of vibrancy. For example, playing the music of their youth can release surprising displays of joy and vitality that, as with the laborer in the poem, might seem like a miracle. Poetry might well have the same effect.

The Poet and the Poem

Gillian Clarke is a prominent Welsh poet and playwright who was brought up speaking English. She has been honored for her work by being named the third National Poet of Wales and awarded the Queen's Gold Medal for Poetry.

Her poetry is studied by students throughout the United Kingdom, and her work has been translated into ten languages. She has written sixteen books.

In seeking permission to use Clarke's poem in this book, I contacted her directly. Without contract, negotiation, fees, or hesitation, she replied, "Do use it. That's what poetry is for."

"Do ye the little things," I thought.

Chapter Seventeen

TRANSCENDENCE IN BODY AND MIND

LINES COMPOSED A FEW MILES ABOVE TINTERN ABBEY (EXCERPT)
by William Wordsworth

These beauteous forms,
Through a long absence, have not been to me
As is a landscape to a blind man's eye:
But oft, in lonely rooms, and 'mid the din
Of towns and cities, I have owed to them,
In hours of weariness, sensations sweet,
Felt in the blood, and felt along the heart;
And passing even into my purer mind
With tranquil restoration:—feelings too
Of unremembered pleasure: such, perhaps,
As have no slight or trivial influence
On that best portion of a good man's life,
His little, nameless, unremembered, acts
Of kindness and of love. Nor less, I trust,
To them I may have owed another gift,
Of aspect more sublime; that blessed mood,
In which the burthen of the mystery,
In which the heavy and the weary weight
Of all this unintelligible world,
Is lightened:—that serene and blessed mood,
In which the affections gently lead us on,—
Until, the breath of this corporeal frame

And even the motion of our human blood
Almost suspended, we are laid asleep
In body, and become a living soul:
While with an eye made quiet by the power
Of harmony, and the deep power of joy,
We see into the life of things.

. . .

And I have felt
A presence that disturbs me with the joy
Of elevated thoughts; a sense sublime
Of something far more deeply interfused,
Whose dwelling is the light of setting suns,
And the round ocean and the living air,

. . .

All thinking things, all objects of all thought,
And rolls through all things.

Not long ago, I was chatting with some friends out on the deck. The day was surprisingly warm for late autumn. My attention drifted towards the Carolina jasmine draped across the pergola when I heard their conversation turn angrily towards politics, about which we were always arguing.

I heard the blast of a distant trumpet calling me to war. Instead of firing into the melee, I said, "Let's not talk politics today."

The sun shone through the Carolina jasmine, still nursing a few late blooms, and I slipped back into my transcendent reverie. We had a pleasant afternoon, uninterrupted by discord. I realized that I had changed a long-standing reflexive pattern of behavior. To paraphrase neurologist Viktor Frankl, a space had opened up in my mind between stimulus and response, and in that space I was able to make a thoughtful decision.

That experience comes to mind in connection with "Tintern Abbey," in which Wordsworth revisits a natural setting last seen five years earlier at age twenty-three, when he was feeling troubled. Viewing this scene again sends Wordsworth into a reverie or transcendent state in which his present thoughts and feelings mingle with those felt five years earlier and the effects this scene had on him in the intervening years.

Tintern Abbey is simply the port of entry into his reverie and search for lost time, much as the tea-soaked madeleine was for Proust. This poem presents a stream of consciousness over a hundred years before the great exponents of that craft emerged in the twentieth century.

Note how elements of consciousness shift between the physical and emotional, the contemplative and lively, just as we have seen in "Daffodils." Also, see if you feel any changes in your own state of awareness, emotional or physical, as you read the lines excerpted above.

After describing the landscape, familiar to him from his earlier visit—the rolling waters of mountain springs, the lofty cliffs, trees, and hedgerows—Wordsworth goes on to express gratitude for the salutary effects of his earlier trip during the five years past when he has been "in lonely rooms, and 'mid the din of towns and cities." He has felt these effects physically in the form of "sensations sweet," as well as in the blood and heart, which have provided him with "tranquil restoration" in hours of weariness. The physical aspects of transcendence often refresh and reinvigorate.

Once again we see the elements that make Wordsworth a unique poetic healer. He has a marvelous ability to perceive his environment, feel its effects on his body and mind, and translate those effects into words so as to enable the reader to experience them as well and derive their attendant benefits.

Wordsworth then chronicles the emotional aspects of his transcendent state, such as "unremembered pleasure." He observes that feeling good helps us be good to others in "little, nameless, unremembered, acts / Of kindness and of love."

The poet goes on to explore the mind-body effects of the experience:

> Of aspect more sublime; that blessed mood,
> In which the burthen of the mystery,
> In which the heavy and the weary weight
> Of all this unintelligible world,
> Is lightened.

Here the poet marvels at the mystery of how such an experience of nature can relieve life's burdens. Then he shifts back to his body, where it seems as though the motion of the blood and breath are "almost suspended." Even as the body settles down, however, the mind awakens with joy and insight:

> While with an eye made quiet by the power
> Of harmony, and the deep power of joy,
> We see into the life of things.

In the second excerpt, which occurs a little further down in the poem, the poet describes "the joy / Of elevated thoughts; a sense sublime." This brings to mind the pleasure of observing the ordinary elements of nature, which become extraordinary when filtered through the eyes of a master poet:

the light of setting suns,
And the round ocean and the living air.

In "Tintern Abbey," Wordsworth communicates many elements that are found in states of transcendence: physical relaxation, renewal and revitalization, improved mood, mystical experience, profound insights, and elation which merges with wondrous elements of the cosmos, just as in the quote by Lao Tzu included in the chapter on "Daffodils."

Takeaways

✘ **Getting in touch with nature can benefit consciousness and improve your life.** Nature has powerful effects on both body and spirit.

✘ **There is a relationship between our responses to poetry and to the natural world.** Nature inspires poetry, which in turn deepens our appreciation of nature.

✘ **Recollections of nature and poetry can be a continuing source of healing, inspiration, and joy long after our initial experience.** The intertwined sound and meaning of the poem stays in mind and body and strengthens our experience of what the poem describes.

Chapter Eighteen

THE POWER OF DARK AND LIGHT

✿ THERE'S A CERTAIN SLANT OF LIGHT
by Emily Dickinson

There's a certain Slant of light,
Winter Afternoons —
That oppresses, like the Heft
Of Cathedral Tunes —

Heavenly Hurt, it gives us —
We can find no scar,
But internal difference —
Where the Meanings, are —

None may teach it — Any —
'Tis the seal Despair —
An imperial affliction
Sent us of the Air —

When it comes, the Landscape listens —
Shadows — hold their breath —
When it goes, 'tis like the Distance
On the look of Death —

I first encountered this poem when it fell out of a letter I opened. It was 1981, and I was a junior psychiatric associate at the National

Institute of Mental Health (NIMH), opening thousands of letters
from people all over the United States who had responded to a news-
paper ad seeking people with recurrent winter depressions. At the
time, the condition of seasonal affective disorder (SAD) had not yet
been recognized, and there was a fair amount of skepticism about
the idea. So when Dickinson's poem tumbled out of one of the let-
ters, I appreciated it not only for its artistry, but also as validation of
the condition I was to study for much of my professional life.

"A certain Slant of light": what is it about the light in winter that
some people find oppressive? Some might say shorter days or grey
skies, but few would likely comment on "a certain Slant of light."
Yet it is this angle of the sun to the earth that is the very essence of
winter, as the earth tilts away from the sun in its annual orbit. So, in
the very first line, we see elements of what makes Emily Dickinson
a great poet: originality of insight, and the ability to penetrate to the
core of a concept in just a few words.

The second two lines reveal another astute observation: A direct
link between the outside world and an internal response. We learn
that the "certain Slant of light" oppresses her and reminds her of the
"Heft of Cathedral Tunes."

The next stanza begins with a mysterious oxymoron: "Heavenly
Hurt." Is Dickinson implying that some aspects of religion may be pain-
ful? Or does she mean, more simply, that cathedrals are dark places,
where somebody with SAD might feel depressed? I for one recall long
hours of sitting in a dark synagogue, longing to be playing outdoors.

Dickinson goes on to observe that although the pain of the win-
ter afternoon is real,

> We can find no scar,
> But internal difference —
> Where the Meanings, are —

The first line reminds me of the poignant regrets that patients with emotional problems often express—that there is no external sign to indicate their pain. As a consequence, they do not get the type of understanding their suffering warrants, which would be forthcoming if they had a cast on their leg or were missing a limb. At a deeper level, they themselves often don't validate the legitimacy of their own suffering as they might if they could find a scar.

Yet Dickinson is not bound by convention and trusts her inner experiences regardless of what others might think or feel. She is in tune with that part of herself that registers "internal difference — / Where the Meanings, are." At the time when Dickinson was writing, in the late nineteenth century, scientists had not yet discovered where meanings (or emotional responses) are registered in the brain. Now there is considerable evidence that emotions are localized to certain brain regions, for example pleasure to the nucleus accumbens and fear to the amygdala.

After identifying this hidden pain, relating it to light, and suggesting a deep-seated place where the pain is registered, she begins the next stanza with: "None may teach it — Any —."

At the time Dickinson was writing, nobody knew about SAD; therefore none could teach it. But to someone who was in tune with her own feelings, including the effects of light on mood, like the poet herself, anybody could teach it.

Dickinson goes on to describe it:

> 'Tis the seal Despair —
> An imperial affliction
> Sent us of the Air —

The feeling of oppression arrives like a letter embossed with a seal marked "Despair," like an affliction sent by an emperor.

The mysterious last stanza captures the sense of suspended animation that accompanies the paralysis of winter depression and the difficulty of remembering what it was like when it passes.

If Dickinson felt "heavenly hurt" on winter afternoons, how did she feel at other times of year? Fortunately we have some clues in her poems. Consider spring, for example:

> I cannot meet the Spring unmoved —
> I feel the old desire —A Hurry with a lingering, mixed,
> A Warrant to be fair —

We see here a tension between the urge to move forward and the inertia of wanting to stay behind, a mixture of hurry and lingering seen also in the opening lines of T. S. Eliot's famous poem *The Waste Land,* in which he observes how April is "the cruelest month . . . mixing memory and desire."

For both Dickinson and Eliot, spring is a tricky season. Just as it is a time of adjustment in nature, so it is for many people.

If Dickinson feels any ambivalence about spring, it disappears in summer as she compares herself to a drunken bee:

> Inebriate of Air — am I —
> And Debauchee of Dew —
> Reeling — thro' endless summer days —
> From Inns of Molten Blue —

Takeaways

✖ **Experience the light around you**. Experience how the light changes across the day and with the seasons, how it is softened by grass and trees and greenery, intensified by vast skies and desert, and reflected off rivers, lakes, and oceans. An awareness of the changing light can add joy and drama to every day.

✗ **Experience how changes in light, weather, and your physical environment influence your mood.** On dreary days, when it is difficult to go outdoors, notice how bringing extra light into your environment can increase your energy and spirits. Conversely, even when your indoor light is adequate, notice how time spent outdoors, especially when combined with exercise, can be bracing and enlivening. If you have troubles with the changing seasons, there is now an extensive literature that can help you address them.

✗ **Observe how bright light in the morning can get you going and help you start the day with a spring in your stride.** Likewise, soft light in the evening can help you wind down and get a good night's sleep. Correctly used, exposure to bright light and darkness at different times of day can strengthen your circadian rhythms. Internal clocks, which respond to the timing of light and darkness, govern these daily rhythms and influence many functions that can make your daily activities more efficient and enjoyable. In fact, there is a biological clock in every cell in the body, all of which are controlled by a master clock in the brain.

The Poet and the Poem

Dickinson's poetry was unconventional when she wrote it and even now is so distinctive that her poems are readily recognizable. They are short and untitled, with characteristic punctuation—notably, long dashes instead of commas and periods—and idiosyncratic capitalization. Moreover, her rhyme scheme is unusual for its mixed use of regular and slant rhymes—words that almost rhyme but are just a little off.

Much has been written about Emily Dickinson. She was born in 1830 to a prominent family in Amherst, Massachusetts, was surrounded by friends and family, but never married. Her paternal grandfather founded Amherst College, and her father, a successful lawyer, went on to become treasurer of the college. Emily was the middle child in this close-knit family, with an older brother, Austin, and a younger sister, Lavinia.

Although she wrote prolifically (eighteen hundred poems in all), only ten of them were published during her lifetime, heavily edited to conform to the conventions of the day. Her poems are startlingly original, passionate, and confessional, which stand in stark contrast to her secluded life.

She was apparently not always so isolated, writing at age twenty, "Amherst is alive with fun this winter . . . Oh, a very great town this is." But she appears also to have been subject to depression.

Dickinson had close friends, but her most affectionate relationship was with her sister-in-law Susan Gilbert, to whom she wrote hundreds of letters. In one, written in 1852, she wrote:

Susie, will you indeed come home next Saturday, and be my own again, and kiss me . . . I hope for you so much, and feel so eager for you, feel that I cannot wait, feel that now I must have you—that the expectation once more to see your face again, makes me feel hot and feverish, and my heart beats so fast . . . my darling, so near I seem to you, that I disdain this pen, and wait for a warmer language.

Dickinson's much discussed tendency to seclusion started shortly thereafter, and the very next year she wrote, "I do not go far from home." That tendency deepened to the point that she would greet friends from the top of the stairs or from behind half-closed doors.

While different psychiatric explanations for her withdrawal have been suggested (and psychiatric diagnoses made postmortem are essentially conjectures), I would suggest that her symptoms are typical of agoraphobia. For people with this condition, venturing out is associated with anxiety, so they tend to avoid going outdoors. Nowadays this condition is eminently treatable by cognitive behavior therapy, sometimes along with medications.

Dickinson died of kidney disease at age fifty-five. After her death, her sister found hundreds of poems written over the years. Since the first volume of her poems appeared in 1890, Dickinson's reputation has soared, and she is now regarded as one of the greatest American poets. Two other of her works appear in this collection (see chapters 25 and 49).

Chapter Nineteen

IN PRAISE OF DIVERSITY

PIED BEAUTY
by Gerard Manley Hopkins

> Glory be to God for dappled things—
>   For skies of couple-colour as a brinded cow;
>   For rose-moles all in stipple upon trout that swim;
> Fresh-firecoal chestnut-falls; finches' wings;
>   Landscape plotted and pieced—fold, fallow, and plough;
>   And áll trádes, their gear and tackle and trim.
>
> All things counter, original, spare, strange;
>   Whatever is fickle, freckled (who knows how?)
>   With swift, slow; sweet, sour; adazzle, dim;
> He fathers-forth whose beauty is past change:
>   Praise him.

About 150 years ago a Jesuit monk who had taken the customary vows of poverty, chastity, and obedience quietly wrote some of the most memorable, original, and brilliant poems of the nineteenth century. I have included two of his most famous poems, both short, powerful, and crafted with the intricate beauty of a Fabergé egg. (The second poem is in the following chapter.)

Hopkins innovated what he called *sprung rhythm*, turning away from the other types of rhythms used by great poets. As we have seen, these often consist of feet containing two syllables, the second of which is usually accented. In sprung rhythm, Hopkins accents the first syllable and allows a variable number of beats in each foot. I encourage you to read his poems aloud, which will bring out the effect of their unusual rhythms, powerful alliteration, and word combinations.

"Pied Beauty" starts with a simple line reminiscent of a hymn: "Glory be to God for dappled things."

For a Jesuit priest to praise the Lord in a poem would be nothing out of the ordinary, but why for "dappled things"? For that matter, what *are* "dappled things"? The dictionary defines *dappled* as "marked with spots or rounded patches." That is consistent with the title of the poem, in which two words are strangely juxtaposed: "pied," which means having two or more different colors, and "beauty." What is beautiful about being dappled?

This theme continues through the first stanza, in which the poet extends his blessing to other creatures that bear this feature: a "brinded" cow, meaning one with patchy coloring, and trout that have rose-colored moles on their skin. The word "moles" is often used to describe skin elevations that may signal illness. We often feel a certain gut-level aversion to such elevations, probably out of fear of contagion. Yet here we are led to see the beauty of naturally stippled "trout that swim."

In the second stanza, Hopkins goes on to include things (and, we can infer, people) who are different or unusual in some way. Consider the four adjectives in the first line and note how carefully they are chosen. "Counter" means "opposite," as in someone who takes an opposite position or point of view or someone who leads an alternative lifestyle. "Original" could mean someone who thinks or acts differently, which might be unwelcome in a system that expects people to conform to certain norms. "Spare" connotes something or someone who is redundant, extra, or unnecessary. Finally, "strange" is someone or something that could be off-putting, because he, she, or it seems alien or perhaps threatening. Hopkins praises all these outcasts.

In the second line, Hopkins extends this category to whatever is "fickle," which the dictionary defines as "changing frequently, especially as regards one's loyalties, interests or affection," a quality not generally admired in a world that values the steadfast; and "freckled," which brings us back to the theme of different colors. Then Hopkins adds in parentheses, almost as a throwaway, "Who knows how?" acknowledging that we don't know how things or people come to differ from one another in their appearance or nature.

Hopkins then praises the endless variety of opposing attributes like 'swift, slow; sweet, sour; adazzle, dim,' created by God, 'whose singular beauty is past change.

Hopkins ends the poem very simply with two words: "Praise him," which echo the opening line, thereby closing the circle on the poem as a hymn.

Although I first read this poem many years ago, I still marvel at how much Hopkins has packed into these eleven short lines. My understanding of the poem has deepened gradually over time, perhaps as the understanding of diversity has evolved in me personally and in our culture over the past several decades. When I first read the poem, I thought that Hopkins was simply finding beauty in unexpected places. And he is. But he is specifically celebrating the beauty of diversity. By "dappled," he means not only of different colors but things that won't fit simply into one category because they are out of the mainstream, ambiguous, indeterminate, and different. Perhaps Hopkins felt that difference, unacceptable and suppressed in many societies (including nineteenth-century Britain), and yearned for the acceptance (and even celebration) of diversity that is beginning to emerge today. We are slowly waking up to the vast spectrum of human experience and its profuse range of identities, cultures, ethnicities, expressions of gender and sexuality, that make today's society more interesting and successful.

It is clear that this short poem is informed by deep thought on the part of the poet. He has looked into nature and perhaps himself and has extracted a central truth over a century before the rest of the world caught up with him. I should add that different cultures have been quicker or slower to catch up with modern Western ideas of diversity, and some hardly have at all. Even today people who fall outside accepted norms risk persecution or death in certain cultures. Many of these cultures pray to God, though, one might suspect, not in praise of "Pied Beauty." For the millions of people who have read the poem in the years since it was written, it has perhaps served as a stealth message: "You are all creatures of God, beautiful in your own way."

Takeaways

✘ **For those of you who feel different in some way, you are not alone.** Diversity is part of nature, and different creatures will thrive in different conditions. In fact, some people who have been considered outcasts have made critical contributions to the arts, sciences, and other areas.

✘ **For those of you who succeed in the mainstream because you have qualities that are generally admired and rewarded, remember that not everybody has those advantages.** Try to appreciate differences among individuals. Also recognize that people are not all one way or another. They are often mixtures of different qualities—dappled.

✗ For those of you who are different in some way from the mainstream, remember that being different sometimes gives you a privileged perspective on a situation or problem, and potential solutions, discoveries, and inventions. So make the most of your differences, and enjoy their advantages. Also, seek out people who will appreciate those differences and help you create an environment in which you can thrive.

Chapter Twenty

A PLEA TO SAVE THE NATURAL WORLD

꧁ INVERSNAID

by Gerard Manley Hopkins

This darksome burn, horseback brown,
His rollrock highroad roaring down,
In coop and in comb the fleece of his foam
Flutes and low to the lake falls home.

A windpuff-bonnet of fáwn-fróth
Turns and twindles over the broth
Of a pool so pitchblack, féll-frówning,
It rounds and rounds Despair to drowning.

Degged with dew, dappled with dew
Are the groins of the braes that the brook treads through,
Wiry heathpacks, flitches of fern,
And the beadbonny ash that sits over the burn.

What would the world be, once bereft
Of wet and of wildness? Let them be left,
O let them be left, wildness and wet;
Long live the weeds and the wilderness yet.

Inversnaid is a small village in the Highlands of Scotland in which
the poet spent some time. The first three stanzas describe different

views of a powerful mountain stream and its wild, rustic surround-
ings, just as an artist might paint three different pictures. In the
first, the river is seen rushing down; in the second, we see it churn-
ing up a pool, and the third shows the countryside through which
the waters rush. Note how the tone and rhythm changes across the
first three stanzas—fast and rollicking in the first stanza, slow and
ponderous in the second, and vibrant in the third.

The language is sprinkled with Scottish terms such as "burn,"
meaning "brook"; "coop," an enclosed hollow; "comb," meaning
"water running freely"; and "braes," which are hills. We also see
some compound words invented by Hopkins. "Rollrock" conveys
a sense of a stream so powerful that it rolls rocks along its course,
which reminds him of a high road with its traffic. Likewise, "heath-
packs" refers to the heather packed down, and "beadbonny" gives a
sense of an ash tree bedecked with beadlike berries.

Hopkins goes even further, creating brand-new words such as
"twindles" and "flitches." "Twindles" may be a compound of "twists"
and "dwindles," according to the poet's notebook jottings. I can't
find any reference to "flitches" of fern, but I remember once walking
across a field of bracken without socks and feeling the sharp fronds
cutting my ankles before springing back into place, and thinking,
"Ah, those are flitches. They flick and twitch and make my ankles
itch."

If you think of the first three stanzas as three paintings, con-
sider how their colors and movements vary: the first dark but ener-
getic; the second with its bonnet of brown froth whirling down into
a black pool; and the third, the bright countryside, decorated by the
"beadbonny ash" atop the burn.

In the last stanza, Hopkins imagines a world without such natu-
ral splendor and issues a heartfelt plea to save the wildness and wet,
the weeds and the wilderness.

Even before we had any studies on climate change, this visionary poet could imagine a world bereft of such treasure. He had experienced pollution from the Industrial Revolution and understood human nature well enough to realize that people might not sufficiently value our natural environment, so he pleads with them to leave it unspoiled.

Takeaways

✗ **Do whatever you can to preserve our natural environment.** If that was important in Hopkins' time (the nineteenth century), it is critical now.

✗ **Try not to give in to despair.** Sometimes the task of protecting the environment seems so huge that it is easy to give up. Besides joining environmental groups, it is possible to do small things on one's own. For example, recycle, plant trees, and maintain a garden, however small. To paraphrase poet-songwriter Joni Mitchell, don't pave paradise and put up a parking lot.

The Poet and the Poems

Gerard Manley Hopkins (1844–1889) was born into a well-to-do British family in what is now Greater London, the eldest of nine children. His father, a successful businessman, was also a published poet, and his mother was the daughter of a London physician. The family valued culture, and many of his siblings became successful in the arts.

At age eight, Hopkins was sent to board at an excellent local school, from which he was admitted to Balliol College, Oxford. He studied classics there and did so brilliantly that one of his colleagues called him "The Star of Balliol." Besides his gift for poetry, Hopkins also was a skilled artist and musical composer.

Despite his brilliance, Hopkins led an unhappy life. He suffered from recurrent episodes of depression and was perhaps bipolar. As you can see, many successful poets have suffered from mood disorders, a topic studied most notably by psychologist Kay Redfield Jamison, whose landmark book *Touched with Fire* explores the connection between creativity and mood disorders.

Some of Hopkins' poems chronicle his pitiful depressions. One of his six "terrible" sonnets, for example, begins:

> I wake and feel the fell of dark, not day.
> What hours, O what black hours we have spent . . .

For depressed people, the morning hours are often worst, so waking into such a state is an ordeal even before the day begins. We will explore this idea further when we examine Roethke's "The Waking" (chapter 39).

In contrast to these "terrible sonnets," some of Hopkins' poems radiate ecstasy—for example, "The Windhover," a sonnet that begins:

> I caught this morning morning's minion, king-
> dom of daylight's dauphin, dapple-dawn-drawn Falcon, in his riding . . .

Compounding the unhappiness resulting from his mood disorder, Hopkins had a lifelong tendency to deprive himself of things that could give him joy or comfort. In school, for example, he deprived himself of water until he collapsed. At Oxford, he converted to Catholicism and became a Jesuit, thereby forgoing the emotional support of his large, vibrant Anglican family. Becoming a Jesuit involved taking vows of poverty, chastity, and obedience. At one point, he burned all his poems after he "resolved to be a religious" and gave up writing poetry almost completely for the next seven years.

Hopkins published few poems during his lifetime, and we have his lifelong friend Robert Bridges to thank for making his poems available to the public after his death.

Hopkins spent his last years as a priest in Ireland, sad to be away from England and his friends, and he felt like a failure. Yet by some mystery, the pied beauty of his mind delivered him a gift on his deathbed, to judge by his last words, spoken as he lay dying of typhoid fever at age forty-four: "I am so happy," he said, "I am so happy. I loved my life."

Chapter Twenty-One

THE IMPORTANCE OF BEING NEEDED

STOPPING BY WOODS ON A SNOWY EVENING
by Robert Frost

Whose woods these are I think I know.
His house is in the village though;
He will not see me stopping here
To watch his woods fill up with snow.

My little horse must think it queer
To stop without a farmhouse near
Between the woods and frozen lake
The darkest evening of the year.

He gives his harness bells a shake
To ask if there is some mistake.
The only other sound's the sweep
Of easy wind and downy flake.

The woods are lovely, dark and deep,
But I have promises to keep,
And miles to go before I sleep,
And miles to go before I sleep.

This famous poem came to mind unexpectedly during a clinical session with a woman who was telling me that she had no reason or desire to live any longer. She was roughly my age, highly accomplished, and beloved by family and colleagues; to an outsider, she might have seemed to have everything to live for. Yet as we spoke about her feelings of depression and hopelessness, none of that seemed reason enough to stay alive. She had preselected a site in downtown Washington, D.C., where she could drive off a bridge without her seatbelt on and have an accident that was sure to kill her and nobody else. What could I say to her to make a difference? That's when I thought of Robert Frost's classic poem.

On the surface, the poem may seem simple. In four short stanzas of four lines each, Frost tells the story of a man riding through the countryside in a horse-drawn carriage on a snowy evening. He stops, stands by the roadside, and looks at the snow falling into the woods. Then he decides to get back into the carriage and head on to his destination. In other words, not much happens—or so it seems.

The poem is readily accessible; all its words would be easily understood by the average high school student. There is something comforting about this absence of fancy language. It makes you feel as though a friend or neighbor is talking to you. The language, though spare, is gorgeous. Consider the poet's description of what he hears apart from his horse's harness bells:

> The only other sound's the sweep
> Of easy wind and downy flake.

In just two lines Frost conveys to us the sound and feel of the wind and goose feather snowflakes. Those lines bring us to the last stanza, where a shift occurs:

The woods are lovely, dark and deep,
But I have promises to keep,
And miles to go before I sleep,
And miles to go before I sleep.

To my mind, this last stanza holds the key to the life-enhancing and healing powers of the poem. At one level, the poet's dilemma is common to all of us. "The woods are lovely, dark and deep" suggests that he is tired, would like to rest there a while, but needs to move on. It is the type of internal gearshift we routinely make in everyday life. That is how this segue is often interpreted: as though he is saying to himself, "It's been a lovely evening, but I have to get home." But the psychiatrist in me wonders whether there may be more happening here.

Consider the connection between the first and second line. What is the relationship between the woods being "lovely, dark and deep" and the promises the poet has to keep? Something is going on in the poet's mind that is implied but not stated. So the reader is left to fill in the gap, and it is this mystery, I believe, that draws us back again and again to the poem and makes it endlessly fascinating.

In trying to understand what other people are thinking, we generally use what has been called "theory of mind," which has been defined as "the ability to interpret one's own and other people's mental and emotional states, understanding that each person has unique motives and perspectives." As psychotherapists, we routinely employ this theory to build mental models of what may be going on in our patients' minds, which helps move the therapy forwards.

Such models often include things left unsaid, perhaps even outside the patient's awareness. Let us suppose for a moment that someone in therapy were to say to me: "I was riding along in my horse-drawn carriage the other night, when suddenly, in the middle of nowhere, I stopped and looked into the dark woods as the snow was falling. My little horse seemed to sense that there was something wrong, because I don't usually stop in the middle of nowhere without a farmhouse near. I was very tired, but I kept staring into the distance as the woods filled up with snow, thinking, 'These woods are lovely, dark and deep.'"

I might well ask, "Did you perhaps wish to lie down and fall asleep in those woods and let the snow cover you?"

I would not be surprised to hear, "That thought did cross my mind."

I might ask, "What stopped you from doing so?"

And the answer might be, "I have promises to keep."

A friend told me a story about her father, who in later life developed a severe alcohol problem. One snowy evening, drunk and depressed, he went walking into the woods, tripped over a log, and landed on the snow-covered ground. He thought how peaceful it would be to just lie there and let the snow cover him. The cold numbed him, and at that moment he felt as though there would be no suffering in ending his life that way. Then he remembered that he had promised to pay for his granddaughter's college education, and the thought bothered him. If he allowed himself to get buried, who would take care of her tuition? She was a clever girl, and it was important that she reach her potential. And how could that happen without his help? That was when he hauled himself up off the ground and slowly lumbered back to the house, took off his wet clothes, lay down on the couch, and fell into a deep sleep. He couldn't end his life, not while he had promises to keep.

The Dalai Lama and social scientist Arthur C. Brooks have pointed out that older people who don't feel useful to others are three times as susceptible to early death as those who feel useful. Their conclusion: "We all need to be needed."

When you promise something to someone, you recognize that the person needs you in some way. You feel needed, if only to fulfill the promise. Perhaps that is how the poet felt when he was standing and staring into those dark woods. He had promises to keep, he was needed, so he'd better get a move on.

That brings me back to the suicidal woman I mentioned above. Though brilliant, accomplished, and financially secure, she felt she had no reason to go on living. After all attempts to dissuade her from ending her life had failed, I resorted to a psychiatrist's Hail Mary: would she contract with me that she would let me know in real time if she was feeling actively suicidal, and give me the chance to see if together we could make a plan to prevent her from taking her life? She responded with a wry smile and pointed out something that had many times occurred to me about the apparent absurdity of the so-called suicide contract:

"If I'm willing to leave behind everything dear to me," she said, "why should a contract with you hold any water?" She had me there, of course, but quickly bailed me out. She told me how her previous psychiatrist (since deceased) had responded when she had posed that question to him. "'I know you wouldn't break such a contract,' he had said. 'You wouldn't do that to *me*.' And of course," she added, "he was right." She had a promise to keep, and it was not in her nature to break a promise.

I wonder if much of what has made "Stopping by Woods on a Snowy Evening" so dearly loved and meaningful to generations is unwritten but implied. Frost has left to our imagination what transpires in the poet's mind in that shift between "The woods are lovely, dark and deep" and "But I have promises to keep." The suggestion I offer above may be only one of many possible interpretations. No doubt the reader can conjure other scenarios to fill that space. But the central elements are likely to be there: the weariness, the struggle to carry on, the promises that bind us to those who need us, that bind us to life; the pain of exhaustion, and our profound need for sleep.

Takeaways

✘ **Most of us need to be needed if we are to find a sense of purpose in life.** If you don't feel needed, find some person or cause who could use what you have to offer and appreciate it.

✘ **Incidentally, it doesn't have to be a person. It could be an animal that needs you.** I have had many patients tell me that they would not commit suicide because they would not trust anyone else to properly take care of their dog or cat.

✘ **Likewise, it could even be a society or establishment to which you have a special sense of loyalty or commitment.**

✘ **Understand the value of contemplating nature in helping you sort out your thoughts.** Whether it is a field of daffodils, a "darksome burn," a certain slant of light, or a neighbor's woods filling up with snow.

✘ **Consider the promises you have to keep to yourself as well.** Why should you promise yourself less than what you promise anyone else?

✘ **Finally, be sure to get a good night's sleep.** The world may look different in the morning.

Chapter Twenty-Two

THE CHOICES WE MAKE

THE ROAD NOT TAKEN
by Robert Frost

Two roads diverged in a yellow wood,
And sorry I could not travel both
And be one traveler, long I stood
And looked down one as far as I could
To where it bent in the undergrowth;

Then took the other, as just as fair,
And having perhaps the better claim,
Because it was grassy and wanted wear;
Though as for that the passing there
Had worn them really about the same,

And both that morning equally lay
In leaves no step had trodden black.
Oh, I kept the first for another day!
Yet knowing how way leads on to way,
I doubted if I should ever come back.

I shall be telling this with a sigh
Somewhere ages and ages hence:
Two roads diverged in a wood, and I—
I took the one less traveled by,
And that has made all the difference.

The quality of our lives—success or failure, triumph or disaster, happiness or misery—is in large measure a function of the choices we make. Frost's poem presents us with an archetypal image of a binary choice: a fork in the road. This apparently simple poem is a great favorite, arguably the most read poem of the last century.

Frost is on record as referring to this poem as "tricky," and it is its trickiness that may provide some of its charm. He describes two divergent roads, one that he takes and one that he leaves behind. The title of the poem is "The Road Not Taken," but the concluding line refers to the road he *did* take. Juxtaposing these two roads highlights a profound truth: every choice we make in life involves both gain and loss, the choice we make and the one we leave behind.

One endearing aspect of the poem is that the poet lets us in on the small processes that go on in his mind both in making the choice and reflecting on it afterwards. On encountering the fork in the road, he immediately recognizes that he has to choose one road or the other; he cannot choose both. But which one? Perhaps the universality of such a dilemma is one reason this poem is so popular.

Frost cursorily describes how he makes his choice. He looks down one road, then chooses the other, but doesn't give a good explanation as to the reason for his choice—and may not really know. Perhaps we generally have a tendency to choose the second of two options presented to us. Maybe it gives us a sense of agency. No, we won't take *this* one, we'll take *that* one instead. Psychologists could test that theory if they have not already done so.

In addition, there is a fascinating body of evidence that people often make choices based on subliminal cues of which they are not even aware. After making his choice, Frost begins to rationalize it to himself and to the reader. Perhaps the second one had a better claim, he argues: "Because it was grassy and wanted wear."

But he goes on to contradict that argument by observing:

> Though as for that the passing there
> Had worn them really about the same,
>
> And both that morning equally lay
> In leaves no step had trodden black.

He seems to have some regret at having to give up the first option (for which the poem is named), as is so common after one has made a choice, so he consoles himself by pointing out: "Oh, I kept the first for another day!"

At some level, though, he acknowledges he is kidding himself:

> Yet knowing how way leads on to way,
> I doubted if I should ever come back.

Storyteller that he is, he may already be thinking about how he plans to talk about the choice in years to come, with a sigh, perhaps remembering the road he had to forfeit. And the story he will tell will be:

> Two roads diverged in a wood, and I—
> I took the one less traveled by,
> And that has made all the difference.

Any major choice is a commitment, at least to some extent, because even if you change your mind later, the new moment of choice and its circumstances will be different—and so will you.

Opportunity cost, a concept used in business, applies equally to other aspects of life. By making a choice, we forfeit alternatives: when we choose to invest in A, we may forfeit the opportunity to invest in B and vice versa. Recognizing this, business managers have a maxim: If the choice is easily reversed, you can make it quickly. If it is hard to reverse, take more time to think it over. The principle is useful in daily life as well.

If the poet thinks he will be telling the story of his choice "ages hence," we might conclude that it was an important choice. In that case, it seems as though he made it rather quickly. But there is evidence that even when it comes to important decisions, some of us go with our gut rather than by careful measurement and consideration.

Once the poet makes his choice and commits himself to it, he can choose whether to focus on the road not taken (as in the title of the poem) or the road he chooses (as in the next to last line of the poem). In life, as in the poem, however, we may to a greater or lesser extent keep both choices in mind. Concluding by declaring that choosing the road less traveled had made all the difference suggests that in the end, the poet is pleased with his choice.

I once had the treat of hearing the distinguished paleontologist Stephen Jay Gould discuss this poem. He took issue with Frost's last line, arguing, as others have done, that Frost was being melodramatic by emphasizing that taking the road less traveled by had made all the difference. After all, Gould said, the poet himself pointed out that the two roads had been worn about the same and were equally untrodden. How then could he legitimately claim that he had taken the road less traveled by?

My perspective differs from that of a paleontologist. I work with people who are examining their lives, not with tectonic evolutionary changes. They struggle with the many important choices they have to make—what career or job to pursue, where to live, and whom to love and marry.

So I am with Frost here. Each person's story is unique, and whatever road a person takes ends up being the road less traveled by, because no one else has traveled exactly that way before, and, for better or worse, it *can* make all the difference. You encounter different opportunities, challenges, and problems, meet different people, and establish different relationships. The life you lead is, to a large extent, a result of the choices you make.

Takeaways

✘ **Make your choices carefully, because they determine the type of life you will lead.**

✘ **In general, the bigger the decision—and the harder it is to reverse—the more time it is worth taking over.** This might include whether to get married, whom to marry, your career, and where you choose to live.

✘ **When it comes to big decisions, it is often useful to seek the advice of people you respect to see how their opinions mesh with yours (and one another's).** This is called *triangulating*, where you are at the apex of the triangle and your consultants are at the other corners.

✘ **In the end, of course, you have the ultimate say.** After all, it is *your* life, and you will reap the rewards and bear the consequences of whatever course you choose.

The Poet and the Poems

Robert Frost was born in 1874 in San Francisco, where he lived until age eleven, when his father died. He then moved with his mother and sister Jeanie to Lawrenceville, Massachusetts, where he went to high school. Although he spent some years studying, first at Dartmouth and later at Harvard, he didn't graduate because of health concerns.

Frost went on to marry his co-valedictorian at Lawrenceville High School, Elinor White. They tried their hand at farming, unsuccessfully, for twelve years, then decided to move to England in the hope that Frost would find a better reception for his poetry, That turned out to be wise, and, shortly after arriving there, they found publishers for his first two books of poetry: *A Boy's Will* and *North of Boston*.

When Frost and Elinor returned to the United States in 1914, after the start of World War I, Frost's reputation was already on the ascendant. He and his family settled in New England, which provides the landscape for many of his poems, including the two featured here. What followed was a dazzling career as a poet, which included four Pulitzer Prizes (the most for any poet), thirty-one Nobel Prize nominations, and forty honorary degrees.

Despite his success, Frost had more than his share of tragedy in his life. Of the six children he had with Elinor, only two survived him. Psychiatric illness ran in the family. One son, Carol, committed suicide, and one daughter, Irma, developed mental illness that required commitment to a mental hospital. He also had to commit his sister Jeanie to a mental institute in 1920, where she stayed for nine years until her death. Frost and Elinor both suffered from bouts of depression.

I didn't know about Frost's history of depression when I first read "Stopping by Woods on a Snowy Evening," but it is consistent with my interpretation of the poem.

In both of the poems given here, Frost shows his capacity to describe apparently ordinary events and decisions while riding or walking in the countryside and to extract profound insights from them. In this regard, he joins the other great poets featured in this section, who had the ability to look deeply into nature and share with us their unique insights into universal situations.

Chapter Twenty-Three

THE FORCE OF LONGING

SEA FEVER
by John Masefield

I must down to the seas again, to the lonely sea and the sky,
And all I ask is a tall ship and a star to steer her by;
And the wheel's kick and the wind's song and the white sail's
   shaking,
And a grey mist on the sea's face, and a grey dawn breaking.

I must down to the seas again, for the call of the running tide
Is a wild call and a clear call that may not be denied;
And all I ask is a windy day with the white clouds flying,
And the flung spray and the blown spume, and the sea-gulls
   crying.

I must down to the seas again, to the vagrant gypsy life,
To the gull's way and the whale's way where the wind's like a
   whetted knife;
And all I ask is a merry yarn from a laughing fellow-rover,
And quiet sleep and a sweet dream when the long trick's over.

By the time of his death, John Masefield (1878–1967) had arguably
been the most celebrated living poet in the United Kingdom for
thirty-seven years. He had been the nation's poet laureate under four

monarchs and had written numerous collections of poems, plays, and works of nonfiction. Yet the work for which he is perhaps best known is the short poem shown above. Read it out loud and see if it doesn't make you want to pack your bag immediately and rush down to the sea.

The title "Sea Fever" is perfect. Imagine if he had called it "Sea Passion" instead. The sense and beat would have been retained, but we would have missed the physical intensity of "fever"—the sweat of the poet's urge and urgency to get to the sea. Masefield amplifies this intensity by the repeated opening refrain: "I must down to the seas again." Think of what it means when you repeatedly command yourself to do something: usually you very much want to do it, but something keeps getting in the way. So there is an implied tension between what you desperately long to do and whatever is holding you back. We don't know what that might have been for the poet—or if or when he ever got back to the sea—which adds mystery and tension to the poem.

In the first stanza we encounter the phrase "the lonely sea and the sky." Here, being alone does not convey the painful isolation that it does elsewhere in other poems in this book, notably in "Not Waving but Drowning" (chapter 47). Instead we feel the poet's *solitude* as part of his adventure—steering the tall ship alone with only a star to guide him. All around there are signs of life familiar to a seasoned seaman—the wheel's kick, the wind's song, the white sail shaking. Everything is alive and moving. The sea's face is covered with mist, the grey dawn is breaking. You have a sense that to the experienced mariner, all these signals are crucial because his life may depend on them.

In the second stanza the running tide is calling to him with a call "that may not be denied," bringing to mind the sirens' call to Odysseus as he wends his way home to Ithaca. Again, all the poet is asking for are the sounds, sights, and sensations of the sea, animated and in perpetual motion.

The final stanza introduces a new theme: "the vagrant gypsy life." There is a sense here of wanting to get not only to the sea but also to a life free of the responsibilities of the workaday world, to be unfettered, like the gull and the whale. The sharpness of the wind slashing the skin "like a whetted knife" communicates a sense of feeling fully alive rather than the pain such an image might otherwise convey.

The last two lines pack a vigorous punch. In the penultimate line we see the first reference to another human being, "a laughing fellow-rover," who can spin "a merry yarn" perhaps as well as the poet himself. The poet's love of stories and storytelling is evident in this affectionate image. In the last line, Masefield presents us with the images of sleep and a sweet dream. The very last words—"when the long trick's over"—convey a peaceful sense of death. The words "long trick" evoke an image of a long life, full of fun, yet demanding the skill and mastery of a conjurer. The word "over" is accurate but not melodramatic: just what one might expect from an old salt. It simply says, "Life has been astonishing, but now it's over. So go to sleep and exit with a sweet dream."

Elsewhere in this book, notably in "An Irish Airman Foresees His Death" (chapter 43) and "High Flight" (chapter 33), adventure and excitement carry with them inevitable danger and probable early death. Not so here. In this poem, Masefield integrates his love of adventure and of the sea with the "long trick" of a life fully lived. Since the question of whether the poet will return to the sea remains unresolved, the poem leaves us with the force of longing that drives and compels people in all walks of life.

The poet uses many special effects in this masterful poem:

1. Variable rhythm, which gives you a feel for the pitch and roll of a ship at sea.

2. Many one-syllable words, which convey a sense of urgency consistent with the poet's longing.

3. Alliteration, as in "the wheel's kick and the wind's song and the white sail shaking."

4. Repetition: "And all I ask . . ."

5. Movement words in almost every line, which convey a sense of the sea as a place that is constantly teeming and vibrating with life.

6. An appeal to all the senses: the smell and taste of the saltiness of the "flung spray and the blown spume"; the sound of "the seagulls crying"; and the feel of the wind "like a whetted knife."

7. An appeal to emotions: we can feel (and share) the poet's excitement of being at sea, enjoyment of a merry yarn, and desire for a sweet dream and ultimately, the sense of serenity at life ending on a peaceful note.

Takeaways

✘ Live life fully, pursuing your dreams and integrating your sense of adventure with your long-term goals.

✘ It is possible to live a life of adventure without risking your life.

✘ It is a comfort to think of your life as a life well lived.

✘ The force of longing is a powerful motivator. After calculating risks and rewards, take that force seriously.

The Poet and the Poem

The poem is deeply informed by Masefield's personal knowledge of the sea. He had an unhappy childhood and education. He was born in 1878, and his mother died when he was six years old. Seven years later, his father died after suffering a nervous breakdown that required being institutionalized. Masefield was sent to stay with an unwelcoming aunt and attended a harsh school. At age thirteen, he entered officer training, and at age sixteen he boarded a ship bound for Chile.

While at sea, he took comfort in prodigious reading and writing, for which he had plenty of time. He enjoyed the natural wonders encountered on his voyages, such as flying fish, porpoises, and a rare lunar rainbow. In addition, he developed a love for storytelling. Tired of sailing and eager to become a writer, he jumped ship in New York City at age seventeen to pursue his dream.

Masefield worked odd jobs in the New York area, never losing his passion for reading. In 1897, at age nineteen, he returned to Britain in a desperate state. As he wrote, "I landed in England with about six pounds and a revolver. I was going to try to get myself a job as a clerk (I knew nothing of business). Failing that I was going to shoot myself. I was desperately ill and sick, I hadn't the strength to stand more hardships."

In England Masefield's fortunes changed. At age twenty-three, he met his wife-to-be Constance de la Cherois Crommelin, and the following year published his first collection of verse: *Salt-Water Ballads*. The couple were married and had two children, a daughter and a son, who was killed in action in World War II.

Although Masefield went on to be one of the most successful British poets of the twentieth century, on a personal level, he suffered several tragedies, including the early death of his parents and the loss of his son. He cared for Constance lovingly as she suffered through her last year before her death in 1960. He died six years afterwards, in 1967, at age eighty-eight, and was buried in Westminster Abbey.

Only later was the following note discovered, addressed to his "Heirs, Administrators and Assigns," with sad instructions as to how to deal with his remains:

> Let no religious rite be done or read
> In any place for me when I am dead,
> But burn my body into ash, and scatter
> The ash in secret into running water,
> Or on the windy down, and let none see;
> And then thank God that there's an end of me.

Chapter Twenty-Four

FINDING HOPE IN NATURE

THE DARKLING THRUSH
by Thomas Hardy

> I leant upon a coppice gate
>   When Frost was spectre-grey,
> And Winter's dregs made desolate
>   The weakening eye of day.
> The tangled bine-stems scored the sky
>   Like strings of broken lyres,
> And all mankind that haunted nigh
>   Had sought their household fires.
>
> The land's sharp features seemed to be
>   The Century's corpse outleant,
> His crypt the cloudy canopy,
>   The wind his death-lament.
> The ancient pulse of germ and birth
>   Was shrunken hard and dry,
> And every spirit upon earth
>   Seemed fervourless as I.
>
> At once a voice arose among
>   The bleak twigs overhead
> In a full-hearted evensong
>   Of joy illimited;
> An aged thrush, frail, gaunt, and small,
>   In blast-beruffled plume,

Had chosen thus to fling his soul
   Upon the growing gloom.

So little cause for carolings
   Of such ecstatic sound
Was written on terrestrial things
   Afar or nigh around,
That I could think there trembled through
   His happy good-night air
Some blessed Hope, whereof he knew
   And I was unaware.

Although this poem was written over a century ago, in 1900, it raises a question that is as relevant today as it was then: where can we find hope in a world that so often seems desolate?

The first two stanzas are bleak, full of imagery of death: "spectre-grey" frost, "the Century's corpse," the cryptlike clouds, and the "death-lament" of the wind. It comes as no surprise to learn that the poem was initially titled "By the Century's Deathbed." As Hardy looks out over the landscape in the closing days of the nineteenth century, it seems to reflect his own fervorless mood.

In the third stanza, the poem takes a sharp turn, with the sound of a tiny, weather-beaten, and disheveled thrush, unprepossessing, but with a beautiful song. Hardy's immortal description of the bird contrasts starkly with the desolate tone of the first two stanzas.

The thrush's song transforms the poet's spirit in a way reminiscent of Shakespeare's description of the exhilarating song of the lark in sonnet 29:

(Like to the lark at break of day arising
From sullen earth) sings hymns at heaven's gate.

Here, just as with sonnet 29, the joy of hearing the thrush's song is heightened by the bleakness of the first two stanzas. Hardy, like Shakespeare, was skilled at creating dramatic effects. In fact, the term "cliffhanger" originated from one of Hardy's serialized works of fiction, in which the hero was left literally hanging from a cliff at the end of an episode. We see Hardy's dramatic skill in evidence here as well.

Hardy did well to jettison the initial, funereal title of the poem in favor of one suggesting hope: "The Darkling Thrush." Despite his gloom, Hardy allows for the possibility that the thrush may know of some cause for hope of which he is unaware. Something about the bird's song, notwithstanding its "blast-beruffled plume," allows the poet's mind to remain open to that possibility.

It has often been said that pessimists are in general more realistic than optimists. That would certainly be true of anyone who made a gloomy forecast about the world at the end of the nineteenth century, inasmuch as in the following fifty years there would be two world wars, a historic epidemic, a great depression and the Holocaust. So Hardy was not wrong to be pessimistic. Nevertheless, no harm was done by the spell of the thrush's song, which instilled in Hardy the possibility of hope, and provided joy and inspiration to generations of readers.

As in all the poems in this section that speak to responses to the natural world, little may seem to happen externally, yet much happens in the poet's mind. And so gifted is a great poet in the capacity to process those inner experiences and communicate them verbally in ways that are both pleasing and profound that the reader is left similarly transformed.

Imagine if you asked someone without Hardy's genius, leaning upon a gate on a midwinter's day, what he was thinking. The response might easily be, "It's dreary out there, a nasty way to end the century. Then a bird started singing and cheered me up no end. Now how about a cup of tea?" Instead, here we are, over a century later, marveling at Hardy's masterpiece.

Takeaways for All Poems in This Section

✘ **To fully appreciate nature, be mindful of its sights and smells, but don't forget its sounds.** Listen to the crickets, cicadas, and even the bullfrog croaking by the pond, but above all the birds. We have evolved alongside them, and perhaps our brains have become wired to respond to their movements and sounds with joy and hope.

✘ **Look for signs of hope in the natural world and elsewhere.** They will buoy up your spirits.

The Poet and the Poem

Thomas Hardy (1840–1928) was born in Dorset, in the southwest of England, into a working-class family. According to biographer Michael Millgate:

> As a sickly child, not confidently expected to survive into adulthood and kept mostly at home, Hardy gained an intimate knowledge of the surrounding countryside, the hard and sometimes violent lives of neighboring rural families, and the songs, stories, superstitions, seasonal rituals, and day-to-day gossip of a still predominantly oral culture.

Hardy's formal education ended at age sixteen, when he was apprenticed to an architect, but he continued to educate himself privately. Though successful in his first profession, his real passion lay with literature and, self-taught, he became highly successful as both a poet and popular novelist. As a poet, he had a powerful influence over the poets of subsequent generations, including W. H. Auden, Dylan Thomas, and Robert Frost. He was twice nominated for the Nobel Prize in Literature.

Hardy's first love was Emma Lavinia Gifford, whom he married four years after meeting her on an architectural assignment. Emma helped Hardy with his fledgling literary career, and the couple moved between London and Dorset as he started writing novels, which became famous but controversial as they challenged aspects of Victorian morality. He always seemed to value his poetry more highly, however, and diverted his creative energies to poetry in later life.

Hardy and Emma became estranged, but continued to live together for many years in the same house until her death in 1912. A few years later he married Florence Emily Dugdale, but continued to obsess over his failed relationship with Emma, even writing poems about his continued devotion to her. Like many poets, Hardy suffered severe depressions.

Florence, thirty-eight years his junior, was a devoted wife and attended to his care, comfort, and privacy into his old age. He dictated his last poem to her just before he died at age eighty-eight.

But Hardy never forgot Emma. When she died, he inscribed a wreath to her with the words, "From her lonely husband with the Old Affection." When Hardy died, his body was buried in Westminster Abbey, alongside other great British poets, but, according to his wishes, his heart was buried, as Emma had been, in the churchyard of his native parish.

To See the World in a Grain of Sand

The poets in this section show the rare ability to look at nature in a novel way and extract profound insights from it. In "Daffodils" and "Tintern Abbey," Wordsworth shows us how scenes of natural beauty can have a profound influence on our state of consciousness. Dickinson connects "a certain Slant of light" to mood regulation. Hopkins is inspired by dappled creatures and natural beauty to extol diversity and environmental protection. In a walk or ride through the countryside, Frost finds profound life lessons, while in his urgent longing to go back to the sea, Masefield recreates a world unknown to many of us. And finally, there is Hardy, gloomy at the end of the nineteenth century, finding hope in the song of a thrush.

The brilliance of these poets bring to mind William Blake's famous words:

> To see a World in a Grain of Sand
> And a Heaven in a Wild Flower
> Hold Infinity in the palm of your hand
> And Eternity in an hour

PART THREE

The Human Experience

This being human is a guest house.

—Jalaluddin Rumi

Chapter Twenty-Five

THE POWER OF HOPE

"HOPE" IS THE THING WITH FEATHERS
by Emily Dickinson

> "Hope" is the thing with feathers —
> That perches in the soul —
> And sings the tune without the words —
> And never stops — at all —
>
> And sweetest — in the Gale — is heard —
> And sore must be the storm —
> That could abash the little Bird
> That kept so many warm —
>
> I've heard it in the chillest land —
> And on the strangest Sea —
> Yet — never — in Extremity,
> It asked a crumb — of me.

To me, this poem seems like the embodiment of hope. As I read it now, for the nth time, I still ponder the secret to its comforting and therapeutic powers, short and slender as it is, much like the imaginary bird it describes.

Birds have been connected with hope at least since biblical times, when, as we are told in Genesis, Noah's dove returned with a freshly plucked olive leaf in its mouth, indicating that the waters had subsided. Noah and his ark had weathered the Flood, along with all its creatures.

It is often a bird's song that inspires hope, as was the case for Hardy's thrush and Shelley's skylark in his famous ode.

Besides the exuberance of their song, birds convey freedom in that they can fly seemingly wherever they want—north or south according to the season, apparently undaunted, or so it seems to us. They have varied, often exquisite, plumage, which inspires hordes of people to rise at the crack of dawn to watch them. They are the descendants of dinosaurs, so we marvel at their survival abilities; somewhere deep down, we suspect that they may well survive our species and inherit the earth. These qualities may engender hope and wonder in us when we hear their song and see them freely going about their lives.

The Thing with Feathers

Why does Dickinson call the creature in the poem "the thing with feathers" instead of simply calling it a bird, even though elsewhere she refers to the creature as such? What do you think? Perhaps it is because she wants to move away from the specifics of a particular bird, like Hardy's thrush, and capture the creature's essential "birdness."

In a way, Dickinson's technique has its counterpart in the world of art. In the nineteenth century, paintings or sketches of birds would generally be realistic, down to their fine feathery details. The darkling thrush's "blast beruffled plume" is an example of a similar technique in poetry.

In the twentieth century, however, Picasso might create the impression of a bird with merely a few brushstrokes. That is what

Dickinson is doing here by describing her creature as "the thing with feathers." Her poem is thought to have been written in 1861, almost forty years before Hardy's. Consider how stunningly modern and original she was for her day, which explains to some extent why she had difficulty getting published at that time.

Dickinson goes on to treat her thing with feathers much as she did her certain slant of light. She wonders what effect it has on the human brain and mind and where it exerts that effect. According to her, the certain slant of light caused an "internal difference—where the Meanings, are," while the thing with feathers "perches in the soul."

Long before neurosurgeon Wilder Penfield began mapping the human brain, electrically stimulating various regions to determine the subjective effects on his patients, Dickinson suggested that there is a location within us (the soul) where hope "perches" and has its comforting effects.

The idea of a creature perching in the soul brings to mind a real bird, not just a "thing with feathers." So we see how Dickinson works her magic. First she is writing about an abstract stylized "thing with feathers," and now about a live creature perching in the soul. She moves fluidly between a birdlike creature, an abstract concept (hope), a region of the brain/soul, and the bird itself. We are clearly in the hands of a conjurer!

Once perched in the soul, the bird sings the tune without words—a tune of pure feeling without cognition. Why do we hope? How do we hope? Hope against hope? We can put words to all these different expressions, but beyond explanations for our feelings, there is the feeling itself—the tune without the words—worthy of our attention in its own right.

In the second stanza, the poet introduces the image of a gale. Like Hardy, this acute observer of nature marvels at the ability of a little bird to withstand foul weather. She notes that hope is sweetest when it is most needed (in a gale), and though small, the bird is not easily deterred (abashed) except by the worst weather ("sore must be the storm").

The second stanza ends on a comforting note. Dickinson's thing with feathers keeps many people warm even in the worst weather. At this point, Dickinson's bird brings to mind the image of a mother, singing without stopping until her child is comforted and pulling up a blanket to keep the child warm. The poet is taking something as abstract as hope and giving it physical attributes that evoke feelings of comfort (like a feather bed or down comforter), along with the attributes of a good parent, who is there when needed most, stays as long as necessary, and hangs in even under the most trying circumstances.

In the last stanza, the poet dons the mantle of authority. She has experienced hope in the coldest and most curious of places ("the chillest land," "the strangest Sea"). Right at the end, the poet becomes personal and writes that in her experience, Hope (like a good parent) has never, even in the most extreme of circumstances, asked even "a crumb" of her.

I can't think of another poem that distills the essence of hope as powerfully as this one. Somehow "the thing with feathers" comes alive through these three short stanzas. Though small, the bird reveals courage, tenacity, and loyalty. It is a small creature with great character, part of who we all are. So without preaching or prescribing, the poet is telling us that we have this precious attribute within ourselves that can see us through life's hardships. Perhaps that is what's most comforting about the poem—to know that within each of us resides the thing with feathers.

Takeaways

✕ **Hope is an important emotion in many situations in medicine.** Doctors and counselors routinely work to help people maintain hope, which can sometimes make the difference between life and death. Dickinson's poem may be of particular value to share and discuss with people in situations where hope is needed.

✕ **Hope can also be a life-saver in dire situations** such as falling overboard, where it may help people hang in long enough to be rescued.

✕ **Hope is contagious and can be a force for good in society by helping us confront difficult problems collectively.**

Even in those circumstances where hope does not make the difference between life and death, it is pleasanter to live with hope than with despair.

Chapter Twenty-Six

WELCOMING YOUR EMOTIONS

THE GUEST HOUSE
by Jalaluddin Rumi
(Translated by Coleman Barks)

> This being human is a guest house.
> Every morning a new arrival.
>
> A joy, a depression, a meanness,
> some momentary awareness comes
> as an unexpected visitor.
>
> Welcome and entertain them all!
> Even if they are a crowd of sorrows,
> who violently sweep your house
> empty of its furniture,
> still, treat each guest honorably.
> He may be clearing you out
> for some new delight.
>
> The dark thought, the shame, the malice,
> meet them at the door laughing,
> and invite them in.
>
> Be grateful for whatever comes.
> because each has been sent
> as a guide from beyond.

In the early phases of writing this book, I encountered a great deal of skepticism about its premise—that poetry can actually heal. It was mildly discouraging to hear people express disbelief in a topic so dear to me, but I had encountered this type of response before in connection with other passions of mine.

In the light of such skepticism, an encounter in Edinburgh made a particularly strong impression on me. I was riding in a car on a balmy summer evening with some friends old and new when someone asked me what my next project would be. When I explained it, I found, to my surprise, that one of the passengers, Ilaria Nardini-Grey, was even more excited about the project than I was.

Ilaria was in her mid-thirties at the time, married with a daughter. As we wended our way through the streets of the old city, Ilaria told us how her life had been changed by Rumi.

About five years before we met, Ilaria was doing well, working in the corporate world in London, and in a long-term relationship. Then her life was disrupted by the death of her father, and she returned to Edinburgh to be with him in his last weeks.

His death threw Ilaria into an existential crisis. Depressed and anxious, she set out on a spiritual journey, and found answers in Rumi's poetry. Reading his poems for the first time while on a train, she experienced "something wonderful." Here is how she describes it:

> As I began to read Rumi's poems, the words just healed my soul. I felt a rush of energy through my body, my hair stood on end. This is what I had patiently been waiting for about life, spirituality, about love, the key to everything. There I was on the train, in tears with everybody looking at me but I didn't care because those were tears of joy, of relief, of "this is it." It was as though my soul had shifted and my heart had opened.

> My life changed from there and wonderful things have hap-
> pened to me since reading Rumi's poems. I believe he is one of the
> great souls and greatest spiritual teachers. He shows us our glory.

Ilaria finds Rumi's writing "accessible, beautiful and healing," and returns to her favorites repeatedly.

She acknowledges that her story sounds "almost magical," but within six months of finding Rumi, she met her husband and decided on a career in coaching. Shortly afterward she became pregnant.

Here's how she sums up the effects of Rumi's poetry on her: "It brought love into my life, first through coaching and helping others, then through my husband and finally through my daughter, whom we named Rumi."

Since her early twenties, Ilaria had been diagnosed with conventional psychiatric syndromes such as panic attacks, depression, and agoraphobia. She dates her recovery from these conditions to discovering Rumi's poems. She acknowledges that "some days are better than others; I'm only human, of course," but her psychiatric syndromes have not returned since that first encounter with Rumi.

A quick web search provides many other examples of people who claim that Rumi's poems have changed their lives. With that in mind, let us examine "The Guest House," one of his most popular poems, to see if we can gain insight into the appeal of this medieval poet.

Before doing so, however, a word about his modern interpreter into English, Coleman Barks. The term *interpreter* is generally used for Barks instead of *translator*, as Barks does not understand Persian (the language in which Rumi wrote) and has used other translations as the basis for his own versions. Although some scholars have taken issue with his interpretations, they are generally regarded as both accessible and beautiful and may be responsible for Rumi's resurgence in the United States.

On a personal note, I called Barks for permission to reprint his version. He gave it to me without fee or fuss in a warm and friendly manner, a quality that may influence his translations and make them more approachable.

The Guest House

The poem opens with a few simple statements:

> This being human is a guest house.
> Every morning a new arrival.

The words have a fresh feel each time I read them. Without preamble they throw you into the action. My associations with guest houses are of charming places where guests are welcome with good cheer and refreshment. So it is, Rumi suggests, that we should welcome the guests that visit us each day—our feelings. One way in which feelings are like the guests in a guest house is that they constantly come and go—a valuable point to bear in mind when unpleasant feelings arrive or when good feelings leave.

In listing these guest-feelings, Rumi mixes them up, so joy sits right next to depression and meanness. That is how emotions are: sometimes they alternate, sometimes they coexist, even if they are opposites. When you visit your childhood home, for example, you may feel joy and sadness at the same time. Nostalgia is a mix of feelings.

Sometimes the visitor comes unexpectedly—a "momentary awareness"—so be prepared, Rumi counsels us. In *Hamlet*, we are told that "sorrows come not as single spies but in battalions." So it is, Rumi tells us, that these guest-emotions may arrive as a crowd of sorrows. Nevertheless, even if they are traumatic, in the wake of such adversity delight may follow.

Then Rumi revisits the dark thoughts of which we are ashamed, like malice. He counsels us to laugh at them and invite them in, to be grateful for what these painful thoughts may bring. They may be guiding us.

Many years ago, when I was in psychoanalysis, one of my analyst's favorite interventions was, "You're not all sweetness and light, you know." Of course I wasn't. Nobody is. But I imagine that I was having trouble accepting the darker emotions within myself, so the analyst was right to point out that I was avoiding these important feelings. Even so, how much kinder it would have been had he followed Rumi's direction and said something like:

> This being human is a guest house.
> Every morning a new arrival.
>
> A joy, a depression, a meanness.

The healing powers in Rumi's poem comes not only from what he says but how he says it, making it clear that we are all in this human condition together.

Takeaways

✘ **Some emotions are painful.** This needs to be acknowledged, because there is a natural desire to deny them, and it can be valuable to label painful feelings as such.

In sonnet 29 (chapter 9), Shakespeare describes feelings of inadequacy, disgrace, discontent, self-abasement, and envy—all painful emotions, viscerally felt and communicated.

Another common and painful emotion is guilt. If you say something that makes someone feel guilty, that person is liable to grow angry and avoid you so as to bypass these painful emotions. Bear that in mind should you choose to say something that might elicit guilt.

Two other painful "guests" that Rumi points out are shame and malice.

✗ Once they are labeled, it is useful to accept painful feelings, which often makes them less painful. We have seen this principle at work in several poems encountered so far. For example:
- "One Art" (chapter 1) tells us to accept loss.
- "Why so pale and wan young lover" (chapter 6) urges the young man to accept the reality of rejection.
- In "Pity me not" (chapter 3), the poet recognizes that she needs to accept her difficulty in aligning her swift mind with a heart that is slow to learn.

✗ Don't just accept your feelings; welcome them. Rumi takes the need for acceptance to the next level, encouraging us to welcome our feelings, even the painful ones, because they may bring us the unexpected gifts of adversity.

✗ Like the guests in a guest house, feelings come and go. This applies to all feelings, both good and bad. Sometimes if you just wait, an unpleasant feeling will pass, though often you can speed it on its way (for example, by acceptance, cognitive corrections, and reaching out to friends and family).

✗ Emotions such as sadness, guilt, and pessimism are often experienced by people suffering from clinical depression. This is one of the most painful conditions people encounter. If you are experiencing these feelings, you should consider seeking help, especially if they are interfering with your ability to function.

✘ Take positive feelings seriously too. For example, if you have the passion to pursue something, don't allow the skepticism of others to stop you. Who knows? You may be right.

Chapter Twenty-Seven

THE HEALING POWER OF RECONCILIATION

⤳ OUT BEYOND IDEAS

by Jalaluddin Rumi

(Translated by Coleman Barks)

> Out beyond ideas of wrongdoing and rightdoing,
> there is a field. I'll meet you there.
>
> When the soul lies down in that grass,
> the world is too full to talk about.
> Ideas, language, even the phrase *each other*
> doesn't make any sense.

Who is right and who is wrong? This question preoccupies many of us from childhood to old age.

A mother consulted me about strife at home between her young son and daughter, both of whom she had instructed to sit in my waiting room until she emerged. Before long a furious neighbor banged at my door to announce that the children had ventured into her garden, where she had found them dangerously close to a pond. The angry mother scolded the older child, who said, "It was his fault. He ran out first, and I went after him to try and stop him." The younger one responded, "She started it! She was so mean. I had to run to get away from her."

There it was. Who was right and who was wrong? So it often is even with adult couples who consult me. They lay out their grievances as though presenting a case before a judge. We see this trope in our society and across different societies. Endless strife, finger pointing, and blaming the other. Who is right, and who is wrong? What is to be done about it?

In his short poem, Rumi cuts through the question of right and wrong and presents us with a vision of what might exist "beyond ideas of wrongdoing and rightdoing." "There is a field," he tells us and makes an offer: "I'll meet you there." It's as though he is willing to make the first move towards reconciliation and invites us to join him. It is a gentle invitation, without preconditions or arm-twisting. Rather, in just a few words he conjures up an enticing scene: souls lying in the long grass, a world too full to talk, and differences of language, ideas, and individual identity that melt away once we put aside ideas of right and wrong. Here Rumi models for us a way to circumvent conflict by reaching out to the opposing party. It is a glorious vision, but does it have any foundation in reality, or is it merely a poet's dream? What do you think?

I would suggest that once again, Rumi's vision embodies a deep truth. In my office I often point out to couples that I am not a judge, and we are not in a court of law. We are trying to find a meeting place where two people can get together, lower their defenses, and try to remember what attracted them to each other in the first place. What do they still have in common, and what shared treasures would they like to protect—such as their shared history and their children?

Therapists commonly assign couples the exercise of asking each party simply to repeat what the other has said. Just the process of repeating the other person's words can help you feel how it is to be inside the other person, as though you are lying together in the long grass. It is also a check to see if you have heard the other correctly and to avoid misinterpretations that commonly occur, especially when feelings run strong.

One of the most memorable encounters of my life was meeting the great writer, neurologist, and Holocaust survivor Viktor Frankl, author of *Man's Search for Meaning.* In the living room of his summer house outside of Vienna, I asked him many questions, all of which he answered candidly and generously. When I asked whether he had forgiven the Germans for the Holocaust, he responded, "I'm not sure I really understand what the word *forgiveness* means. I would rather think of reconciliation, the idea that we need to put aside past grievances and get along with one another." An amazing response from someone whose family had been cruelly killed and who had almost died himself in a death camp.

That same conclusion has been reached in many countries where members of totalitarian regimes had oppressed and tortured their neighbors before the regime changed hands. In my own country of origin, South Africa, after the fall of the cruel system of apartheid, the Truth and Reconciliation Commission was set up to allow those who confessed to their crimes under the apartheid system to receive amnesty. The goal was to allow victims and their torturers to pass one another in the street and do business together without overt aggression, to allow the people to heal their terrible wounds and pursue a common cause.

Whether we think about children squabbling, couples arguing, or political strife, people all over the world have converged on reconciliation as the best solution. Rumi could have told them so.

Takeaways

✖ **In a conflict with someone important to you, decide on your priority—to be right or to get along?** Often you can't have both at the same time.

✖ **Try first to understand, then to be understood.**

✖ **Once there is harmony between you and the other person, there will be time to talk about basic principles on which you can both agree, and how best to adhere to them.**

✖ **If there has been bad blood between people, sometimes a formal process of reconciliation can be helpful.**

The Poet and the Poems

Jalaluddin Rumi (1207–1273) was born in Afghanistan to Persian-speaking parents, but lived most of his life in present-day Turkey. His father was a theologian and jurist. He followed in the same tradition; many of his surviving letters describe how he helped members of his community solve disputes and get loans from one another.

A pivotal incident in Rumi's life occurred in 1244, when he met Shams Tabrizi, about whom Rumi said, "What I thought of before as God I met today in a human being." After that meeting, Rumi began to write his greatest poems. The two men were such close friends for years that Rumi's disciples became jealous. When Shams disappeared, he was believed to have been murdered by Rumi's jealous disciples, or perhaps his son. Rumi searched far and wide for his lost friend but eventually had to accept that Shams was gone. He dealt with his grief by experiencing Shams as part of himself, writing, "his essence speaks through me."

Rumi's poetic production was voluminous; his reputation has grown over the centuries, and thanks to Coleman Barks' renditions, he has sometimes been called America's most popular poet. He was buried close to his father in Konya, Turkey, and his tomb has become a gathering place for thousands of visitors who have been touched by the great poet and healer.

If anyone deserves a place in the pantheon of those who have healed through poetry, it is Rumi.

🌿 TRAVELER, THERE IS NO ROAD
by Antonio Machado

Translated by Mary G. Berg and Dennis Maloney

> Traveler, your footprints
> are the only road, nothing else.
> Traveler, there is no road;
> you make your own path as you walk.
> As you walk, you make your own road,
> and when you look back
> you see the path
> you will never travel again.
> Traveler, there is no road;
> only a ship's wake on the sea.

I recall a conversation I had with a cousin, an elderly widow who had left our native country some years before to settle near her son in Canada. I asked her whether she missed South Africa, to which she replied, "I can't afford to miss South Africa. I have burned my bridges there, so I must make my life here in North America." And she had made a fine life for herself. Her eightieth birthday was attended by dozens of friends, some old but mostly new, in the country she had come to call home.

I tell this story not because it is unusual but because it is so common. In North America, apart from the Native Americans, we were all originally immigrants. Machado's poem—and the lesson embedded in it—is therefore highly relevant to many in the United States, as it is to people all the world over.

All immigrants have a story with common elements: who and what they left behind; what it took to get here (wherever *here* may be); how they were integrated into a brave new world; and longings and nostalgia, intermingled with the excitement, freedom, and opportunities offered by their new home.

Some immigrants may go back to their native countries, disappointed by what they found or for other reasons, but for many, the poverty, tyranny, oppression, danger, or lack of opportunity they left behind makes such a course of action unthinkable. They understand all too well that there is no road back.

I should note here that I was a privileged immigrant, arriving with my medical training and a job lined up for me. Millions of immigrants are not so fortunate. They have to work very hard, often in harsh conditions, to build good lives for themselves.

For those who choose to stay in their adoptive country, the simple but profound realization that my cousin expressed becomes a guiding principle: "I have burned my bridges. I can't go back, so I had better not dwell on how much I miss home and family." It is that principle that Antonio Machado expresses in this short and eloquent poem.

In Machado's vision, there are no bridges to burn. The road that you came by has disappeared like a ship's wake. There is no road. The only road is the road you have made with your footprints. Now your feet are here, and your footprints have disappeared.

Machado, who was a deeply contemplative man, might well have thought of his poem figuratively as well. In other words, each of us travels our own unique road in life as we make our own way. It brings to mind Frost's poem, where the life you lead is determined by which road you take at each fork in the wood. Again, there is no road back. The time has passed. We are at a new place. Options and alternatives have been foreclosed, so we had best focus on the present and the road ahead, not the footprints that have disappeared.

Lines of Machado's poem, initially written in Spanish, were incorporated into a song by the same name, "Caminante no hay camino," composed and made enormously popular throughout the Spanish-speaking world by singer-songwriter Joan Manuel Serrat.

Takeaways

✘ **Acceptance**. We now see a repeated pattern: the first step in handling adversity is acceptance—in this case, of the fact that there is no road back.

✘ **Travel light**. The adage passed down from parent to child among the South Africans I knew (mostly the children of immigrants from Eastern Europe) was: "Education is crucial. Sometimes when you have to emigrate, that is all you have to take with you."

The Poet and the Poem

Antonio Machado (1875–1939) is one of the greatest twentieth-century poets in the Spanish language. His father was a folklorist and his brother, Manuel, was also a poet. Machado was born in Seville in 1875, and spent his childhood there. In 1883 he moved with his family to Madrid.

In 1899 Machado traveled with his brother to Paris to work as a translator, and there he met some of the leading literary figures of the day, including Oscar Wilde. Machado's time in Paris reinforced his resolve to become a poet. He received a doctoral degree in Madrid, attended the Sorbonne, and became a teacher of high school French.

In 1903 Machado published his first book of poetry (*Loneliness*). Much of his writing is tinged with sadness and melancholy. Several volumes followed.

In 1912 Machado married a much younger woman, who died of tuberculosis within a few years of their marriage. Her death inspired him to write a series of poems dealing with his grief.

The Spanish Civil War, which broke out in 1936, separated Machado from his brother, whom he would never see again. Along with his elderly mother, Machado fled to France, where he died. His mother died a few days later.

Chapter Twenty-Nine

AND THOSE YOU LEAVE BEHIND

LETTER TO MY MOTHER
by Salvatore Quasimodo
Translated by Jack Bevan

> *Mater dulcissima*, now the mists are descending,
> the Naviglio thrusts disorderly on the locks,
> the trees swell with water, burn with snow;
> I am not unhappy in the north: I am not
> at peace with myself, but seek
> pardon from no one, and many owe me tears.
> I know you are ailing, live
> like all mothers of poets, poor
> and just in the measure of their love
> for distant sons. Today it is I
> who write to you. . . . At last, you will say, a line
> from the boy who ran away at night
> Poor thing, so ready-hearted,
> one day, someday, they will kill him—
> Yes, I remember that grey stopping place
> for slow trains loaded with almonds, oranges,
> at the mouth of the Imera, the river full of magpies,
> salt and eucalyptus.
> But now I want to thank you
> truly for the wry smile you set
> on my lips, a smile as mild as your own;
> it has saved me pain and grief.

And if now I shed a tear for you,
and all who wait like you and do not know
what they wait for, it does not matter.
O gentle death,
do not touch the clock in the kitchen that ticks on the wall;
all my childhood was passed away on the enamel
of its dial, on those painted flowers;
do not touch the hands, the heart of the old.
Does anyone answer? O death of pity,
death of shame. Goodbye, dear one, farewell my
dulcissima mater.

This poem was extremely meaningful to me as I was leaving South Africa. Each time I read it, often aloud to myself or to a friend, I felt soothing along with sadness, like the mixture of pain and relief you feel when a sore muscle is pressed.

The poet addresses the letter to "*mater dulcissima*," "sweetest mother." He is writing some time after leaving home and has gained the ability to look back and think about how he left, whom he left behind, and what has occurred since then.

In the first line the poet writes, "Now the mists are descending," and moves immediately to a description of the landscape. But as we read further down in the poem, the driving emotional force is his mother's aging. The mists are descending for her as well, which is painful for any adult child to contemplate.

He describes the Naviglio, a river in the north of Italy whose overflowing waters "burn with snow." Later in the poem he recalls another river, the Imera in Sicily, where he was born, which he associates with running away from home and moving north:

Yes, I remember that grey stopping place
for slow trains loaded with almonds, oranges,
at the mouth of the Imera, the river full of magpies,
salt and eucalyptus.

At the beginning of the poem-letter, he tells his mother, "I am not unhappy in the north," although he adds, "I am not at peace with myself." The strong empathy between son and mother that pervades the poem suggests that she might not be surprised at this news, given her son's complexity. He attempts to console her by noting that he has done nothing wrong ("I . . . seek pardon from no one"). On the contrary, he notes, others should be crying for the wrongs they have done him. In other words, he has acted properly towards others. He probably knows his mother well enough to realize that it would make her happy to read that.

Quasimodo imagines how she must have felt when he left, how she feared with a mother's intuition that his ready heart would make him vulnerable to others, who might even kill him. But quickly his empathy shifts to her, and he thanks her for the wry smile he has inherited from her. But though it has saved him grief, it doesn't prevent him from shedding a tear when he contemplates her getting older as she edges closer to death.

In moving lines the poet speaks directly to death, calls it "gentle" and begs it "not to touch the clock in the kitchen that ticks on the wall." Stopping the clock is a tradition performed in some cultures when there is a death in the household. So, the poem pleads with death in poignant lines that I have repeated over and over to myself in years gone by:

Do not touch the clock in the kitchen that ticks on the wall;
all my childhood was passed away on the enamel

of its dial, on those painted flowers;
do not touch the hands, the heart of the old.

At another level, however, stopping the clock could mean stopping time from running inexorably forward. Can death not make an exception in its case? the poet asks, but knows his request is rhetorical. Death doesn't answer requests, and the hands will keep moving across the dial.

At the end, realizing that all his pleas to stop his mother's aging and dying are in vain, he bids her farewell.

Like the poet, I was blessed with a good mother, who did not stop me from emigrating to the north. In fact, she and my father did everything they could to help with the transition. Their parents had emigrated too, so they knew the drill. Get out when you can, and don't make a fuss!

In retrospect, I realize that immigrating even under the best of circumstances doesn't negate your feelings about leaving your family and your home for good. "Letter to My Mother" deals with the feelings for loved ones left behind.

Over time, I saw my elderly mother's health gradually deteriorate. The idea that I would be unable to be at her bedside when she died weighed heavily on me, and I shared that likelihood with her. "Well, there's always the telephone, you know," she replied, ever practical.

So it was, on a visit to Vancouver, I was walking through the vast Stanley Park with its huge trees when I saw a public telephone, which reminded me of her. That was before cell phones worked almost everywhere. I called her. She knew who I was, but not much more than that, and I remembered our earlier conversation. She was dying, I was far away, there was nothing to be done about it, but there was always the telephone and the memory of a loving mother.

As a psychiatrist, it has been my sad lot to hear from many people whose mothers have been troubled to the point that they have not been able to love freely. As I read Salvadore Quasimodo's poem, I think he was not one such person. Even though he has long since passed away, I feel a sense of happiness on his account that he had "*dulcissima mater*," the sweetest mother, who loved him and set him free to make his mark on the world.

Takeaways

✗ If you plan to emigrate or move far away, it is understandable to have feelings of sadness and loss towards those you leave behind.

✗ Do your best to stay in touch with them and help them if you can.

✗ If your children need to emigrate or move far away, let them go.

The Poet and the Poem

Salvatore Quasimodo (1901–1968) was awarded the Nobel Prize in Literature in 1959. He was born in Sicily. In order to become an engineer, he went to technical schools in Palermo and Rome. He studied Latin and Greek, but, unable to afford further study, he took a government engineering job. In 1930, he published his first poems and first book of poetry, *Acque e terre* ("Water and lands").

He rapidly became known in Italian literary circles, moved to Milan in 1938, and began to devote himself entirely to writing. He was a major literary figure in the mid-twentieth century.

Quasimodo married twice: Bice Donetti in 1926 (who died in 1948); and Maria Clementina Cumani, a famous Italian actress and dancer, with whom he had one son. The couple divorced in 1960.

Chapter Thirty

THE IMPORTANCE OF SELF-ACTUALIZATION

ON HIS BLINDNESS
by John Milton

When I consider how my light is spent,
    Ere half my days, in this dark world and wide,
    And that one Talent which is death to hide
    Lodged with me useless, though my Soul more bent
To serve therewith my Maker, and present
    My true account, lest he returning chide;
    "Doth God exact day-labour, light denied?"
    I fondly ask. But Patience, to prevent
That murmur, soon replies, "God doth not need
    Either man's work or his own gifts; who best
    Bear his mild yoke, they serve him best. His state
Is kingly. Thousands at his bidding speed
And post o'er Land and Ocean without rest:
They also serve who only stand and wait."

John Milton was a hugely influential English poet, widely acknowledged as a genius. Nowadays his most important contributions, such as his masterpiece *Paradise Lost*, are not widely read by the general public because they are considered too long and difficult. This small gem, however, enables us to appreciate the brilliant and profound mind of this celebrated poet.

In the first line, the poet introduces the subject of his reflection—his blindness, which has come on in midlife. He focuses on a particular problem it presents: his inability to use his one talent and thereby serve God.

The talent to which Milton is referring can be understood in different ways: his ability to write, and his ability to serve God. According to a parable in the New Testament (Matthew 25:14–30), before going on a journey, a master gave three servants different amounts of money (five, two, and one talents, which were units of currency at the time, representing enormous amounts of money), each according to his ability, to tend in his absence.

When the master returned, the servants who had received five and two talents had put the money to use and doubled its value. The third servant, afraid of what the master would do if he lost the money, hid it in the ground and had no profit to show for it. The master took away this servant's one talent from him and gave it to the one with the most talents.

In the sonnet, Milton says that "one Talent . . . is death to hide." He wonders whether he will be adversely judged for not having worked full days given his blindness: "Doth God exact day-labour, light denied?"

A personified patience responds: "God doth not need / Either man's work or his own gifts"; those who "bear his mild yoke" serve him best. The sonnet concludes with the famous line: "They also serve who only stand and wait."

You may recognize this as a Petrarchan sonnet (see page 16), in which the poet states his problem in the octet, and resolves it in the sestet.

I have included it here not only for its excellence but because it discusses two important topics.

The first is self-actualization.

Milton's observation that it is "death to hide" a talent raises the idea of self-actualization as formulated by the psychologist Abraham Maslow, who wrote: "A musician must make music, an artist must paint, a poet must write, if he is to be ultimately at peace with himself."

Maslow's widely cited hierarchy of needs, often represented as a pyramid with horizontal stripes, indicates human needs in order of importance. At the bottom of the pyramid are basic physiological needs; next comes safety; then love and a sense of connection; then esteem; and right at the top, after all the other needs are fulfilled, comes self-actualization. In working with my clients, I have come to realize how important self-actualization is. Sometimes it can feel like "that one Talent which is death to hide."

Self-actualization is not confined to famous people or super-achievers. Most of us have some talent, no matter how great or small, that is painful to hide and a joy to express. I will never forget Minnie, a middle-aged woman from my hometown, who baked a unique kind of ginger cookie—crunchy on the outside and moist on the inside—for which she became famous in the community (I can smell and taste them even as I write). Everyone identified Minnie with those cookies, and she would often introduce herself with pride as the woman who baked them. This is just one of the endless examples of talents which have to be expressed if a talented person is to feel fulfilled.

The other important theme in Milton's sonnet is belief in a kindly higher power.

He experiences relief when he feels freed from the guilt of not properly serving God.

Guilt is a painful feeling, so feeling released from guilt (a state of grace) is generally accompanied by relief and even euphoria. Some religious teachings encourage you to feel that there is something good about your existence even without doing anything to justify it. In the words of the American philosopher Abraham Joshua Heschel,

"Just to be is a blessing. Just to live is holy."

Often, unburdening yourself of painful feelings such as guilt and inadequacy can free you up and make you more effective. In fact, Milton found ways to continue to write by dictating his work to various scribes. He wrote some of his most important work, including *Paradise Lost*, after he went completely blind.

Takeaways

✘ **Recognize the importance of expressing whatever talent you have that cries out for actualization**. This does not have to be a talent that makes people rich or famous. It can be whatever makes you feel fulfilled, recognized, or appreciated.

✘ **Don't be too hard on yourself**. Do whatever you reasonably can to accomplish a task. If there are obstacles, acknowledge them and try to find a way around them—or ask someone to help you. In the meanwhile, try to adopt an encouraging voice towards yourself.

✘ **Recognize that the time for productivity may pass, and that just being a good person may have to be enough**.

The Poet and the Poem

John Milton (1608–1674) was a polymath who, despite being struck by blindness in midlife, is recognized as one of the greatest writers in the English language. He lived to the age of sixty-five, which was an unusually long life for the time, when the average life span was forty years. Encyclopedic in his learning, he had command of multiple languages, traveled widely, held high political office, and wrote some of the most celebrated poems in literature.

In his writings, Milton also took controversial political positions that included advocating divorce, the abolition of the Church of England, and the execution of Britain's King Charles I.

Milton was imprisoned for publishing his beliefs and might even have been executed had it not been for the intervention of powerful friends and family. He traveled on the European continent and in Florence met Galileo, who was under house arrest. He married three times and had five children.

Milton became blind by 1652, after which he had to dictate his writings for others to transcribe. It is at this time that he wrote "On His Blindness."

PSALM 23
A Psalm of David

> The LORD *is* my shepherd; I shall not want.
> He maketh me to lie down in green pastures: he leadeth me
>   beside the still waters.
> He restoreth my soul: he leadeth me in the paths of
>   righteousness for his name's sake.
> Yea, though I walk through the valley of the shadow of death,
>   I will fear no evil: for thou *art* with me; thy rod and thy
>   staff they comfort me.
> Thou preparest a table before me in the presence of mine
>   enemies: thou anointest my head with oil; my cup runneth
>   over.
> Surely goodness and mercy shall follow me all the days of my
>   life: and I will dwell in the house of the LORD for ever.

No collection of poems that offer consolation would be complete without including at least one psalm. The 150 psalms in the Old Testament, many of which (like this one) are attributed to King David, have long been associated with healing. They are often read to those who are ailing physically or mentally to offer comfort.

If you were to pick one psalm as an example of this comforting quality, Psalm 23 would be a top contender. The words and phrases from the King James Version (used here) are particularly beautiful, and the imagery especially poetic.

Psalm 23 presents a shepherd, an image that is sustained through the first three verses. In the same spirit as we saw in Milton's poem, the Lord is portrayed as an entirely positive force. In the very first verse, the poet says that he shall not want. In other words, under the care of the Lord, all the poet's needs will be met.

First the poet addresses his physical needs: the need to sleep comfortably (in green pastures) and to walk in a peaceful setting (still waters). The Lord also makes it easy for the poet not to stray: "He leadeth me in the paths of righteousness for his name's sake."

Then comes perhaps one of the most memorable verses in all the psalms: the representation of death as a shadow falling across us as we walk through a valley. But even there the poet fears no evil, because he senses that God is with him. The image of a rod, which elsewhere may be associated with punishment, is here a source of comfort, as is a shepherd's staff.

Now the shepherd feeds the poet, preparing a table even in the presence of his enemies. In other words, the Lord's protection enables the poet to eat comfortably even though his enemies are close at hand. The Lord goes on to elevate the poet by anointing his head with oil—a ceremony that turns an ordinary person into a king or priest. At this point, the poet is bathed in a sense of abundance, beautifully expressed in four simple words, "My cup runneth over," which has entered regular language. In the last verse, the poet expresses confidence in the future as he continues along his spiritual path: "Surely goodness and mercy shall follow me all the days of my life: and I will dwell in the house of the Lord for ever."

In sharing with us his joy in God's role in his life, the poet presents us with a totally comforting picture of this relationship, without the threats and punitive elements found in some religious writings. Small wonder that Psalm 23 is such a perennial favorite.

One personal anecdote in relation to this poem occurred when our Latin class was asked to translate the sentence about the valley of the shadow from English to Latin. I translated it in the subjunctive mood as: "Though I *may* walk through the valley of the shadow of death." Our Latin teacher, Dr. Elena Thomas, a brilliant Italian woman with a thick accent and a sharp wit, challenged the translation. "What are you doing using the subjunctive mood?" she demanded. "You *are* walking through the valley of the shadow of death! We all are! There is nothing subjunctive about it!" She was right, of course. There was more than bad grammar involved in my mistake. I was trying to distance myself from the prospect of my own death.

I became acutely aware of the "valley of the shadow" some years later, after a brutal attack almost killed me and landed me in a ward in the same hospital where I was serving as a medical intern. Elena came to visit (we were now on first-name terms) and was kind and solicitous.

"How are you feeling, Norman?" she asked.

"I feel stupid."

"*Why* are you feeling stupid?" I can still hear her Italian accent with the emphasis on the word "Why."

"It was stupid of me to be parking late at night in a lane with my girlfriend," I replied.

"Ah, Norman. Parking with a girlfriend in a car late at night is what life is all about!"

I felt greatly comforted.

In the years that followed, whenever I returned to South Africa to visit my family, I would catch up with Elena. I saw her age, as one does when you see people at long intervals over many years. She became blind, but her fiery spirit remained undaunted.

David, a South African friend, kept in touch with her as her health declined and visited her in the hospital, where she was suffering from her last illness. She had all her wits about her right up till the end at age eighty-eight. On his last visit to her, she asked him, "What's the matter?"

"I'm worried about you," he said.

"Everyone's got to die," she said, "it's no big deal."

A remarkable teacher, she remained true to the lesson she taught me in her high school Latin class, a lesson that transcended grammar and spoke to a fundamental truth about life. We all have to die. She held on to that truth fifty years later in the hour of her death. We *are* all walking through the valley of the shadow of death. It's a scary prospect, for which we can use any comfort we can find.

Takeaway

✘ If you are feeling tired, sick or despondent, you may find renewal, hope and comfort in the lines of Psalm 23, or any of a number of other psalms.

Chapter Thirty-Two

THE THRILL OF DISCOVERY

ON FIRST LOOKING INTO CHAPMAN'S HOMER
by John Keats

Much have I travell'd in the realms of gold,
    And many goodly states and kingdoms seen;
    Round many western islands have I been
Which bards in fealty to Apollo hold.
Oft of one wide expanse had I been told
    That deep-brow'd Homer ruled as his demesne;
    Yet did I never breathe its pure serene
Till I heard Chapman speak out loud and bold:

Then felt I like some watcher of the skies
    When a new planet swims into his ken;
Or like stout Cortez, when with eagle eyes
    He star'd at the Pacific—and all his men
Look'd at each other with a wild surmise—
    Silent, upon a peak in Darien.

In the first line of this famous poem, Keats sets the scene of the action: the isles of Greece, the great poet Homer, and the translation of his works by George Chapman, first published in 1616. By "the realms of gold" Keats means the ancient world, where gold refers not only to the sun-filled isles but also to the golden works that flowed from them. The bards of the time showed loyalty to the sun god Apollo, and among these bards, the "deep-browed" Homer reigned supreme. His great epics, the *Odyssey* and the *Iliad*, in which angry Apollo played a key role, were familiar to Keats.

The present poem celebrates a translation that Keats had just read for the first time, which so greatly excited the young poet that he was impelled to write a sonnet expressing his sense of discovery and wonder at experiencing Homer's great works afresh.

Keats' excitement brings to mind another story from ancient Greece. The great physicist and mathematician Archimedes was struggling with a problem: how to determine whether the king's newly acquired crown was made of pure gold, as advertised, or had been alloyed with a cheaper metal.

To solve the problem, Archimedes needed to determine the crown's density, which required knowing both its weight and its volume. Its weight was easy to measure, but nobody at the time knew how to measure the volume of an unevenly shaped object—until Archimedes climbed into the most famous bathtub of all time. As he sank into the water, he noticed that the level in the bathtub rose, and the answer suddenly came to him. By dipping the crown in water and observing the volume of water displaced, he could establish its volume and thus discover its density. So excited was he, that he ran down the streets of Athens—stark naked, so the story goes—exclaiming "Eureka!", meaning "I found it." He put the crown to the test and, unfortunately for the king and whoever had made his crown, the density was too low, which meant that the denser gold had been mixed with a less dense (and cheaper) metal.

This vignette captures the wonder of discovery and the irrepressible urge to share this excitement with others, which Keats communicates in this classical Petrarchan sonnet (See page 16).

Even though the poet had read other translations of Homer (presumably those of Dryden and Pope), never had he experienced the freshness of Chapman's version ("its pure serene"). Keats almost shouts out his excitement at the end of the octet: "Till I heard Chapman speak out loud and bold."

This volta sets the stage for the sestet: the wonder of discovery. In his excitement, Keats reflects on other discoveries that he imagines must surely have evoked similar feelings. In referencing "some watcher of the skies," Keats was probably referring to the astronomer Sir William Herschel, who had recently discovered the planet Uranus. He follows that with the apocryphal story of "Cortez" first sighting the Pacific from a mountaintop in the province of Darien in Panama. In fact, Keats was confusing two conquistadors. He meant Vasco Núñez de Balboa, the first European to discover the Pacific, rather than Hernán Cortés, who conquered the Aztec empire in Mexico, but even after the mistake had been pointed out to him, he left "Cortez" in the poem, perhaps because it scans far better that way.

In both instances, Keats communicates not only the discoveries, but the sense of amazement and wonder that must have accompanied them. We can almost feel the astronomer's thrill as "some new planet drifts into his ken," or the conquistador staring at the Pacific for the first time "with eagle eyes," while his men silently stare at each other "with a wild surmise." These are Keats' associations to his excitement at first looking into Chapman's Homer.

This poem came to mind when I was working as a junior psychiatrist and researcher at the National Institute of Mental Health in Maryland. My colleagues and I had recruited a cohort of people who had reported becoming depressed every winter. When they entered the study, they all looked fine, and skeptical colleagues questioned whether they would get depressed when winter arrived. Right on schedule, as the days shortened, the study subjects began to report the symptoms of what we later called seasonal affective disorder. At a certain point we were ready to take the key step: to expose the patients to bright environmental light and see if they responded.

I vividly recall one of the first patients to respond to light therapy, coming into our research unit, smiling broadly and telling us that she couldn't remember feeling so happy before, especially in winter. The nurses on the unit stared at each other, if not in wild surmise, then at least with great delight, and certainly not silently. At that moment, I thought of Keats' poem and of the experience of wonder that is one of life's great sources of delight. Nowadays I try to cultivate that feeling in response to experiences both great and small, which enhances the joy of being alive.

Takeaways

✖ **Be prepared to experience wonder every day and everywhere you go.** If you are open to the possibility, you can find wonder and delight in more places than I can name. Here are a few: sunset; twilight; falling in love; the birth of a child; watching her or him grow up; live theater; an exciting sporting game (for example, the Chicago Cubs winning the World Series in 2016, after a 108-year drought); plying your art or trade or profession and seeing people benefit from it. The opportunities for wonder are boundless and ubiquitous.

✖ **Consider discovery as one source of wonder.** As you see, the poet's "discovery" was simply coming across a fresh translation of a classic work. For another type of person, a meaningful discovery might arise from an entirely different event. Finally, if you are a scientist like Archimedes, you may discover a law of nature while soaking in your bathtub, but I suggest you wear a robe before running through the city streets.

The Poet and the Poem

John Keats (1795–1821) is regarded as one of the greatest British poets, even though his life was short and his body of work correspondingly less voluminous than that of many of his peers. Yet he is credited with writing some of the finest poems in the English language, including "Ode on a Grecian Urn," "Ode on Melancholy," and "Ode to a Nightingale."

Keats, the oldest of four children, lost both parents at a young age. His father, a livery stable keeper, was trampled to death by a horse when Keats was eight; his mother died of tuberculosis six years later.

Keats was educated at Enfield School, whose headmaster took a paternal interest in orphaned boys, and the headmaster's son, Charles Cowden Clarke, became a good friend. Both father and son encouraged Keats in his literary ambitions.

Keats left school early and graduated as an apothecary, but his love was for poetry. When he was twenty-five, he met Leigh Hunt, an influential editor, who published "On First Looking into Chapman's Homer," commonly regarded as Keats' first mature poem.

The circumstances in which Keats wrote this famous sonnet are well documented. Clarke first brought Chapman's translation to Keats' attention. The two friends sat up all night reading the translation, with Keats shouting out his delight in response to certain passages. Keats left at daylight and by ten o'clock in the morning, Clarke found the sonnet, more or less as you see it above, on his breakfast table.

The poem, written in 1816, has since become a great classic. Consider what a genius Keats must have been to compose such a masterpiece in a few hours after a night without sleep. He was twenty-one years old at the time and had only five more years to live.

Keats packed into those five years all the energy that a young genius in a hurry could muster: publishing another volume of poetry; going on a walking tour of England and Scotland; caring for his brother Tom, sick with tuberculosis; and falling in love with Fanny Brawne.

Before long, however, Keats contracted tuberculosis, and his health deteriorated so badly that his doctor ordered him to go to a warm climate for the winter. He went to Rome with his friend, the painter Joseph Severn, who nursed him devotedly. Keats died in his friend's arms and was buried in Rome in 1821 under a tombstone bearing the following words, as per his request: "Here lies One whose name was writ in Water."

Chapter Thirty-Three

THE ENDURING THRILL OF THE MOMENT

HIGH FLIGHT
by John Gillespie Magee Jr.

Oh! I have slipped the surly bonds of Earth
And danced the skies on laughter-silvered wings;
Sunward I've climbed, and joined the tumbling mirth
Of sun-split clouds—and done a hundred things
You have not dreamed of—wheeled and soared and swung
High in the sunlit silence. Hov'ring there,
I've chased the shouting wind along, and flung
My eager craft through footless halls of air . . .

Up, up the long, delirious, burning blue
I've topped the wind-swept heights with easy grace
Where never lark, or ever eagle flew—
And, while with silent, lifting mind I've trod
The high untrespassed sanctity of space,
Put out my hand, and touched the face of God.

Flying is represented in several poems in this collection, its exuberance frequently paired with its danger. Think of Icarus spreading his wings of wax and feathers, so carried away with delight that he flies too close to the sun and crashes (chapters 5 and 44). But perhaps the present poem is the purest representation of the thrill of human flight in all of poetry. In fact, *Air and Space Magazine* declared "High Flight" to be the most enduring of aviation poems.

The first line is perhaps most famous and oft quoted: "Oh! I have slipped the surly bonds of Earth."

President Ronald Reagan quoted it after the tragic explosion of the *Challenger* shuttle in 1986. The former actor did justice to the great line (which is all I remember from his speech). The idea that the "bonds of Earth"—its gravitational force—are "surly" is in itself novel. For most of us, having our feet firmly planted on the ground is a source of comfort and assurance. For this aviator-poet, however, it is unwelcome, something to be slipped, like detention or an unpleasant social engagement. The world "surly" echoes Shakespeare's sonnet 29 (chapter 9), which refers to the lark arising from "sullen" earth.

This poem was written to celebrate Magee's having set a new record height for the World War II Spitfire fighter. How scary it must be to hurtle through the sky so fast that a wrong move can be fatal! For this poet, however, it held nothing but delight.

Despite the modern subject of the poem, you may recognize that it is, once again, a Petrarchan sonnet (see page 16). The octet is festooned with joyful images—"laughter-silvered wings," and "the tumbling mirth / Of sun-split clouds." The poet-pilot is obviously having fun, wheeling, soaring, hovering, and chasing the wind. The octet ends with the phrase "footless halls of air," reminding us that only the air is supporting him.

At the end of the octet, where the volta usually occurs, we see an ellipsis, which, I suggest, represent the shift in the pilot's intentions from flying low, close to the clouds, to breaking the record for the highest flight ever recorded with that plane up to that time.

The sestet begins with: "Up, up the long delirious burning blue."

Happiness now turns into euphoria as the poet realizes that he has flown higher than even the most powerful birds can. The last three lines describe the essence of a peak experience:

> And, while with silent, lifting mind I've trod
> The high untrespassed sanctity of space,
> Put out my hand, and touched the face of God.

To get some sense of how Magee might have felt to fly above the clouds in a Spitfire and then surge upwards, I consulted with Ben Berman, a pilot who has been flying with a major airline for decades. According to Berman:

> It's a special experience for pilots to break through the clouds and smash into them, to fly just above the clouds, with the prop cutting into the tops and the plane skimming them. It's called "being on the top." You really feel your speed at 6,000 to 15,000 feet because you're so close to these solid-looking masses that then give way.
>
> If you plan to fly higher, you're only able to enjoy the experience for a few seconds because you're actively monitoring the plane and its responses. You are referencing the nose and wingtips with the horizon, monitoring the rate of climb, pitch attitude and air speed. You are rapidly switching between functions.

Berman considers it a bold and potentially hazardous move on Magee's part to fly as high as possible. He explains first the thrill of it, then the hazards:

> To get a record, you'd have to be careful not to exceed the maximum height for the plane. You start out as a zoom climb and might want to shout "Yeah!" But there's work involved.

You'd have to know what level you are targeting in order to remain below service ceiling. Remember, it's the air that's holding you up, and the higher you fly, the thinner the air gets. As the air gets thinner over the wings, you can stall, and the plane can fall out of the sky.

Berman agrees with speculations that the euphoria of Magee's flight might have been fueled by hypoxia, which can occur when a pilot flies so high that the oxygen mask fails to compensate for the low oxygen levels in the cockpit.

The poet's euphoria is accompanied by grandiosity. He boasts, "I've . . . done a hundred things you have not dreamed of" and that he's flying where no birds can. Like Icarus, he revels in the delight of flying as high as he can and takes us along for the exuberant ride. In so doing, Magee has crystallized the thrill of the moment and preserved it for all time.

One can view "High Flight" as a "peak experience" as defined by psychologist Abraham Maslow, who recognized such experiences as states of ecstasy accompanied by certain ways of thinking (as discussed in chapter 4). According to Maslow, during peak experiences, "the world is only seen as beautiful, good, desirable and worthwhile." Peak experiences may be viewed as highly valuable, something that lends meaning to people's lives, and often take on a religious sense, as we see in the last line of the poem.

Sometimes in seeking peak experiences, however, people may endanger themselves by taking excessive risks. In his final thought on Magee's "High Flight," Berman quoted an expression well known to aviators: "There are old pilots and bold pilots, but no old, bold pilots."

Takeaways

✘ **Peak experiences can be valuable and important to the person having them. (See also "Lullaby," chapter 4.)** In ordinary life, peak experiences typically happen when we fall in love, get married, have our first child, or accomplish something important to us.

There are brain neurotransmitters responsible for feelings of joy and happiness, including dopamine, serotonin, and endorphins.

✘ **Be careful of peak experiences.** Brain pathways responsible for high levels of joy or exuberance did not evolve so as to be activated too often or too powerfully. In certain instances they may lead us to take dangerous and unnecessary risks.

The Poet and the Poem

Pilot officer John Gillespie Magee Jr. was an American serving with the Royal Canadian Air Force. He was born in China in 1922 to an American father and a British mother, both missionaries. He moved to England with his mother at age nine and went to Rugby School, where he aspired to become a poet like former Rugby alumnus Rupert Brooke. He emulated Brooke's style and won a school poetry prize for his poem about the burial of Brooke's body in Greece after he had been killed in World War I.

Magee visited the United States and, unable to return to Britain because of the outbreak of World War II, finished his schooling there. He declined a scholarship to Yale, choosing instead to enlist in the Royal Canadian Air Force in 1940. He trained to become a pilot officer and returned to Britain, where he learned to fly a Spitfire.

In 1941, Magee began to fly combat missions. In occupied France, Magee's four-ship section was engaged by the Luftwaffe, and he was the only member of the party to survive. At the end of 1941, in his tenth week of active service, Magee was killed flying a Spitfire during a training accident in which he collided in midair with another young pilot. He completed his famous poem "High Flight" a few months before his death, after the record 33,000-feet flight.

He was only nineteen at the time.

Chapter Thirty-Four

THE LONG REACH OF TRAUMA

THE SENTENCE

by Anna Akhmatova

Translated by Judith Hemschemeyer

> And the stone word fell
> On my still-living breast.
> Never mind, I was ready.
> I will manage somehow.
>
> Today I have so much to do:
> I must kill memory once and for all,
> I must turn my soul to stone,
> I must learn to live again—
>
> Unless . . . Summer's ardent rustling
> Is like a festival outside my window.
> For a long time I've foreseen this
> Brilliant day, deserted house.

I came across this poem thanks to Nancy Nersessian, a professor of cognitive science at Georgia Tech University, who had submitted it to former U.S. poet laureate Robert Pinsky's Favorite Poem Project.

"The Sentence" addresses a critical emotional problem—the psychological consequences of trauma—and is of special interest to me because it deals with post-traumatic stress disorder (PTSD), a huge mental health problem.

The poem begins by connecting two curious phrases: "the stone word" with "my still-living breast," conveying a mixture of life and lifelessness. "Never mind," the poet says to reassure herself, "I will manage somehow," like a parent comforting a child. As adults, however, we realize that we don't say "never mind" unless there is in fact something to mind.

In the second stanza, the poet gives herself a strange set of instructions for the day: to kill memory once and for all, to turn her soul to stone, and to learn to live again. These instructions raise more questions than they answer. Can you "kill memory," and if you could, would it be a good thing to do? Certainly the desire to "live again" seems healthy, but how might she learn to do so? And what kind of life would it be if she were to turn her soul to stone?

The last stanza starts with a word of hope: "Unless . . ." raising the possibility that maybe she can spontaneously feel better with "Summer's ardent rustling," which is "like a festival outside my window." But the poem ends on a pessimistic note. Although the day is brilliant, the house (normally a haven and source of comfort) is deserted.

To anyone familiar with PTSD, the emotions expressed in this poem will be quite familiar. Symptoms of PTSD include several elements mentioned here: (1) numbness and detachment; (2) avoidance (a wish to kill memories); (3) a sad mood; and (4) a markedly decreased interest in activities.

I spoke to Dr. Nersessian and asked her why, of all Akhmatova's many poems, she chose this particular one. It resonated most strongly, she said, because it helped her understand her brother David, with whom she had always been close. Here is what she had to say about him:

> David graduated as a commissioned officer at the young age of nineteen, and was sent to fight in Vietnam. When he was growing up, he had so many dreams, so many things he wanted to do. . . . He was somebody you always noticed because he was always lively and full of energy.
>
> When he came back from Vietnam, however, he didn't have any life in him. He had become addicted to heroin in Vietnam but, with the help of treatment, he had managed to kick the addiction. His other problems, however, never went away. He always had flashbacks, nightmares. He married, had children . . . but he was always a broken man.

The Vietnam War ended in 1975, and David lived till 1997. Yet Nersessian dates his emotional death to July 4, 1970. Here's how she describes it:

> He had been out on a mission and he was very, very tired. And he decided to ask a friend Billy Sullivan if he would walk point for him that day. And when Billy Sullivan walked point, he was killed. And David never, never recovered from that. He always thought that he should have died that day and every 4th of July after that he had a terrible time.

Dr. Nersessian found comfort in Akhmatova's words, which she felt expressed her brother's long struggle to deal with this traumatic memory.

The last stanza of the poem reminds me of many veterans after they return from the battlefield. Although they may be greeted by the pageant of civilian life, their inner numbness prevents them from enjoying it. The day may be brilliant, but the house is deserted. That was part of David's story as well.

PTSD is an enormous problem among U.S. veterans, currently accounting for twenty-one suicides per day. As of the time of writing, suicide has killed more veterans than all the direct casualties in both the Iraq and Afghanistan wars. The majority of current veteran suicides result from the Vietnam War, indicating that the problem doesn't just get better on its own.

In the aftermath of trauma, some of the symptoms of PTSD derive from unconscious memories in a brain defending itself against the overwhelming impact of trauma, but at a disastrous cost. Some PTSD therapists believe that avoidance prevents therapeutically processing the trauma.

Treating PTSD

There are several approaches currently used to treat PTSD in both veterans and civilians, though they are often only partially effective. None of them involves trying to "kill memory," which most experts would agree would be unhelpful at best and perhaps harmful.

Here is a partial list of some better-known treatments for PTSD in veterans:

1. Cognitive behavior therapy (CBT), including two special types of CBT: cognitive processing therapy (CPT) and prolonged exposure (PE).
2. Eye movement desensitization and reprocessing (EMDR), in which people are encouraged to scan their eyes from left to right while remembering a traumatic event.

3. Interpersonal therapy, which involves building up personal connections.

4. Present centered therapy (PCT), a verbal therapy in which people are encouraged to focus on the present and allow past traumas to recede into the background.

5. Transcendental Meditation (TM).

Transcendental Meditation for PTSD

Most of what I have learned about combat-related PTSD comes from my work on the effects of TM on veterans suffering from this disabling condition: casualties of World War II, Vietnam, Afghanistan, and Iraq. Several of these veterans have been my friends. One of them, the late Jerry Yellin, chronicled his World War II experiences, PTSD, and recovery with the help of TM.

In his memoir *The Resilient Warrior*, Yellin describes his life as a fighter pilot in the Second World War, where "I quickly became familiar with death." He flew nineteen long-range missions over Japan from Iwo Jima with eleven other young pilots, none of whom returned home. As he puts it, "Life for me from 1946 to 1975 was empty. The highs I had experienced in combat became the lows of daily living. I had absolutely no connection to my parents, my sister, my relatives, or my friends." Despite marriage and the birth of four sons, Jerry continued to suffer. As he writes:

"I couldn't find contentment, any reason to succeed, any connection to anyone that had meaning or value. I was depressed, unhappy, and lonely even though surrounded by my family."

Jerry suffered for thirty years until learning TM. After a few weeks of practice, he says, "I felt a connection to my inner self. My anger and resentment began to dissipate, and a calmness that I never knew before became apparent, not only to me but to my family as well. As time progressed I found myself thinking differently about the world around me, and found a direction that had been missing in my life."

Observations such as these led my colleagues and me to systematically study the effects of TM on PTSD. We conducted a promising controlled study at the VA San Diego Healthcare System, and a large-scale multi-center study is currently underway.

Can Poetry Help PTSD?

In a 2018 *New York Times* op-ed piece entitled "What Kept Me From Killing Myself," acclaimed novelist and Iraq War veteran Kevin Powers wrote about how the written word saved his life. He had returned home with disabling symptoms of PTSD. He was depressed, suicidal, and numbed himself with alcohol.

Here's how he described the beginning of his recovery:

One day, for some reason, I picked up "The Collected Poems of Dylan Thomas" and found that the following oft-quoted lines of Thomas's provided me with a moment of, for lack of a better word, grace: "These poems, with all their crudities, doubts, and confusions, are written for the love of man and in praise of God, and I'd be a damn fool if they weren't." . . .

For the first time in a long while I recognized myself in another, and somehow that simple tether allowed me to slowly pull myself away from one of the most terrifying beliefs common to the ailment I'm describing, that one is utterly alone, uniquely so, and that this condition is permanent.

In an interview with Powers, I asked him what was so special about the words of Dylan Thomas that were the fulcrum of his recovery. He replied:

I think it was his bravery and vulnerability, an acknowledgment of flaw and insufficiency, but also a celebration of the effort, the attempt and the desire. So . . . being the kind of person who wants to engage with the world but accepting that the best-case scenario is to do it imperfectly is reassuring. Even though Dylan Thomas has a reputation as being one of the greats of the twentieth century, he acknowledges a kind of humility and modesty along with a kind of daring.

In this short and powerful piece, Powers describes how the right words, presented in the right way, at the right time, can provide a crucial thread that enables readers to find their way out of painful estrangement into the company of their fellow human beings.

A 2019 *Wall Street Journal* article reported on the use of poetry as therapy being conducted at the James J. Peters VA Medical Center in the Bronx, New York. One veteran in the program requested the poem "Invictus," about overcoming extreme adversity, which he remembered from the past (see chapter 38). Reading it aloud helped fortify his resolve to keep on fighting his illness.

This anecdotal evidence reinforces the idea that poetry may have a role in helping people with PTSD and other afflictions.

Takeaways

✘ **The mind and body remember trauma for many years.** Sometimes for a person's whole life, even though victims may not be able to recall traumas consciously.

✘ **It is important to recognize the symptoms of PTSD in yourself or a loved one. PTSD can have major consequences in the lives of trauma victims and their families—and it is treatable.**

✖ There are many ways to help people with PTSD, as listed above.

✖ Literature in general and poetry in particular can help people with PTSD by letting them know that they are not alone in their suffering.

The Poet and the Poem

Anna Akhmatova (1889–1966), whose literary career spanned sixty years, was one of the greatest Russian poets of the twentieth century. Born to an aristocratic family in a wealthy suburb of St. Petersburg, she was educated at a girls' school. Although she entered law school in Kiev, she decided to pursue an early talent for poetry instead.

She came to the attention of the poet Nikolai Gumilyov, who promoted her poetry and spent years pursuing her romantically. Finally, after seven years, Akhmatova agreed to marry him. While on honeymoon in Paris, she met the famous artist Amedeo Modigliani, with whom she developed a friendship.

Akhmatova became a leading literary figure in bohemian St. Petersburg, famous for her beauty and charisma. Her life changed with World War I and the Bolshevik Revolution. Akhmatova's poetry now no longer focused on love, but on politics. Unsurprisingly, she fell foul of the totalitarian regime, but chose to stay in Russia despite her friends' pleas for her to leave. She divorced her husband (by whom she had a son) as well as her next husband.

During her many years as a leading Russian intellectual, Akhmatova experienced multiple traumas, including the two World Wars and the horrors of the Stalin era. The litany of indignities, hardships, and losses to which she was subjected is hard to imagine. She suffered from multiple physical illnesses, was treated as an enemy of the state, had her poems banned, and saw friends and close relatives imprisoned and exiled to the gulag. Her son spent most of his youth in labor camps and was imprisoned several times, finally being sent to Siberia for seven years. Her former husband, Gumilyov, was sent to prison, where he was shot, and many people she knew met similar fates.

Akhmatova would stand in line for hours to deliver food for her son and plead on his behalf. She describes this experience in a famous preface to her masterpiece, "Requiem," which goes as follows:

> In the terrible years of the Yezhov terror, I spent seventeen months in the prison lines of Leningrad. Once, someone "recognized" me. Then a woman with bluish lips standing behind me, who, of course, had never heard me called by name before, woke up from the stupor to which everyone had succumbed and whispered in my ear (everyone spoke in whispers there):
>
> "Can you describe this?"
>
> And I answered: "Yes I can."
>
> Then something that looked like a smile passed over what had once been her face.

As you see, there is probably no poet better qualified to write about trauma and its aftermath than Akhmatova. Her twelve-line poem "The Sentence" gives us a glimpse into the mind of this brilliant woman, her art, and the devastating consequences of trauma.

Chapter Thirty-Five

THE DANGER OF ANGER

A POISON TREE
by William Blake

I was angry with my friend;
I told my wrath, my wrath did end.
I was angry with my foe:
I told it not, my wrath did grow.

And I waterd it in fears,
Night & morning with my tears:
And I sunned it with smiles,
And with soft deceitful wiles.

And it grew both day and night.
Till it bore an apple bright.
And my foe beheld it shine,
And he knew that it was mine.

And into my garden stole,
When the night had veild the pole;
In the morning glad I see;
My foe outstretched beneath the tree.

This poem reminds me of Duncan, a highly successful middle-aged businessman whose anger caused problems for him both at home and in business. Duncan's anger took many forms. He would get furious when he felt provoked or insulted, his face turning so red that his wife worried he would have a stroke. He often misinterpreted other people's neutral actions and motivations as hostile and demolished many relationships under the wrecking ball of his rage.

Duncan developed a vendetta against a business associate whom I will call Jimmy Green. At every session he would decry Green's latest outrages and detail strategies for getting even with him. I explained to him the dangers to himself of living in a state of perpetual anger, but to no avail.

They say that revenge is a dish best served cold, and Duncan was certainly able to wait before dishing his out. But he was also given to sudden outbursts of rage. For example, he could not tolerate being cut off in traffic. Once after this happened, he shifted lanes so his car was alongside that of the offending driver. When they stopped at the next red light, he opened his window and spat into the man's face before speeding off.

According to a Chinese proverb, before you plan revenge, you had best dig two graves. The years of anger caught up with Duncan, who had a heart attack, required bypass surgery, and suffered other stress-related illnesses. Such problems are common in people with anger problems. In fact, one panel of cardiologists rated chronic anger as a risk factor for cardiovascular disease as serious as smoking and unhealthy eating.

With that clinical vignette in mind, let me return to Blake's poem. The first stanza sets the stage for the rest and in four simple lines provides a powerful antidote for toxic anger: talk to yourself. The poet is capable of settling his anger down by addressing it directly, as he decides to do when angry with a friend. He doesn't choose to do so when dealing with an enemy, however, so his anger grows. Which course he chooses to take is a conscious decision.

When he doesn't "tell" his anger, he actually cultivates it as one might a fruit tree:

> And I waterd it in fears,
> Night & morning with my tears.

Hypocritically, he dissembles, pretending to be friendly:

> And I sunned it with smiles,
> And with soft deceitful wiles.

The enemy is deceived by the poet's strategy, which bears a shining fruit that tempts him into the garden to steal and take a bite out of it. The next morning, the poet is glad to see the corpse of his enemy stretched out beneath the tree.

Although the poet is represented as guilty by setting a trap for his enemy, the latter is guilty of trespassing and stealing the apple. Blake sets up a morally complex scenario. But our focus here is on anger and its potential consequences.

Like every emotion, anger does have value in certain circumstances. Aristotle pointed out the distinction between healthy and unhealthy anger as follows:

Anybody can become angry, that is easy; but to be angry with the right person, and to the right degree, and at the right time, and for the right purpose, and in the right way, that is not within everybody's power, that is not easy.

All too often, however, we encounter malignant anger: a knee to the neck, a baby shaken, someone casually shot to death. Less dramatically, we see daily cases of road rage, bullying, and online persecution. Fortunately, much can be done for people with anger management problems—including having them read Blake's poem.

The basic idea behind "A Poison Tree" has its modern counterpart in the "Legend of Two Wolves," which has been attributed to the Cherokee or Lenape Indians. In one popular version, a conversation occurs between a grandson and a grandfather in which the grandson says (perhaps based on a dream) that there is a battle going on inside him between two wolves, one that is all good and one that is all bad. He asks his grandfather which wolf will win the battle. The grandfather replies, "The one you feed."

I suspect that Blake, who might have anticipated this parable, would have approved of the answer, perhaps adding, "And the one you talk to."

Takeaways

✖ **Be careful when and how you express anger.** When appropriate in degree, method of expression, and chosen object, anger can be useful. When excessive, unreasonable, and misdirected, it can have dire consequences for both angry people and their victims.

✖ **Angry people need first of all to recognize that they have an anger problem.** This is often difficult, because the angry person usually rationalizes and dismisses the anger as justified by the circumstances, thereby disclaiming responsibility. It is valuable to realize that regardless of the validity of the anger, it can still be a problem in its own right.

✘ **In trying to help an angry person, I often find it useful to involve a person's partner or suggest group therapy with other people with anger problems.** Anybody who is being abused (as is often the case with partners of angry people) can often benefit from help as well.

✘ **Strategies that may help angry people include cognitive behavior therapy, meditation, yoga, and exercise.**

The Poet and the Poem

William Blake (1757–1827) was born in London to James and Katherine Blake. He was marked as unusual from early childhood, when he described having visions. At four he saw God "put his head to the window;" at nine he saw "a tree full of angels." His parents saw that he was different from other children and educated him at home. At age ten Blake said he wanted to become a painter, so his parents sent him to drawing school. At age twelve he began writing poetry. From these early beginnings, Blake went on to become a successful engraver, painter, and poet.

In 1789 he published *Songs of Innocence*, his most popular collection, and, five years later, *Songs of Experience*, both printed with illustrations. "A Poison Tree" was published in *Songs of Experience*.

Blake was revolutionary in his thinking and wrote against oppressive systems such as the English monarchy, eighteenth-century political and social tyranny, and the authority of church and state.

In 1800 Blake's patron William Haley invited him to the coastal town of Felpham, where he lived and worked until 1803. There he taught himself Greek, Latin, Hebrew, and Italian, which inspired him to write several epic poems.

Blake was a kind person. He taught his wife Catherine to read, write, draw and even experience his visions, in which she unquestionably believed for the forty-five years of their marriage. He also trained his younger brother, Robert, to draw, paint and engrave. When Robert became ill in 1787 and died, probably of tuberculosis, Blake saw his brother's spirit rise up through the ceiling, "clapping its hands for joy." He believed that Robert's spirit continued to visit him and provide him with inspiration. Blake and Catherine had no children.

Despite Blake's genius and prolific output, he never made a good living, but was supported emotionally and financially by friends. Despite his material poverty, Blake's work lives on. His paintings and sketches are displayed in the foremost galleries, and his poems are widely read. As we see from "A Poison Tree," his writing still feels fresh and relevant centuries after the ink dried on his page.

PART FOUR

A Design for Living and the Search for Meaning

This above all: to thine own self be true.

—William Shakespeare

Chapter Thirty-Six

PRINCIPLES FOR A GOOD LIFE

POLONIUS' ADVICE TO LAERTES
by William Shakespeare
From *Hamlet*, act 1, scene 3

> Yet here, Laertes! aboard, aboard, for shame!
> The wind sits in the shoulder of your sail,
> And you are stay'd for. There; my blessing with thee!
> And these few precepts in thy memory
> Look thou character. Give thy thoughts no tongue,
> Nor any unproportioned thought his act.
> Be thou familiar, but by no means vulgar.
> Those friends thou hast, and their adoption tried,
> Grapple them to thy soul with hoops of steel,
> But do not dull thy palm with entertainment
> Of each new-hatch'd, unfledged comrade. Beware
> Of entrance to a quarrel, but being in,
> Bear't that the opposed may beware of thee.
> Give every man thy ear, but few thy voice;
> Take each man's censure, but reserve thy judgement.
> Costly thy habit as thy purse can buy,
> But not express'd in fancy; rich, not gaudy;
> For the apparel oft proclaims the man,
> And they in France of the best rank and station
> Are of a most select and generous chief in that.
> Neither a borrower nor a lender be;
> For loan oft loses both itself and friend,

(continued)

And borrowing dulleth edge of husbandry.
This above all: to thine own self be true,
And it must follow, as the night the day,
Thou canst not then be false to any man.
Farewell: my blessing season this in thee!

This scene from *Hamlet* takes place as Laertes, Polonius's son and Hamlet's friend, is about to set sail for France. In this famous speech, the father uses this opportunity to give his son advice. An erudite friend, on looking over the table of contents for this book, said, "I don't think you want to include Polonius in a book about helpful wisdom. He was, after all, a foolish busybody with little credibility."

I agree with his assessment of the old man, and it has always been a paradox to me how Shakespeare chose to put such wise lines in the mouth of a foolish man. Was the playwright showing us that people are complex—that foolish men can offer wise advice? Or did Shakespeare put himself in the mind of a father (which he was) and conjure up these excellent parental guidelines that he simply couldn't resist using, even if they had to come out of the mouth of a fool? We will never know. In any event, I have included the speech here because it is full of useful insights elegantly expressed, which I have actually used in my own life and my work with clients.

The father starts with the words:

And these few precepts in thy memory
Look thou character.

In Shakespearean English, "character" means *write*. So Polonius means, "Write these precepts down in your memory." It is easy to miss this, because the advice that follows refers to elements of character as we understand the word nowadays. Anyway, let's see what we can take away from his advice.

"Neither a borrower nor a lender be." This advice has been particularly useful to me. My mother used to say, "If you lend money to a friend, consider it a gift." With the benefit of experience, I now understand what she meant. Someone who needs to borrow money from a friend may not be able to pay the loan back, and other creditors will generally take precedence. That can put a strain on friendship, as the borrower often feels guilty and will want to avoid the lender.

I once loaned money to a friend who, in all fairness, signaled to me that he would not soon be in a position to repay it. Some years passed, during which a strain developed in the friendship. A keystone birthday of his arrived, and as a gift, I forgave the loan, which cleared the air between us. Since then, if a friend has needed money and I have been able and willing to part with it, I have made it clear that it is a gift, not a loan.

Polonius also advises Laertes not to borrow money, for "borrowing dulls the edge of husbandry." In other words, if money is readily available to you through borrowing, you will have less incentive to figure out ways to manage your finances yourself.

Ever the consummate dramatist, Shakespeare leaves the most important piece of advice for last: "This above all: to thine own self be true." This piece of advice sounds so modern that it seems almost like a cliché. Yet Shakespeare appears to have been the first person to write it. In classical times, the words "Know thyself" were inscribed at the oracle of Delphi. Shakespeare has taken the ancient dictum a step further.

Nowadays every self-help guide worth its publisher's advance must surely incorporate this piece of advice in some form. Here is Shakespeare's reason for it:

> And it must follow, as the night the day,
> Thou canst not then be false to any man.

It is curious that Shakespeare, a writer-actor who created and played so many parts, should have so valued being true to oneself. It reminds me of actor Hugh Jackman, whom I interviewed for my book *Super Mind* on his experience with TM. I asked him how he could reconcile being authentic as a person with having to put on the many masks required of an actor. He responded:

> I'm an actor, so a lot of my life is putting on other masks and other personalities and looking into them. But, of course, for the actor the real power is finding authenticity no matter what character you're playing—and being. You cannot really move forward as an actor until you understand who you are as a person, and understand yourself. . . . so I think that actors in particular—but anyone in the creative field—would call authenticity the Holy Grail.

Takeaways

✘ **Be authentic.**

✘ **Don't be impulsive.** Use good judgment in speech and action. Be careful about speaking your mind; if your thoughts are extreme, be slow to act on them.

✘ **Listen to everyone, but be judicious in what you say and reserve judgment**. There have been times in history when it has been very dangerous to say the wrong thing to the wrong person, but listening to others has always been good policy. Although the stakes may not be as high nowadays, listening has these advantages: (1) you get more information; (2) others appreciate the chance to speak and be heard. In relationships, it is usually good to have a balance between listening and speaking so that both parties feel that their thoughts are valued.

✗ **Distinguish between tried and trusted friends and untested new ones.** Hold tight to trusted friends: "Grapple them to thy soul with hoops of steel." But don't waste your time on every new and inexperienced person who comes your way.

✗ **Be slow to enter combat, but if you have to, be sure to act in such a way that your opponent takes you seriously.**

✗ **Dress properly, according to your means and situation.** "For the apparel oft proclaims the man."

✗ **Beware of lending to, or borrowing from, friends.**

Chapter Thirty–Seven

REMAINING STEADY THROUGH
LIFE'S UPS AND DOWNS

 IF

by Rudyard Kipling

> If you can keep your head when all about you
>   Are losing theirs and blaming it on you,
> If you can trust yourself when all men doubt you,
>   But make allowance for their doubting too;
> If you can wait and not be tired by waiting,
>   Or being lied about, don't deal in lies,
> Or being hated, don't give way to hating,
>   And yet don't look too good, nor talk too wise:
>
> If you can dream—and not make dreams your master;
>   If you can think—and not make thoughts your aim;
> If you can meet with Triumph and Disaster
>   And treat those two impostors just the same;
> If you can bear to hear the truth you've spoken
>   Twisted by knaves to make a trap for fools,
> Or watch the things you gave your life to, broken,
>   And stoop and build 'em up with worn-out tools:
>
> If you can make one heap of all your winnings
>   And risk it on one turn of pitch-and-toss,
> And lose, and start again at your beginnings
>   And never breathe a word about your loss;

If you can force your heart and nerve and sinew
   To serve your turn long after they are gone,
And so hold on when there is nothing in you
   Except the Will which says to them: "Hold on!"

If you can talk with crowds and keep your virtue,
   Or walk with Kings—nor lose the common touch,
If neither foes nor loving friends can hurt you,
   If all men count with you, but none too much;
If you can fill the unforgiving minute
   With sixty seconds' worth of distance run,
Yours is the Earth and everything that's in it,
   And—which is more—you'll be a Man, my son!

This immensely popular poem was rated first by a large margin in the 1995 BBC survey of the U.K.'s favorite poems, and many have told me how much it has meant to them.

Nevertheless, Kipling is now a controversial figure because he was a proud British colonialist, who supported policies unacceptable by today's standards. That said, let us look at the poem for what we can learn from it.

Like the previous poem, "If" consists of advice from a father to a son, who, in Kipling's case, was thirteen at the time. The poem describes the things he needs to do to inherit "the Earth and everything that's in it." The last line, in which the poet holds out to his son what was then perceived as the highest achievement—"you'll be a Man"—dates the poem and its sexist era. I include "If" here, however, because of what it can teach us.

Triumph and Disaster

The two lines that have been most useful in my practice are:

> **If you can meet with Triumph and Disaster**
> **And treat those two impostors just the same . . .**

In the jumble of life's successes and failures, there is a natural inclination to exaggerate the significance of these fluxes of fortune in both directions. For example, people who are lucky enough to have a windfall, like winning the lottery, may be careless in their exuberance and run through their money. Conversely, people who suffer misfortune may feel as though all is lost, become depressed, and be unable to help themselves recover. Thinking of triumph and disaster as "impostors"—separate from yourself—can help you treat the problem practically, not personally. And research shows that these two impostors often turn out to be less impactful (in either direction) than predicted.

At a cognitive level, people often mistake strokes of luck for strokes of genius, or runs of bad luck as signs of inherent deficiency. The impostor image allows us to separate out those elements of triumph and disaster that are outside our control from those that are the results of our own efforts or mistakes. Such an approach offers a good framework for dealing with the ups and downs of life.

In a moving reading of "If" on the Internet, the actor Michael Caine recalls his father reading it to him when he was a child and declares the poem one of his favorites, especially the lines about triumph and disaster. They remind him of life as an actor.

Much of the poem promotes good, solid values, such as self-confidence, patience, and honesty. In addition, Kipling flags two other valuable traits: dogged tenacity and equipoise (the careful balance of countervailing forces), which reflect prevailing philosophies of the two countries that most influenced Kipling: imperial Britain and India.

East Meets West: The Stiff Upper Lip Meets the Bhagavad Gita

To some degree "If" reflects the stoicism and stiff-upper-lip attitude inculcated into British children, particularly boys from the upper class, from an early age during the heyday of the British Empire. This attitude was necessary for building an empire on which the sun never set, but involved emotional costs. Children, especially in the upper classes, were expected to endure punishment and harsh circumstances without complaint.

On the other hand, the Indian writer Khushwant Singh considered "If" to be "the essence of the message of the Bhagavad Gita in English." Fascinated at how this Hindu sacred text might have influenced Kipling, who spent many years in India, I consulted Judy Booth, who has lectured on the Gita. She has helped me understand some of the connections between the poem and the sacred text.

Consider the corresponding quotes from "If" and the Gita:

> **If you can keep your head when all about you**
> **Are losing theirs and blaming it on you . . .**

> Established in Yoga, O winner of wealth, perform actions, having abandoned attachment and having become balanced in success and failure, for balance of mind is called Yoga. (Bhagavad Gita 2.48)

The second quote emphasizes the balance between action and non-attachment that pervades both "If" and the Gita. In several lines Kipling advises us to temper our impulses by being open to competing considerations. For example: (1) "Trust yourself even when all men doubt you," but "make allowance for their doubting too." In other words, don't discard their input. (2) Allow yourself to take on a high profile ("talk with crowds") but don't let it go to your head ("keep your virtue"). (3) Hobnob with royalty if you like, but don't lose your "common touch." Similarly, the Gita tells us, keep your equilibrium; stay in balance.

Incidentally, *Yoga* in the sacred text means Unity or Oneness, not doing the downward dog on a yoga mat.

Here is another comparison: Kipling's "If neither foes nor loving friends can hurt you" with the Gita's exhortation:

> Distinguished is he who is of even intellect among well-wishers, friends and foes, among the indifferent and the impartial, among hateful persons and among kinsmen, among the saintly as well as the sinful. (Bhagavad Gita, 6.9)

And finally:

> **If you can make one heap of all your winnings**
> **And risk it on one turn of pitch-and-toss,**
> **And lose, and start again at your beginnings**
> **And never breathe a word about your loss . . .**

> You have control over action alone, never over its fruits. Live not for the fruits of action, nor attach yourself to inaction. (Bhagavad Gita, 2.47)

I have found this quote from the Gita particularly useful because it succinctly describes an interplay between action and inaction in our efforts. In reality, inaction often requires us to avoid becoming overattached to a goal. On the other hand, the verse advises against becoming detached to the point of giving up on your goal altogether.

The Kipling verse uses the game of "pitch-and-toss" to illustrate the importance of persevering (not attaching yourself to inaction). The game consists of throwing coins at a wall. Whoever throws the coin that lands closest to the wall collects all the coins. Kipling is using the game as a metaphor for goals in general.

I see a major problem in Kipling's approach here. He doesn't include a phase of contemplation between the first and second round of the game—a time to reflect on what went wrong, reconsider your strategy and do things differently the next time. This problem was to play out tragically later in Kipling's life.

Another curiosity about this verse is its denigration of breathing "a word about your loss." Here the stiff upper lip enters the picture again—a warning against complaining and showing weakness. Although this attitude might have been helpful for people to stifle their feelings in building an empire, it is stressful to suffer in silence. In addition, it prevents you from getting helpful advice from others when you may need it most. Those who can solicit advice from respected colleagues or friends, then use it, are at a huge advantage in life.

Takeaways

✘ **Remain as calm as possible in a crisis.** That doesn't mean fiddling while Rome burns; just try not to get overwhelmed so you can act most effectively.

✘ **Don't overreact to things.** Behaviors such as good sleep, exercise, meditation, and spending time with friends and loved ones may help in this regard.

✘ **Take other people's thoughts and feelings into consideration.** If you do, they are more likely to cooperate, and who knows? They may actually have something to offer.

✘ **Don't reciprocate bad behavior.** It is unlikely to advance your cause. Although it may sometimes be satisfying to create a drama, it is unproductive and may sabotage your mission.

✘ **Be as resilient as you can.** To some extent, resilience is an innate ability, but like all abilities, it can be cultivated.

✘ **Balance attachment and detachment (or non-attachment).** Do your best in your work and relationships, but recognize that there may sometimes be a value in detachment—for example, from a bad relationship, a bad job, an unpromising venture, or an addictive substance or behavior. Incidentally, there is a subtle but important difference between detachment (actively removing attention or interest) and non-attachment (not engaging).

The Poet and the Poem

Rudyard Kipling (1865–1936) was a celebrated journalist, novelist, poet, and short-story writer. Born in India, he lived there till age five, returning for a further seven years at age eighteen. His father, John Lockwood Kipling, was a professor of architectural sculpture in Bombay. His mother, Alice MacDonald, was known for her beauty and vivacity.

After age five, Kipling was sent to England (as was the practice with many British colonials), along with his sister, then age three. There they were raised by paid guardians in an atmosphere that, in its sheer meanness and cruelty, might have come straight out of a Dickens novel.

A welcome annual reprieve came in the form of Kipling's month-long visits with his aunt in London. In 1878, he went to a college founded by army officers to provide an affordable public school education. On graduating he returned to India, where he landed jobs for local newspapers. He soon distinguished himself as a wildly productive story writer.

In 1889 Kipling traveled across North America, visiting most of the major cities between San Francisco and Boston. One highlight of his trip was meeting Mark Twain. He then crossed the Atlantic and settled down in London. There he met famous authors and soon became famous too for his originality and productivity. In the next twenty-five years, he published three novels, four volumes of poems, and twelve volumes of short stories, essays, sketches, and the enormously famous *Jungle Books*. No less a literary giant than Henry James wrote of him, "Kipling strikes me as personally the most complete man of genius that I have ever known." In 1907, at age forty-two, Kipling was the youngest person ever, and the first English writer, to win the Nobel Prize for Literature.

In 1891 Kipling went on a voyage around the southern hemisphere and arrived in Lahore to learn that his close friend Wolcott Balestier had died. He immediately returned to London and at once married Balestier's sister Caroline. It is unclear what prompted this rapid decision in the wake of his friend's death. But he and Caroline remained married for the next forty-four years, though not always happily.

In the United States, the Kiplings tried to establish roots in Vermont but didn't feel at home there and returned to England, finally settling in Sussex. Health problems required Kipling to winter in

South Africa, where he became engaged in supporting the British colonial cause.

When World War I came, Kipling strongly supported the Allies and was keen that his son should seek active service. John Kipling attempted to enroll first in the Royal Navy and then in the army, but was rejected both times because of severe short-sightedness. His father, unwilling to accept that outcome, pulled strings to get him into the army against medical advice. John Kipling was sent to France, where he was killed in action. One can only imagine how the bitter knowledge of his role in the tragedy must have haunted the father.

In applying twice for admission to military service, John Kipling had twice bet everything on a game of pitch-and-toss, and twice he had lost. It would seem to have been the sensible thing to conclude (as did two medical evaluators) that John Kipling was unsuitable for active service and perhaps could have helped the war effort in some other way. But for his father the stiff upper lip won the day, with tragic consequences.

Despite Kipling's flaws, many of which were a function of his place and time, he was a genius. His poem "If" has given many people hours of enjoyment and contemplation. I hope it provides some measure of the same for you.

Chapter Thirty-Eight

NEVER GIVE UP

INVICTUS
by William Ernest Henley

> Out of the night that covers me,
>> Black as the pit from pole to pole,
> I thank whatever gods may be
>> For my unconquerable soul.
>
> In the fell clutch of circumstance
>> I have not winced nor cried aloud.
> Under the bludgeonings of chance
>> My head is bloody, but unbowed.
>
> Beyond this place of wrath and tears
>> Looms but the Horror of the shade,
> And yet the menace of the years
>> Finds and shall find me unafraid.
>
> It matters not how strait the gate,
>> How charged with punishments the scroll,
> I am the master of my fate,
>> I am the captain of my soul.

In "If," Kipling addresses ways to behave in the face of various life circumstances such as triumph and disaster. "Invictus" deals only with extreme disaster: hardship, misfortune, and agony, with nobody to help but one person—yourself. We can hope that we will never be in such dire straits as to need Henley's advice. Yet this poem has been widely appreciated and is perhaps the best known of all its author's works. It appears that many people can relate to its words.

The first stanza epitomizes what is now commonly known as "the dark night of the soul." It starts a pattern that will be repeated across the other three stanzas: two lines that sketch grim circumstances, a transitional line, and a triumphant final line. In the last stanza, the last two lines are both triumphant.

The final line of the first stanza, referencing "my unconquerable soul," inspired the poem's title, "Invictus," which is Latin for *unconquered*.

The second stanza refers to the "fell clutch of circumstance," leaving specific details to the imagination. The word "clutch" evokes a visceral sense of being grabbed or strangled, while "fell" in this context means *evil*. The line, "I have not winced nor cried aloud," reflects the stiff-upper-lip attitude that we saw in "If." What would be the harm of wincing or crying aloud? you might ask. Perhaps the poet doesn't want others to see that torture is having an impact on him. Or maybe he thinks it would weaken his resolve and capacity to resist the onslaughts of fate. In a similar vein, the poet seems to register some satisfaction in not having bowed his head (shown defeat or servitude) even when it has been "bloodied."

The third stanza looks to the future, "beyond this place of wrath and tears," and sees only "the Horror of the shade." Again, the poet heightens the atmosphere of terror and dread by leaving details to the reader's imagination.

The final stanza looks to whatever the grim future may hold. "How strait the gate" alludes to Matthew 7:13: "Because strait is the gate, and narrow is the way, which leadeth unto life, and few there be that find it." Here it seems to mean: no matter how difficult it is to pass through the narrow gate, the speaker will prevail. "No matter how charged the scroll" refers to how many punishments are in store. It is curious that the poet doesn't seem to take into account the possibility that there might be some good things on the scroll. In fact, the whole poem is suffused with unmitigated pessimism about everything except his ability to withstand it. The unfortunate reality, however, is that for some people life is like that.

One such person was Nelson Mandela, who was imprisoned for twenty-seven years for defying the South African apartheid government. Eighteen of those years were spent on Robben Island, a rocky fortress jutting out of the sea and visible from Cape Town, much as Alcatraz is visible from San Francisco. Mandela used to recite "Invictus" to himself and his fellow inmates to maintain their courage and strength in order to survive the hardship and indignity of the harsh prison conditions.

A 2009 movie called *Invictus* portrayed Mandela after he had been freed from prison following the fall of apartheid, helping to broker peace between blacks and whites in the South African rugby team as they faced their English opponents in a game they went on to win. When Mandela (known to his followers as Madiba) died in 2013, President Barack Obama gave the eulogy, which he concluded as follows:

> And when the night grows dark, when injustice weighs heavy on our hearts, or our best laid plans seem beyond our reach—think of Madiba, and the words that brought him comfort within the four walls of a cell:

It matters not how strait the gate,
How charged with punishments the scroll,
I am the master of my fate,
I am the captain of my soul.

That gives you some sense of the reach and influence of this poem almost 150 years after it was written. The last two lines are justifiably famous and often quoted even by people who are not in extreme situations. For those who face terrible hardship, this short but powerful work occupies a unique niche in the genre of poetry that can heal and inspire.

There is a long list of famous people who have quoted or paraphrased lines from the poem, including Winston Churchill. During the Invictus Games, an international sporting event for wounded veterans, the poem was quoted on the masthead of their website. Given the reach of "Invictus," it is fair to say that few poems can claim to have had as much influence or done as much good as this one, particularly for people in extraordinarily challenging situations.

Takeaways

✗ **In circumstances of extraordinary adversity, a poem can make a huge difference.** "Invictus" is one such poem.

✗ **When no one else is available, it can sustain your morale to remember that one person is always at hand who understands you and has your interests first and foremost at heart—yourself!**

✗ **Often things may seem worse than they are.** Always look for angles to supplement the help you provide for yourself. A combination of independence and seeking help often works best. Often people want to help you more when they see how hard you have worked to help yourself.

The Poet and the Poem

William Ernest Henley (1849–1903) was a British critic, editor, and poet. Like many other poets in this collection, he is best remembered for one poem: "Invictus."

The depth of suffering expressed in this poem came from his own life. From age twelve, Henley was never entirely free from pain and poor health as a result of tuberculosis. His illness, aggravated by his father's poverty, caused breaks in his education. After high school, Henley moved to London, where he earned a marginal living through journalism. Tuberculosis in his left leg required amputation just below the knee, after which he walked with the aid of a wooden prosthesis and crutches. He became the model for Long John Silver in *Treasure Island*, written by his friend Robert Louis Stevenson.

The disease next spread to his right foot and, once again, doctors advised him that amputation was the only remedy. This time, however, Henley refused to accept the advice and traveled from London to Edinburgh to be treated by the famous surgeon Joseph Lister. The treatment required nearly two years in hospital, but Lister helped Henley save his right foot. Henley used the time in hospital profitably, studying literature and languages and writing poetry.

Robert Louis Stevenson paints this vivid picture of Henley, whom he first met when the latter was in hospital: "The poor fellow sat up in his bed, with his hair and beard all tangled, and talked as cheerfully as if he had been in a King's Palace."

After being discharged from hospital Henley found work at a magazine through Stevenson's connections, which enabled him to marry a woman he first met in hospital, Hannah Johnson Boyle. They set up home in London. Even though Henley was poor, his widowed mother and four brothers looked to him for financial support. The Henleys had only one child, a daughter, Margaret, who died of meningitis at age five—yet another severe blow to him.

Henley wrote prolifically for magazines. He had a forceful personality and was a brilliant talker, which drew people to him. In 1889 he became editor of the *Scots Observer*, a weekly journal. His editorial gifts and his ability to find and nurture young talent became legendary. He edited the writings of Hardy, Kipling, and Yeats, the last of whom wrote that he "made us feel always our importance, and no man among us would do good work or show the promise of it, and lack his praise."

Although some scholars have derided "Invictus" for its bravado, such critiques overlook the tremendous suffering that gave birth to it and the countless people to whom it has brought comfort. In 1902, Henley fell from a railway carriage, which caused his latent tuberculosis to flare up, and he died the following year at age fifty-three.

Despite a long illness, amputation, severe pain, the death of his only child, and chronic poverty, Henley achieved much in his life, writing several volumes of poetry. His substantial body of work has largely been forgotten, but "Invictus" lives on as a gift to those who suffer deeply and need to look to themselves for inner strength.

Chapter Thirty-Nine

PUTTING ONE FOOT IN FRONT OF THE OTHER

THE WAKING

by Theodore Roethke

I wake to sleep, and take my waking slow.
I feel my fate in what I cannot fear.
I learn by going where I have to go.

We think by feeling. What is there to know?
I hear my being dance from ear to ear.
I wake to sleep, and take my waking slow.

Of those so close beside me, which are you?
God bless the Ground! I shall walk softly there,
And learn by going where I have to go.

Light takes the Tree; but who can tell us how?
The lowly worm climbs up a winding stair;
I wake to sleep, and take my waking slow.

Great Nature has another thing to do
To you and me; so take the lively air,
And, lovely, learn by going where to go.

This shaking keeps me steady. I should know.
What falls away is always. And is near.
I wake to sleep, and take my waking slow.
I learn by going where I have to go.

"The Waking" is a villanelle, like "One Art" (see chapter 1). It deals with a different adversity from the type we saw in "If" and "Invictus." In those two poems, adversity comes from outside, whereas in "The Waking" the adversity is internal. For millions of people, just waking up and getting going is a challenge. Let us look at three important lessons that the poet teaches us, using his own observations.

Lesson One:
I Wake to Sleep, and Take My Waking Slow

This line encapsulates a profound insight. The poet is not waking to a state of full alertness, but to a state that feels something like sleep. He has learned that it will take time before his brain comes fully online, so he adjusts his expectations and slowly goes about the actions that will help him wake up. For people who tend to wake up slowly, rushing themselves, or, worse still, being rushed by others, is likely to provoke distress. Although I have often heard such observations from patients, never before have I seen them so concisely and eloquently expressed. Such morning difficulties are reported by people with depression, neurological diseases, chronic fatigue syndrome, and hangovers, to give just a few examples.

Lesson Two:
I Learn by Going Where I Have to Go

The classical approach to psychotherapy (also known as psychoanalytic or psychodynamic psychotherapy) advocates probing the psyche for insight (cognition), which then guides the appropriate action. In this model of the mind, thought or cognition is at the top of the therapeutic hierarchy. An alternative approach holds that "insight follows action"—an observation often shared in Twelve Step groups.

This is what line 3 expresses: The poet does what he needs to do and learns by doing so.

Lesson Three:
We Think by Feeling. What Is There to Know?

We have seen thinking subordinated to action. Here thinking takes a second blow, as it is subordinated to feeling as well. Aside from feeling, the poet asks, what is there to know? Although some have made this observation recently, it must have seemed novel when Roethke put it forward in the early 1950s.

Years earlier, the eighteenth-century feminist writer Mary Wollstonecraft wrote, "When we feel deeply, we reason profoundly." Earlier still, the philosopher Blaise Pascal wrote, "The heart has its reasons of which reason knows nothing." These observations appeared to contradict the classical dictum of Descartes, who famously said, "I think therefore I am," putting cognition right at the top of the mental pyramid. This premise was challenged in recent years by neuroscientist Antonio Damasio in *Descartes' Error*, in which he buttressed the opinions of Wollstonecraft and Pascal with evidence gathered from patients with injuries to the prefrontal cortex of the brain, a region influential in decision making.

Many other lines in this poem are more obscure, open to different interpretations. Here the poet may be indirectly expressing his internal state, which is one of vagueness and ambiguity. Also, he is leaving room for the reader to interpret what he means, thereby giving the poem an intriguing air of mystery, a puzzle for the reader to figure out.

Recognizing the subjective nature of interpreting ambiguous lines, I'll offer my take on just a few:

"I hear my being dance from ear to ear."

This line might seem curious to anyone unfamiliar with bipolar disorder. All of a sudden a person who is struggling to wake up hears his being dancing! How can that be? To me, it looks like a so-called mixed state, in which a person can feel slowed down at one moment and sped up at another (or both simultaneously).

> **This shaking keeps me steady. I should know.**
> **What falls away is always. And is near.**

The poet seems to be struggling to hold onto himself physically and cognitively. Once again, morning shakiness could be part of a neurological condition or related to heavy drinking. How does shakiness keep a person steady? Perhaps knowing that he is shaky causes the poet to be more careful and hold on to things. The next sentence begins with "What falls away." People who are shaky may well be afraid of falling, so the fear of falling may be ever present. Or, in another frame of reference, we may always retain elements of what has fallen away—past relationships, past abilities now lost, past strengths and capacities.

I encourage you to enjoy this and the other evocative mysteries in this short poem.

It offers valuable insights to all who "wake to sleep" and need to take their waking slow. Yet in my opinion, its brilliant insights have enormous relevance to everyone.

Takeaways

✖ If you have a hard time waking up in the morning, be sure to seek help, as it may be related to a treatable condition, such as a sleep disorder, depression, a neurological problem, or the effect of drugs (prescribed or non-prescribed).

✗ Regardless of the reason, start the day slowly, and take things at a pace that is right for you.

✗ Sometimes taking a wise action can precede the development of insight. As people in Twelve Step programs say, "Do the next right thing."

✗ Your feelings can be an important source of information about significant things going on in your world. Respect your intuition, which may often lead you to insights much more quickly than waiting for your thinking to catch up.

✗ Pay attention to mystery and wonder in the world around you and to what it can teach you.

The Poet and the Poem

Theodore Roethke (1908–1963) is considered by many to be one of the greatest American poets of the twentieth century. He won the 1950 Pulitzer Prize for Poetry for the book *The Waking*, which contains the present poem, and two National Book Awards for poetry (in 1959 and 1965) for other collections. He taught at the University of Washington from 1947 until his death in 1963. Here he was considered a great teacher and inspired a generation of poets, including Jack Gilbert, whose poem "Failing and Flying" is featured in chapter 5.

Roethke was born in 1908 in Saginaw, Michigan, to Otto and Helen Huebner Roethke. His father and uncle ran a huge set of greenhouses, owned by his father, a German immigrant. Roethke spent many hours in the greenhouses, as well as on a game sanctuary maintained by his family. Remembering these settings, he recalled, "I had several worlds to live in, which I felt were mine. One favorite place was a swampy corner of the game sanctuary where herons always nested." He often included images of the greenhouse and nature in his poetry. "The Waking" makes several references to nature, such as:

> Great Nature has another thing to do
> To you and me; so take the lively air.

And

> Light takes the Tree; but who can tell us how?
> The lowly worm climbs up a winding stair.

Here Roethke is marveling at two scenes from nature: the way an intense beam of light can appear to capture a tree; and the tenacity of a lowly worm in climbing up a winding stair. Here we see how flashes of natural settings enliven the poet struggling with his morning lethargy.

Roethke's tranquil childhood came to an end at age fourteen, when his father and uncle clashed, leading to the sale of the family greenhouses. His father developed cancer, and his uncle committed suicide. Shortly afterwards his father died.

Roethke entered the University of Michigan in Ann Arbor, graduating magna cum laude. Later, while teaching at Michigan State University, he suffered his first psychiatric breakdown, which required hospitalization. Roethke subsequently described this as "a mystical experience." It also appears to have been the emergence of his bipolar disorder, which was to afflict him intermittently throughout his life. His psychiatric problems were compounded by heavy drinking. He lost his position at Michigan State but went on to complete his master of arts degree.

Roethke's poetry seemed to gain momentum after his bipolar diagnosis. His first book of poems, *Open House*, appeared in 1945, followed by *The Lost Son and Other Poems* in 1948. His growing success led to a permanent position at the University of Washington. He had dalliances with female students, which these days would have not have passed muster. He went on to marry Beatrice O'Connell, a former student, in 1953. Although Roethke didn't inform her of his history of psychiatric illness before marriage, she continued to support him and his work. He died unexpectedly of a heart attack at age fifty-five while swimming in a pool near Seattle.

Chapter Forty

SHOULD YOU REACT OR PROACT?

WAITING FOR THE BARBARIANS
by Constantine Cavafy

Translated by Edmund Keeley and Philip Sherrard

What are we waiting for, assembled in the forum?

    The barbarians are due here today.

Why isn't anything going on in the senate?
Why are the senators sitting there without legislating?

    Because the barbarians are coming today.
    What's the point of senators making laws now?
    Once the barbarians are here, they'll do the legislating.

Why did our emperor get up so early,
and why is he sitting enthroned at the city's main gate,
in state, wearing the crown?

    Because the barbarians are coming today
    and the emperor's waiting to receive their leader.
    He's even got a scroll to give him,
    loaded with titles, with imposing names.

Why have our two consuls and praetors come out today
wearing their embroidered, their scarlet togas?
Why have they put on bracelets with so many amethysts,
rings sparkling with magnificent emeralds?
Why are they carrying elegant canes
beautifully worked in silver and gold?

Because the barbarians are coming today
and things like that dazzle the barbarians.

Why don't our distinguished orators turn up as usual
to make their speeches, say what they have to say?

Because the barbarians are coming today
and they're bored by rhetoric and public speaking.

Why this sudden bewilderment, this confusion?
(How serious people's faces have become.)
Why are the streets and squares emptying so rapidly,
everyone going home lost in thought?

Because night has fallen and the barbarians haven't come.
And some of our men just in from the border say
there are no barbarians any longer.

Now what's going to happen to us without barbarians?
Those people were a kind of solution.

In this highly original poem, Cavafy conjures up a scene reminiscent of ancient Rome. It feels as though the curtain is going up at an opera, in which the players are dressed in gorgeous clothes, bejeweled and accoutred with silver and gold accessories. The audience (and in this case the reader) is ready for high drama, which unfolds as a dialogue between two choruses, one that asks questions and one that provides answers. There is a sense that the first voice comes from ordinary people, eager to find out what is going on in highly unusual circumstances. The response comes perhaps from better informed neighbors or officials.

The poet makes it clear from the outset that everybody is waiting for the barbarians to arrive. All the unusual behaviors among the rank and file, the senators, the emperor in attendance, the fancily dressed consuls and praetors are there for one reason only. They are waiting for the barbarians.

This operatic scene is absurd in many ways. Why would people wait for the barbarians to invade and perhaps kill them instead of putting up some kind of fight or running away? Why would they put their best jewels on display for easy plunder rather than hiding them? It would be an understatement to say that they were overdressed for the occasion. Even as we enjoy the grand spectacle and the beautiful costumes and sets that the poet vividly describes, we smile at the irony created by this theater of the absurd.

There are also signs that the crowd is poking fun at the senators and the emperor, who is waiting with a scroll to give to the leader of the barbarians. What use would the barbarians have for a scroll "loaded with titles, with imposing names?" When the poet writes that the barbarians are "bored by rhetoric and public speaking," all of us who have been on the receiving end of such speeches might well nod and smile in sympathy.

Then comes the denouement! There are no barbarians. One might think the people of the city would rejoice, but no, they've become serious. They are leaving the streets, lost in thought. Finally, the poet delivers the last two lines that are worth the price of admission:

Now what's going to happen to us without barbarians?
Those people were a kind of solution.

The poet has teased us by setting up such dramatic expectations, then deflating them with a stupendous anticlimax. It is reminiscent of Ernest Thayer's "Casey at the Bat."

The last two lines remind us how often people think about their lives and organize their plans and actions in terms of some outside threat or demand. Removing those external factors can leave them with a sense of loss and force them to think about their own priorities and make their own decisions.

In my professional work, I have had occasion to refer to this famous poem from time to time in questioning whether a client might not do better to be proactive rather than reacting to some external circumstance. An example that comes to mind is a retired lawyer who became entangled in a squabble with the head of his homeowners' association about various administrative actions. Emails between the two of them flew to and fro at all hours of the day and night, gobbling up his days and interrupting his sleep.

I referred him to Cavafy's poem. Was he going to organize his life around the ongoing feud with the head of the homeowners' association, or would he rather find better ways to spend his golden years? I like to think that the poem gave him some food for thought.

On a grander scale, how often do we and our leaders blame outsiders (such as immigrants) for problems of our own creation or look elsewhere for answers that lie within ourselves?

Cavafy's "Waiting for the Barbarians" has influenced many artists to create works by the same name or related names, including a novel by the Nobel Prize–winning South African author J. M. Coetzee and an opera by Philip Glass.

It is the mark of a great work of art that it retains relevance across eras and continents. And so it is with this poem, written in Egypt at the end of the nineteenth century, as it relates to modern life and events on different continents.

Takeaways

✗ **You have a limited number of days, so use them wisely.** As author Annie Dillard wrote, "How we spend our days is, of course, how we spend our lives."

✗ **When given the option to react to a provocation or opportunity, ask yourself what would be the best way to spend your time and energy.** Catch yourself when you spend time on other people's priorities and reevaluate your plans in light of your own priorities.

Chapter Forty-One

IT'S THE JOURNEY THAT MATTERS

ITHAKA
by Constantine Cavafy
Translated by Edmund Keeley

As you set out for Ithaka
hope your road is a long one,
full of adventure, full of discovery.
Laistrygonians, Cyclops,
angry Poseidon—don't be afraid of them:
you'll never find things like that on your way
as long as you keep your thoughts raised high,
as long as a rare excitement
stirs your spirit and your body.
Laistrygonians, Cyclops,
wild Poseidon—you won't encounter them
unless you bring them along inside your soul,
unless your soul sets them up in front of you.

Hope your road is a long one.
May there be many summer mornings when,
with what pleasure, what joy,
you enter harbors you're seeing for the first time;
may you stop at Phoenician trading stations
to buy fine things,
mother of pearl and coral, amber and ebony,

(continued)

sensual perfume of every kind—
as many sensual perfumes as you can;
and may you visit many Egyptian cities
to learn and go on learning from their scholars.

Keep Ithaka always in your mind.
Arriving there is what you're destined for.
But don't hurry the journey at all.
Better if it lasts for years,
so you're old by the time you reach the island,
wealthy with all you've gained on the way,
not expecting Ithaka to make you rich.

Ithaka gave you the marvelous journey.
Without her you wouldn't have set out.
She has nothing left to give you now.

And if you find her poor, Ithaka won't have fooled you.
Wise as you will have become, so full of experience,
you'll have understood by then what these Ithakas mean.

I came to this poem on the recommendation of two good friends, who independently told me that it was one of the poems to which they have frequently returned over the course of their lives because of its capacity to heal, inspire, and delight. Given such recommendations, how could I resist hastening at once to read this famous poem by Cavafy? The word *read* doesn't do justice to the experience of consuming "Ithaka," a poem so full of sensory delights—visual images and "sensual perfumes."

In this poem Cavafy gives the reader advice about making a journey—life's journey—using the *Odyssey* as a template. Homer's epic portrays Odysseus's long journey from the Trojan War to his home, the island of Ithaka (or Ithaca) off the western coast of Greece. The mythological characters to which Cavafy refers are Poseidon, god of the sea, who bears a grudge against Odysseus, and sundry vicious giants.

At the beginning of the journey, Cavafy recommends that the reader set out with a positive attitude and a long view:

Hope your road is a long one.

Cavafy encourages the reader to look on life as an adventure. Take a positive attitude, he recommends. Life will give you what you bring to it. Of course, we all know that one can (and does) encounter monsters along the way, but Cavafy admonishes the reader to watch out for the monsters within. He is perhaps a bit overoptimistic in suggesting that you will encounter no monsters as long as you bring none along with you. But let's allow him some poetic license, considering the delightful journey on which he guides us.

The poet takes time to pause over delights encountered along the way: exotic things to buy in settings much richer and more interesting than online shopping, vivid experiences, and master classes from Egyptian scholars.

Cavafy recommends that we should not hurry the journey, but take our time to relish the experience. Let us not worry about what we accumulate, he advises: although we might be old and poor by the time we reach Ithaka, we will nonetheless be rich in the experiences, knowledge, and wisdom that the journey has given us.

I can do no better to illustrate the power of "Ithaka" to help people than relate the experience of two of my friends, Liz and Patrick.

Liz's Story

Liz, a lawyer and policy expert, has returned to "Ithaka" many times over the course of her life, usually when looking for inspiration about life's journey, drawn especially by its visual delights. For her, the poem communicates two special lessons: first, "look at the beautiful things and don't let the crummy things get in the way," she says. She recalls a favorite aunt, who embraced "whatever was good in life." Out of the blue, she would buy tickets for the ballet or the theater, enlivening times that might otherwise have been dreary or discouraging. When she reads the poem, Liz remembers these unexpected pleasures.

As Liz thinks of "Ithaka," she recalls a trip she took with her husband to Naples, Italy, many years ago. At that time, much about the city was shabby, having fallen into such disrepair that the casual tourist walking through its streets, observing the buildings, might have come away unimpressed. But with an enthusiastic native Neapolitan friend as tour guide, all sorts of hidden delights were revealed: a charming courtyard with a fountain, surrounded by ordinary buildings; a dazzling fresco in a church; a modest but inviting restaurant that accurately boasted of having invented the famous pizza margherita. These were just a few of the unexpected delights that popped out of the dreariness thanks to their knowledgeable guide. It reminds her of Cavafy's "Ithaka," an expert guide to unexpected beauty and charm. He teaches the same lesson they learned from their friend in Naples: be sure to enjoy the beautiful things as you travel. The poem always reminds her to do so.

Although she is a goal oriented professional, "Ithaka" reminds her that "it's not just where you're going but the journey itself that matters."

Patrick, a publisher, writer, and painter, has his own "Ithaka" story.

Patrick's Story

I first encountered "Ithaka" many years ago in a literature course. Because "Ithaka" is the story of a journey filled with adventure and reward, it had a pleasantly unsettling and exciting impact on my young mind. I savored the poem, but, impatient to begin my own journey, I quickly forgot it.

Much later, in the middle of my life, things went seriously off the rails, and I became profoundly depressed. I had been rejected by a woman I thought I loved. I was living in a city far from home, where I had few friends. I was working at a job which didn't interest me. I felt lost, utterly alone, and a failure. My life's journey seemed fruitless, and the road before me promised nothing. Nothing I could see offered meaning or satisfaction. I was preoccupied with blaming—bad luck, others, mostly myself. Not even the smallest of life's pleasures—the warmth of a sunny day or the earthy taste of a glass of wine—held any interest. I remember the experience of a beautiful sunset and thinking, "So what? Why doesn't this give me any pleasure? Why is it that I just don't care about anything?"

One evening I was wandering aimlessly around a secondhand bookstore, killing time after another hopeless day at work. I didn't want to go home where there was no one waiting for me. I don't know why I picked up a slim volume of Cavafy's poetry. I had forgotten "Ithaka"—or thought I had. But when I started to read, "As you set out for Ithaka, / hope your road is a long one," I remembered. It was like stumbling across a friend I had known from long ago. And for the first time since the onset of my depression, I felt some kind of connection. I read it again and again that night.

I thought about the man who had written the poem. He was gay and living in an intolerant society. He surely had his own suffering. While I am neither gay nor surrounded by intolerance, I felt that in some abstract way, the poet and I were fellow travelers; I was not alone. This led me to reflect on my own situation and my own demons in a different way. Over the years since that evening encounter with "Ithaka," I have returned to the poem many times. It is an old message, the story of a long journey home to a place where the door is always open, and there is always a seat at the table.

Takeaways

✘ **Remember to view life as a journey, not just as a goal.** Use your senses. Be alert to visual beauty, colors, jewels, and fragrances. Use your mind as a pathway to pleasure by learning about new things that intrigue you. *Although life may bring you many gifts, don't think of it in merely acquisitive terms.* Even if you arrive at your goal (Ithaka) materially poor, you can still be rich in the experiences and adventures that life has provided.

✘ **Much of what life gives you is in proportion to what you bring to it.**

✘ **Be mindful of the demons within.** They can sometimes be more harmful and difficult to overcome than the monsters you encounter along the way. In fact, sometimes the monsters within can *turn* those we encounter into monsters.

✘ **Think of your goals not simply in terms of whether you achieved them or not, but also for the opportunities they might have afforded you, for example, in the form of friends and travel.**

✗ **Take your time**. A hurried encounter, a rushed meal, conversations always cut short because you are so busy: these prevent you from fully enjoying the journey to Ithaka.

✗ **Don't get too distracted, however, by wayside pleasures.** "Keep Ithaka always in your mind." Whatever your goal is—an intimate relationship, a brilliant career, your art, a family, a discovery that will help humanity. Enjoy the journey, but keep those goals that are important to you in your crosshairs.

✗ **Take care of yourself**. As Cavafy says, "Hope your road is a long one." Nowadays there are many things you can do to improve your chances for a long life. Enjoy staying healthy and the rewards of good health.

The Poet and the Poem

Constantine Cavafy (1863–1933) was the last of seven sons born in Alexandria, Egypt, to immigrants from Constantinople (today's Istanbul). His family was well-off until the death of their father when Cavafy was nine. They set off for England, where they depended on the generosity of relatives, returning to Alexandria when Cavafy was fourteen. Cavafy made Alexandria his permanent home, finding work with the ministry of public works, and enjoying the city's liberal, cosmopolitan atmosphere.

Cavafy started publishing articles and poems in newspapers and journals, many of which revealed his deep interest in the classical world, which is evident in the two poems featured here: "Waiting for the Barbarians" and "Ithaka."

During this time, Cavafy lived with his mother, whom he affectionately called "The Fat One," diligently taking care of her. After

they had dinner together, he would slip out into the streets of Alex-
andria to sample the city's gay life, which became another subject for
his poetry.

After his mother's death, Cavafy moved into an apartment of
his own, stuffed with antiques, where he would entertain guests in
Greek, English, or French. He loved gossiping about people from the
distant past, such as "the tricky behavior of the Emperor Manuel
Comnenus," as his friend E. M. Forster recalled, but his conversa-
tion was expansive, and no subject was too small or large to capture
his attention. Forster gave us the iconic description of this idiosyn-
cratic poet: "A Greek gentleman in a straw hat, standing absolutely
motionless at a slight angle to the universe."

A lifelong smoker, Cavafy was diagnosed with cancer of the
larynx in 1932, which required a tracheostomy. He died a year later,
on his seventieth birthday.

Chapter Forty-Two

HOLD ON TO YOUR DREAMS

DREAMS
by Langston Hughes

> Hold fast to dreams
> For if dreams die
> Life is a broken-winged bird
> That cannot fly.
>
> Hold fast to dreams
> For when dreams go
> Life is a barren field
> Frozen with snow.

It is pageant time in the elementary school, and the children are putting on a performance based on Langston Hughes' famous poem "Dreams." The stage is full of second-graders, some wearing regular clothes, others are dressed in brightly colored garb, adorned with shimmering wings. They are the "dreams." There is music.

A narrator in a long black cloak intones the first line of the Hughes poem: "Hold fast to dreams." The children dance around having fun, each holding on to a "dream." Then comes the next line. The music fades, and the dreams break free of their companions, who sadly exit, followed by the children, leaving the stage bare. Slowly a creature hobbles onto the darkened stage—a "broken-winged bird" struggling to fly.

The next scene follows the second stanza, though this time the scene ends with a lighting change to reveal a barren, snow-covered landscape.

This scene actually took place in a school close to me, but it has probably played out in many schools all over the country.

You might well wonder what this short poem, more suited perhaps to children than to adults, is doing in this collection. The answer is simple: its crucially important message is not represented anywhere else in the book. Our dreams are the vital blueprint for our goals and actions. They sustain us and drive our ambitions and our strivings. As such, it is vital to let children know early on the value of holding fast to their dreams. It is equally important to impress upon adults the necessity of allowing children to do so—and not to let go of their *own* dreams as well.

In this simple verse, Langston Hughes introduces children and adults to the power of poetry to inspire. By keeping the poem short, and the words, meter, and rhyme scheme simple, Hughes has given children a poem to help them learn and remember the importance of holding fast to their dreams.

In a related poem, "Harlem," similarly short and simple, Hughes asks what happens to a dream deferred. The poem is worth reading, because all too often dreams are deferred, especially for disadvantaged groups, with unfortunate and sometimes disastrous consequences, as the following story indicates.

Reginald Dwayne Betts: Saved by Poetry and Dreams

In the mid-Atlantic region at the end of the twentieth century, a sixteen-year-old boy carjacks a man at gunpoint and steals his money. No shots are fired, but within minutes the boy has committed six felonies. He is caught, tried, and sentenced to nine years in prison. Over the next eight crucial developmental years, the young man serves his time in some of the worst prisons in the state as part of the adult population. In these surroundings, this adolescent grows into manhood. The man in question is Reginald Dwayne Betts, who has chronicled some of the horrors he experienced during these years in *A Question of Freedom: A Memoir of Learning, Survival, and Coming of Age in Prison.* I interviewed him for this book.

An intellectually gifted student, Betts was drawn to books since his earliest years and wrote poetry as a child. During his confinement at the Southampton Men's Detention Center in Virginia, Betts spent time in solitary confinement, where it was part of the prison tradition that you could call out for a book. One day, someone slipped Betts a book called *The Black Poets*, which he read avidly. It was a turning point for him. As he put it, "The first time I read poetry that really changed the way I saw or thought about the world was in solitary confinement at the Southampton Correctional Center. That helped open up new worlds for me. I saw the poet not just in a utilitarian way, but as serving art. In a poem you can give somebody a whole world. At that moment I decided to become a poet."

Some poems in particular moved him: "Cutting Greens" by Lucille Clifton put him in touch with feelings of kinship and family; and "Runagate" by Robert Hayden, which describes black men and women running north to escape slavery, and the dangers and hardships they faced. The poem reminded Betts of people who had fought against racial prejudice at a time when few people did.

Through poems such as these, Betts learned about the history of blacks in the United States in a way that communicated both the harsh facts and the painful feelings that went along with them.

When I asked Betts whether he thought poetry could heal, he demurred at first, but reconsidered:

> Poetry does a different job than some other arts. It helps you recognize the ways in which you are broken. And part of being healed has a lot to do with realizing the ways in which you might be broken. Poetry had a huge impact on my life as a vehicle and a means to grapple with the world. *The Black Poets* book was one of many books passed on to me, but it was the one that said what I really needed to hear. It covered ground that I thought was important and engaged my mind in a way that satisfied but also alarmed and troubled me. It gave me an acute awareness of the way other people suffered but also provided me with a means of dealing with suffering. Maybe we often don't talk about the significance of how we deal with suffering. Poetry has helped me to do that.

Throughout our conversation, Betts returned again and again to a poem by Etheridge Knight called "For Freckled-Faced Gerald," which had powerfully affected him. The poem tells the story of a sixteen-year-old prisoner, "thrown in as 'pigmeat' for the buzzards to eat." As Knight describes it, Gerald "didn't stand a chance." It was a foregone conclusion that he would be raped. It is a difficult poem to read, but paradoxically it helped Betts realize that, terrible as his own situation was, others had it worse. As he puts it:

> One of the reasons I talk about "Freckled-Faced Gerald" is because of how it maps to my own life, my own troubles, my own incarceration. From a naïve standpoint it makes sense for a sixteen-year-old kid to think that his suffering is quite singular. But when I read this poem about a kid who was just like me in many obvious

ways, it changed my own superficial understanding of what I was going through. I was not raped in prison. Examples like this have led me to understand that poetry can help you to contextualize your experience. "Freckled-Faced Gerald" allowed me to think differently about who I was and my situation.

Betts' experience with this poem illustrates a principle I have seen many times over. It is not necessarily cheerful poems that comfort and heal, but often poems that express difficulty or suffering. As Betts observes, reading about someone else's pain and struggle can sometimes make you feel better. Perhaps it can give you strength to learn that others who were worse off have survived, or simply that you are not alone in your grief and struggles.

After Betts was discharged from prison, he went on to complete his undergraduate studies and obtain his law degree from Yale University. He has taught poetry to juvenile offenders in prison. When I last spoke to him, Betts was studying to get his PhD in law from Yale.

Takeaways

✘ **Dreams are vitally important**. Every significant plan, achievement, discovery, or creation begins with a dream.

✘ **Hold on to your dreams**. Often things arise that threaten to derail them. These threats can either be external, such as people or institutions that obstruct your dreams, or internal, such as distractions, impulses, temptations or addictions that lead you off track. *Be aware of these external and internal forces so that you can hold fast to your dreams.*

✘ **If you should let go of your dreams, keep your eyes open for a second chance**. Life is full of second chances, but you must be alert to spot and seize them. Broken dreams can sometimes be mended.

✗ Help other people, especially young people, hold on to their dreams, because that will influence not only their future, but the future of our society.

✗ Try not to defer dreams. If you have to do so, find ways to keep them alive.

The Poet and the Poem

Langston Hughes (1902–1967) was a black writer and the leading figure in the Harlem Renaissance in the 1920s. He published his first poem in 1921 and his first book of poetry in 1926. He went on to write multiple books of poetry, prose, and plays, as well as a popular column for the *Chicago Defender*.

Hughes had a complex ancestry. Both of his paternal great grand-fathers were white slave owners in Kentucky, and both of his mater-nal great grandmothers were enslaved Africans. His parents, James Hughes and Carrie Langston, separated soon after his birth, and his father moved to Mexico. Hughes was raised largely by his maternal grandmother, Mary, until she died when he was in his early teens. Hughes then lived with his mother, settling in Cleveland, Ohio.

Hughes was admitted to Columbia University in 1921 but soon left because of racial prejudice among teachers and students. In 1967, shortly after his death, Columbia hosted a memorial, which served as an overdue apology for the university's treatment of him almost fifty years before. Professor James P. Shenton acknowledged, "For a while, there lived a poet down the street from Columbia, and Columbia never took the time to find out what he was about."

Hughes worked at odd jobs and traveled as a crewman on a ship to West Africa and Europe. He returned to the United States, where he met the poet Vachel Lindsay, who was impressed with him and publicized the discovery of a new black poet. Hughes enrolled in Lincoln University, Pennsylvania, where one of his classmates was Thurgood Marshall, who later became a Supreme Court justice. Although Hughes traveled after graduation, he made Harlem his home for the rest of his life. He never married.

Hughes published multiple poetry collections, nonfiction works, plays, short-story collections, and books for children. He received numerous awards and honors.

Langston Hughes' 1967 memorial, according to writer Charlayne Hunter-Gault, "ended as it had begun with Langston Hughes' low, bemused voice—this time telling about how he came from the Midwest to Columbia to go to school, and caused great consternation when he presented himself at Hartley Hall. That was in 1921, and no one of African descent, he says, had ever lived at a dormitory at Columbia. 'There are many barriers people try to break down,' he told an audience. . . . 'I try to do it with poetry.'"

PART FIVE

Into the Night

Do not go gentle into that good night.

—Dylan Thomas

Chapter Forty-Three

SHOULD YOU JUST GO FOR IT?

AN IRISH AIRMAN FORESEES HIS DEATH
by William Butler Yeats

> I know that I shall meet my fate
> Somewhere among the clouds above;
> Those that I fight I do not hate,
> Those that I guard I do not love;
> My country is Kiltartan Cross,
> My countrymen Kiltartan's poor,
> No likely end could bring them loss
> Or leave them happier than before.
> Nor law, nor duty bade me fight,
> Nor public men, nor cheering crowds,
> A lonely impulse of delight
> Drove to this tumult in the clouds;
> I balanced all, brought all to mind,
> The years to come seemed waste of breath,
> A waste of breath the years behind
> In balance with this life, this death.

In this poem, Yeats presents us with a cold analysis of the pros and cons of the dangerous life of a fighter pilot in World War I. Although the speaker has no doubt that he will die in action, he presents a carefully reasoned analysis of the pros and cons of being a fighter pilot. In his concluding lines, he makes it clear that he has done a cost-benefit analysis and has decided to fly nonetheless.

In analyzing his motives for fighting, the airman rejects the usual reasons for going to war, such as fame, duty, love of country, and hatred of the enemy. He recognizes that his own countrymen, the Irish, are unlikely to benefit or lose as a result of the war. These observations reflect long-standing grievances of the Irish against the English.

Why then is he risking his life? Yeats sums it up in a few lines:

> A lonely impulse of delight
> Drove to this tumult in the clouds.

Alongside the thrill of flying all else, past and future, seems meaningless. In peacetime, daredevils make the same calculus when they climb "free solo," without companions, safety equipment, or any artificial aids for support. In the movie *Free Solo*, master climber Alex Honnold scales El Capitan, a three-thousand-foot vertical rock formation in Yosemite National Park. When confronted with the possibility of dying, Honnold responds, "It happens." People weigh the value of thrill versus life-or-death decisions differently.

Yeats' phrase "A lonely impulse of delight" reminds us again of the difference between loneliness and solitude. Some people enjoy being alone, especially in natural and untamed surroundings. Recall, for example, Wordsworth wandering lonely as a cloud or Masefield longing for the lonely sea and the sky.

The Biology of Risk Taking

Personality tests find that some people are more inclined to seek sensations and take risks than others, and these differences correlate with the results of brain imaging studies. It is quite likely that sensation seeking and risk taking are to some extent biologically determined.

Alex Honnold was studied by Jane Joseph, professor of neuroscience at the Medical University of South Carolina, in a functional magnetic resonance imaging (fMRI) scanner. Honnold showed much less reactivity in his amygdala (the brain's alarm center) to shocking or disgusting stimuli compared with a controlled subject.

Connections between the prefrontal cortex (a region important for executive functioning) and other brain areas are slow to develop and may not be fully in place until the mid-twenties. That may explain to some extent the greater tendency of young people to take risks without fully heeding the consequences. It has often been said that old men send young men into war, perhaps intuitively realizing their greater taste for adventure and risk. The morality of this practice has often been questioned. Nevertheless, the risk-taking proclivities of young men and women have often contributed greatly to society. Take for example the young men who scaled the bluffs at Normandy, establishing a crucial beachhead on German-occupied Europe in World War II. Such examples abound in the history of warfare—and in civilian life.

Takeaways

✘ **If you choose to engage in a risky profession and you want to enjoy a long life, be careful.** Remember the adage widely quoted by fliers: "There are no old bold pilots."

✘ **Beware of glamorizing risk, especially when you are young.** If you delay undertaking risky behaviors, as you get older you may be surprised to find that they no longer seem like such a good idea.

✘ **Be particularly careful of what you do in a "hot state," in which people are more likely to take risks.** Psychologists have distinguished between so-called hot and cold states, corresponding to states of high and low levels of arousal respectively. Hot states might include rage, ecstasy, and sexual passion. Studies have shown that in such states people are more likely to do things that they later consider to reflect poor judgment. Drugs and alcohol can induce hot states in which people are more inclined to act impulsively than they normally would.

The Poet and the Poem

Although the poem is written from the perspective of a young daredevil who cherishes "a lonely impulse of delight," the voice has the feel of an old soul. Perhaps that is because Yeats was fifty-three when he wrote it in memory of Major Robert Gregory, the only son of his friend Lady Gregory, Irish poet, dramatist, and folklorist. Yeats also wrote three other poems to commemorate the death of her son.

Major Gregory was a decorated pilot who was killed in action in Italy at age thirty-six. He left behind a wife and three children to join the war effort, which seems like a strange choice for a man who didn't care about those he was fighting for. I wonder what his family thought of the poem, and whether it truly reflects the spirit of the young fighter pilot or rather of a careful, measured, and perhaps disaffected middle-aged man. The detached tone of his imagined thoughts about going to war suggests the latter.

Yeats' poem "When You Are Old" can also be found in this collection (chapter 13). Yeats was one of the most distinguished literary figures of the twentieth century and was awarded the Nobel Prize for Literature in 1923. This short, compelling poem displays his mastery.

Chapter Forty-Four

OR SHOULD YOU BE CAREFUL?

MUSÉE DES BEAUX ARTS
by W. H. Auden

About suffering they were never wrong,
The Old Masters: how well they understood
Its human position: how it takes place
While someone else is eating or opening a window or just walking
    dully along;
How, when the aged are reverently, passionately waiting
For the miraculous birth, there always must be
Children who did not specially want it to happen, skating
On a pond at the edge of the wood:
They never forgot
That even the dreadful martyrdom must run its course
Anyhow in a corner, some untidy spot
Where the dogs go on with their doggy life and the torturer's horse
Scratches its innocent behind on a tree.

In Breughel's *Icarus*, for instance: how everything turns away
Quite leisurely from the disaster; the ploughman may
Have heard the splash, the forsaken cry,
But for him it was not an important failure; the sun shone
As it had to on the white legs disappearing into the green
Water, and the expensive delicate ship that must have seen
Something amazing, a boy falling out of the sky,
Had somewhere to get to and sailed calmly on.

This is one of my favorite poems, not only because it is so full of insights brilliantly communicated, but also because it was the occasion for a pivotal conversation with my son. Not perhaps coincidentally, the poem has as one of its themes the relationship between a father and son.

The poem was inspired by a visit to the art gallery in Brussels for which the poem is named. It is an example of ekphrasis, which is defined as a literary description of, or commentary on, a visual work of art. The work in question here is *The Fall of Icarus* by the Flemish artist Pieter Bruegel the Elder. We have already encountered the Icarus myth in "Failing and Flying" by Jack Gilbert (chapter 5). Let's consider the myth.

The Greek master craftsman Daedalus and his son Icarus are trapped on the island of Crete by the ruling tyrant, King Minos. Daedalus longs for home and, observing that Minos controls the land and sea, realizes that the only way he and his son can escape is via the air. In the *Metamorphoses*, the Roman poet Ovid describes how Daedalus carefully crafts wings out of bird feathers, attaching them with wax. His son stands nearby smiling and playing with the feathers and the wax, interrupting his father's meticulous work, suggesting a warm and tender relationship between father and son.

When the time comes to leave the island, the father becomes serious as he instructs the son to follow him with the famous words:

I warn you, Icarus, to travel the middle course.
If you fly too low, the waves may weigh down your wings.
If you go too high, the sun may scorch your wings.
Stay between both. . . . Follow me!

Like poet-pilot John Gillespie Magee, Icarus can't resist flying high. He flies too close to the sun, which melts the fragrant wax and loosens the feathers. The boy flaps his arms but finds no support from the air and falls. Crying his father's name, he is swept up in the blue sea. Here is how Ovid describes Daedalus's grief:

> The unlucky father, a father no longer, said, "Icarus,
> Icarus, where are you? In what region shall I seek you?"
> "Icarus!" he kept saying: He caught sight of feathers in the waves.
> and cursed his own arts and buried the body in a tomb.

Auden reflects on how suffering can take place anywhere, any time. He's right, of course: children drowning in swimming pools while the family attends to the barbecue, tipping upside down into a bucket of water, or crawling into the driveway when someone is backing up. The opportunities for sudden domestic catastrophe are endless.

Bruegel's *Fall of Icarus* shows a beautiful landscape alongside an emerald green sea, with rocky outcroppings and much activity going on: a ship sailing nearby; a fisherman; a plowman with his horse working the soil; a shepherd with his crook and sheep, staring into the sky (all right out of Ovid). And in the bottom right corner, easy to miss if it's not pointed out, are two splayed legs sticking out of the water. It's Icarus, fallen from the sky, drowning.

Some of the elements in the poem, like the torturer's horse scratching its behind against a tree or dogs going on with their "doggy life," apparently come from other paintings by Bruegel, conflated perhaps in the poet's memory after sweeping through the gallery. The humorous tone of these images highlights the indifference of nature to human suffering.

People and animals around are not only uninterested, Auden points out, but uncaring: "everything turns away / Quite leisurely from the disaster." Even those who may have heard the splash of Icarus falling into the water or "the forsaken cry" pay little heed. It doesn't concern them. Auden wonders how the people on the ship could have failed to see "something amazing, a boy falling out of the sky." Yet they had "somewhere to go and sailed calmly on."

Father and Son

Back to the conversation with my son, Josh. He was a late adolescent, beginning to strike out independently, choosing new friends, and undertaking new activities, as adolescents are wont to do. Josh asked me if he could go to a party in another town one New Year's Eve. His friend Calvin, a trouble-prone teenager, would be driving. I recalled that Calvin tended to get into more than the usual amount of trouble. Once Calvin had driven some friends to an underpass in a dangerous part of town, where he took out a boom box and the group began dancing in the street. Substances were passed around. Josh left and made his way to the subway to come home. He fell asleep in the subway shelter, had his wallet stolen, and was lucky to get back home with the help of a few dollars given to him by the probable thief, who was also waiting for the subway.

As Josh was talking, my mind drifted to my own youthful folly and narrow escape (as described in chapter 31). I must have spaced out, because Josh was staring at me, waiting for an answer. "No," I responded, "no, you can't go."

"Why?" he pleaded. "Why can't I go? It's not far. What can go wrong?"

"You can't go," I said, "because death can happen in an instant. Here, read this poem," and I gave him "Musée des Beaux Arts."

He read it. He understood. And backed off from his request. We all celebrated New Year's Eve together safely and enjoyably.

Some years later, when Josh was in college, he called to tell me they had been assigned the poem in his English course. We both had a good laugh about our exchange years before and how a poem might have saved his life—or not. We will never know, and that's just fine with me.

Imagine how many tourists have passed Bruegel's painting without much thought. But Auden stood, stared, and wondered. The year was 1939, and he understood that the world was on the brink of war and the untold tragedy it would cause. Perhaps that was on his mind as he gazed at the small tragedy depicted in the canvas in front of him, unheeded by those around, and thought deeply about the Old Masters, who knew so much about suffering. Perhaps he wrote this poem to heighten our awareness of tragedy ever lurking at the periphery of our visual field.

Takeaways

✘ **Be mindful of danger, especially if you or people you love are in a vulnerable position.**

✘ **Anticipate danger before it happens whenever possible.** Be sure the gate to the swimming pool is locked and that your children wear their safety equipment.

✘ **If you are a parent confronted by a request that seems dangerous, prioritize safety.** Your job is not primarily to be a friend, but to shepherd your child through the hazards of life, to educate her or him and, yes, to let the child grow into a self-sufficient adult as he or she acquires the necessary skills.

✘ **Remember those who have been lost, and comfort those who are grieving.** How we treat the dying and the dead and those who are left behind is a mark of our humanity.

The Poet and the Poem

This is the third Auden poem in this collection. One was about the loss of a loved one (chapter 11); one was a celebration of a night of loving (chapter 4); and here we see a deep philosophical insight triggered by the work of an Old Master in an art museum. Auden was a poet of such tremendous range that we haven't come near to showcasing the variety of his creative versatility. There is a certain generosity about him that makes his poems feel like gifts.

Auden was generous in life as well. Fellow writers would often seek out his advice and insights. He remained lifelong friends with ex-lovers, even after the romance had long since faded. And he did big favors for strangers anonymously.

Auden wrote not only poems but essays and reviews on a wide variety of subjects, and worked on documentaries and plays. His reputation has grown since his death, and some regard him as one of the greatest poets of the twentieth century.

___

WE REAL COOL
by Gwendolyn Brooks

> The Pool Players.
> Seven at the Golden Shovel.

> We real cool. We
> Left school. We

> Lurk late. We
> Strike straight. We

> Sing sin. We
> Thin gin. We

> Jazz June. We
> Die soon.

At one of her readings, the famous American poet Gwendolyn Brooks introduced this poem as follows, with a tongue-in-cheek reference to how its fame has eclipsed her other poems:

"I guess I'd better offer you 'We Real Cool.' Most young people know me by that poem. I don't mean that I dislike it, but I would prefer it if the compilers and anthologists would assume that I have written a few other poems."

Then she proceeded to introduce the main attraction: a poem that has given its name to a jazz band, has been taught in college, appeared on people's favorite poem lists, provided the central focus for a Broadway play (*Pipeline*) and, most importantly, changed people's lives. Here's how Brooks relates how she came to write the poem:

> I was passing by a pool hall in my community one afternoon during school time and I saw therein a little bunch of boys, I say in this poem seven. And they were shooting pool but instead of asking myself, "Why aren't they in school?" I asked myself, "How do they feel about themselves?" and just perhaps they might have considered themselves contemptuous of the establishment, and I represented the establishment with the month of June, which is a nice, gentle, non-controversial, enjoyable, pleasant, fragrant month that everybody loves. This poem has been banned here and there because of the word "jazz," which some people have considered a sexual reference, which was not my intention—though I have no objection if it helps anybody—but I was thinking of music.

It is surprising to find such a short poem (only twenty-four words long) that delivers such a powerful punch—a sort of jazz haiku. One third of these words consists of the word "we," suggesting that these teenagers are focused mostly on themselves.

They start by bragging, "We real cool," an expression derived from the jazz of the day. Next comes another boast, "We / Left school," thumbing their noses at the establishment. The phrase "lurk late" suggests people hanging around, looking for trouble. When the boys boast, "We / Strike straight," they are presumably referring to their game of pool, but undertones of violence are inescapable. The next two claims, "We / Sing sin," and "We / Thin gin," are nicely ambiguous. Perhaps they are contemplating crime or diluting alcohol? There is menace in the mystery. The poet's disclaimer about "We / Jazz June" is interesting. When I saw *Pipeline*, the actor explicitly played this line as having a sexual meaning.

All the pool players' boasts and bravado deflate in the final devastating lines: "We / Die soon." Here the teenagers acknowledge a sad truth—that many of them will have their lives cut short. They seem to have accepted that and see it as inevitable. But there is nobody around to register the likely tragedy except for a passing poet, who stopped and stared and wrote about it.

Let's consider the tragedy of these young pool players from three vantage points: societal, neurological, and from an individual perspective.

The South Side of Chicago, where Brooks lived most of her life, has been stricken with violence since at least 1960, when "We Real Cool" was written.

Adora Lee, a minister working in the public health field in the poorest areas of Washington, D.C., is all too familiar with the problems of young men growing up in the inner city. She recalls hearing Brooks read "We Real Cool" when Lee was a student at Rutgers University. As Lee recalls, "Gwendolyn Brooks was old at the time, with white hair, but read the poem using language accented in a way that sounded like the young people of the day—reaching out to a new generation."

Lee remembers growing up in the 1950s and 60s in a city in Florida, where her father owned a pool hall. As she says, "Many of the boys did not have much guidance, and pool halls were regarded as cool places, where they could hang out. Their role models were the older guys who ran numbers (an illegal lottery game) and had flashy cars. As you can imagine, young men in those circumstances would be very susceptible to running into trouble that could cost them their lives."

Lee points out that the problems flagged by Brooks continue to trouble young men in underserved areas. She observes:

> They don't have a piece of the American dream. They have a feel-
> ing of forgottenness. They're not invested in society or their fam-
> ilies. They have a sense of early mortality and think, "I'm going to
> die soon, so I may as well live it up now." Men seem more vulner-
> able to these problems than women, perhaps because of a lack of
> male role models.

According to New York University sociology professor Patrick Shar-key, although there has been an overall improvement in the amount of inner city violence since the 1990s, "violence is a fundamental challenge of American cities." In fact, there has been an uptick of violence since 2014.

Exploring the role of adolescence in risk-taking behavior, I spoke with research psychiatrist Jay Giedd, professor of psychia-try at the University of California, San Diego, who confirmed what is well known: that teenage boys have an increased tendency to take risks as compared with girls and older males. Giedd attributes this tendency, which starts at adolescence and continues to about age twenty-five, to changes in brain dopamine systems. He points out that these behavioral trends can be quantified by questionnaires as well as by gambling and betting games.

Adolescent risk-taking behavior appears to be the result of both biological and social influences. Risk-taking is often tied to show-ing off for peers. Researchers studying school children driving out of high school parking lots, for example, have found that a teenage boy will drive out of the lot faster if there are other boys in the car than if he is alone. Likewise, if there are four boys in a car, they will be less likely to wear seatbelts than if there is only one. Interestingly, a boy will drive more slowly if there is a girl in the car. These research observations seem relevant to "We Real Cool," where the seven pool players at the Golden Shovel may egg one another on to the various behaviors they list. It gives additional significance to the repeated use of the word "We."

The man who drew my attention to "We Real Cool" by sending it to the Favorite Poem Project was John. When I interviewed him, he was twenty years old and described himself as coming from "a large, loving, South Boston Irish Catholic family," who were "poor, but we didn't know it." As a high school freshman, at age fourteen, he had already begun to have problems with substance use, mainly alcohol.

When he heard that a family member had been a victim of a violent crime, he felt "completely overwhelmed" and "was on the verge of trouble," preoccupied with how to avenge the vicious act. In retrospect, he believes he had PTSD and used drugs and alcohol to deal with his rage.

An English teacher noticed that there was something wrong with him and kept him late at school. When she heard what had happened, she warned him against taking reprisals, suggesting instead that he start a journal, which he did. His writing quickly took the form of poetry, and with each beat of his poetry he felt "the kind of release you get from punching a heavy bag. There was a rhythm to it." He wrote obsessively—"write, rewrite, go back to it"—full of shame and fear. His teacher would read his work and suggest corrections.

Poetry became a big part of John's life, even as he "got tossed out of three different high schools." In the third school, he talked the journalism teacher into switching the class from journalism to poetry to better engage the students and connect the subject to music. He liked "We Real Cool" because, unlike other poems he had found hard to understand, "We Real Cool" is "blunt and straightforward" and "has a lot to do with rhythm and healing." He was impressed by the accuracy of the poet's portrayal of the "drastic quickness of progression from cutting class in high school to death." Creativity offered relief and directed him away from destructive behaviors, such as violence and drinking, to more creative outlets.

John has found that other young people resonate with "We Real Cool." They say it sounds like hip-hop, has caused them to view poetry differently, and has helped them. John, now in recovery, has a steady job as a health inspector for the city. Acknowledging his debt to "We Real Cool," he says, "Poetry saved my life."

Takeaways

✗ **Advice to parents, teachers, and counselors: detect early signs that a child is having problems and intervene promptly, empathically, and effectively.** Recognize that this will probably be an ongoing project, so be prepared for the long haul. It takes a lot of effort to turn around the trajectory of a child's life, but the potential reward is huge.

✗ **Advice to students: watch out for early signs that you're having difficulties at school or at home and get help.** If you are troubled by feelings of sadness, anxiety, or despair, seek out a professional who can help you. Talk to an adult you trust.

✗ **Consider reading or writing poetry as a way of channeling feelings along constructive pathways.**

✗ **If you are thinking of doing something violent to yourself or others, take a break.** Ask yourself, "Is there anything else I can do instead? Is there anybody I can talk to about this?"

✴ **Remember, poetry and literature teach us that we are not alone.** Whatever problem you are facing, others have faced it before. There may be a solution out there. You don't have to figure it all out yourself.

The Poet and the Poem

Gwendolyn Brooks was born in Topeka, Kansas, in 1917, and grew up in Chicago. Her mother was a schoolteacher, and her father was a janitor who wanted to become a doctor but wasn't able to afford it. Her parents often read to her and encouraged her to do well in school. She was a shy girl who began writing poetry very early. By age sixteen she had already written and published over seventy-five poems. She attended three schools, where she experienced a great deal of racial prejudice, which shaped her understanding of injustice and discrimination in the United States. She decided on going to college for only two years, since her primary interest was writing.

Brooks went on to become one of the most successful American poets of the twentieth century, with multiple books of poetry to her name and many accolades. In 1950 she was awarded the Pulitzer Prize, the first African American to earn that distinction, and in 1968, she was named poet laureate of Illinois. She lived in Chicago nearly all her life, deriving inspiration from the everyday lives of the people of that city. As her reputation grew, she was invited to teach at many institutions, including Columbia University.

Brooks married Henry Lowington Blakely Jr. in 1939, and they had two children, Henry and Nora. She died in 2000 at age eighty-three.

✿ I KNOW I AM GETTING OLD
by Wendell Berry

> I know I am getting old and I say so,
> but I don't think of myself as an old man.
> I think of myself as a young man
> with unforeseen debilities. Time is neither
> young nor old, but simply new, always
> counting, the only apocalypse. And the clouds
> —no mere measure or geometry, no cubism,
> can account for clouds or, satisfactorily, for bodies.
> There is no science for this, or art either.
> Even the old body is new—who has known it
> before?—and no sooner new than gone, to be
> replaced by a body yet older and again new.
> The clouds are rarely absent from our sky
> over this humid valley, and there is a sycamore
> that I watch as, growing on the riverbank,
> it forecloses the horizon, like the years
> of an old man. And you, who are as old
> almost as I am, I love as I loved you
> young, except that, old, I am astonished
> at such a possibility, and am duly grateful.

I recently attended a Zoom high school reunion with my fellow classmates, all around age seventy, most of whom hadn't seen each other for over fifty years. In the weeks running up to the event, we exchanged pictures and videos and greeted one another with words of friendship, such as "You haven't changed a bit," and "You've aged well." This last statement was as close as anyone got to the words "age" and "aging," not to mention the dreaded word "old." In our society that has become a dirty word. For example, when introducing someone to a friend, you might say, "Meet my old friend, Elaine," then rapidly correct yourself to "Well, not really my *old* friend, my long-standing friend." And both of you are likely to smile, a bit embarrassed by the euphemism.

Against this cultural background, Wendell Berry's opening declaration in this poem feels almost courageous: "I know I am getting old and I say so."

Yet as with the person you might mistakenly introduce as an "old friend," Berry quickly qualifies his statement. He doesn't think of himself as an old man, but "as a young man with unforeseen debilities."

Berry has captured a curious aspect of the aging process that unfolds from infancy to senescence. Each stage comes as a surprise as biology plays tricks with the mind and body. Now we are able to climb out of the crib, walk, talk, read. Now new hormones rush through our bloodstream, and all of a sudden we feel a newfound interest in girls or boys or both. Now lots of things happen—families, jobs, careers, and many diversions, joyful or otherwise—and we lose track of time. And before we know it, we are right up alongside Wendell Berry, trying to figure out this new stage, which feels like being "a young man / with unforeseen debilities."

This poem was brought to my attention by a therapist friend, a spry woman in her early eighties, who had given it to several of her clients and friends, with whom it had struck a resonant chord. Uni-

versally they found it helpful that someone had put into words famil-
iar experiences that they had not previously seen so well described.
"Unforeseen debilities" are an unwelcome development of aging.

Berry becomes philosophical:

> Time is neither
> young nor old, but simply new, always
> counting, the only apocalypse.

This concept of time as an arrow moving ever forward is ancient but
remains relevant, especially for older people. But the poet tempers
the implications of this apocalyptic inevitability with a more cheer-
ful spin:

> Even the old body is new—who has known it
> before?—and no sooner new than gone, to be
> replaced by a body yet older and again new.

An older body that has replaced your younger body now feels new.
The poet dodges the challenges of this new body, which may now
require you to hold on to a rail or a helping arm, or the many other
accommodations the new body requires. Instead the poet focuses on
curiosity and fascination with this process.

Berry is intrigued by clouds, which he compares to bodies. Both
change shape over time, and as we age, "clouds are rarely absent
from our sky." Also, vision, memory, and acuity may all become
clouded. And clouds block our view, like a sycamore tree growing on
a river bank. Recall Salvatore Quasimodo's letter to his aging mother
(chapter 29): "Now the mists are descending," The years shorten.
There is no getting away from it. To what can we turn for consola-
tion? Love, perhaps. Berry looks at the person he has loved since

they were young, who is now almost as old as he is, and marvels at the possibility that love can endure even as body and mind decline.

Takeaways

✘ **There is a value in acknowledging that you are getting old.** Self-honesty in this area can help you stay safe and healthy. Many avoidable missteps and disasters can be prevented if people take appropriate measures to catch illnesses early and plan accordingly. Accept that you are less steady on your feet. Overcome the embarrassment of getting older. Use a cane to prevent falls; hold on to railings. If your hearing is less acute, get hearing aids. Ask for help if and when you need it. In short, don't let worries about looking old interfere with your ability to lead your best life.

✘ **Most of us age by degrees.** It is possible to view each new phase of the aging process as an adventure or opportunity, as well as a liability.

✘ **Some recognition of one's shortening timeline is of practical and emotional value in allowing for planning and acceptance.**

✘ **Love can persist into old age and can be a continuing source of joy and comfort.** So can friendship: long-standing friends especially remember you at different stages of your life and can often relate to you more fully than those who have known you only in your older years. But you are never too old to make new friends.

✘ **Hold on to what still gives you joy.** Inventory your moments of delight.

The Poet and the Poem

Wendell Berry, born in 1934, is a man of letters, farmer, and activist for the environment and sustainable farming and against war. Although best known as a poet (with more than thirty collections), he has also written numerous essays and novels.

Berry was the oldest of four children born to John Marshall and Virginia Erdman Berry in Henry County, Kentucky. His father was a lawyer and tobacco farmer, and the families of both parents had been farmers for five generations. After high school, Berry received his BA and MA at the University of Kentucky. He married Tanya Amyx in 1957.

Berry's first volume of poetry, *The Broken Ground*, was published in 1964. His latest collection is *A Timbered Choir: The Sabbath Poems 1979–1997*. These poems reflect Berry's practice of walking out into the countryside on Sunday mornings, one way of observing the Sabbath. In his words, "I go free from the tasks and intentions of my workdays, and so my mind becomes hospitable to unintended thoughts: to what I am very willing to call inspiration." If you enjoyed this poem, you may also enjoy a great favorite, "The Peace of Wild Things," in which he describes retreating to nature as a way of finding inner peace.

Chapter Forty–Seven

THE CRITICAL IMPORTANCE OF COMMUNICATION

NOT WAVING BUT DROWNING

by Stevie Smith

Nobody heard him, the dead man,
But still he lay moaning:
I was much further out than you thought
And not waving but drowning.

Poor chap, he always loved larking
And now he's dead
It must have been too cold for him his heart gave way,
They said.

Oh, no no no, it was too cold always
(Still the dead one lay moaning)
I was much too far out all my life
And not waving but drowning.

This poem intrigues me every time I read it. Consider the first two lines: in line one man is dead; in line two he's lying there moaning. You don't have to have a medical degree to know that dead men don't moan. He is telling the reader (and presumably the people on the beach) that he was not waving but drowning. To the modern reader,

used to cinematic conventions that often employ a voiceover to por-
tray the thoughts of a dead person, this device may be less novel now
than it was when Smith published her poem in 1957. Yet what the
dead man says still fascinates:

> I was much further out than you thought
> And not waving but drowning.

In the second stanza, the poem shifts to the people on the beach,
whose interest in him is casual, almost to the point of callous indif-
ference, reminiscent of the reactions of the onlookers in Auden's
poem about the death of Icarus. After a mild expression of sym-
pathy ("Poor chap") they fatuously observe that "he always loved
larking" (which in Britain means having fun or playing pranks).
They follow up with the obvious, "And now he's dead" and dismiss
the tragedy with the explanation that the water must have been too
cold, causing his heart to "give way." In a not-so-subtle way, they
are shifting the blame to the dead man. He shouldn't have been out
there larking in water that was too cold. In other words, it was the
poor chap's own fault.

This type of reaction is common when people are confronted
with tragedy. We seek explanations to reassure ourselves that the
dead are somehow different from us; we look for some reason to
blame them. They did something wrong, which luckily we are clever
enough to avoid. Also, since it was "their fault," we don't need to
afford them too much sympathy.

Back to the poem. The dead man "speaks" again, responding to
the onlookers:

> Oh, no no no, it was too cold always
> (Still the dead one lay moaning)

I was much too far out all my life
And not waving but drowning.

Here the poet shifts the frame of reference, broadening the dead man's message, as she describes in these comments:

> Perhaps I may read something in the newspaper that disturbs me rather and makes me want to write what I feel. For instance, I read about a man getting drowned once. His friends thought he was waving to them from the sea but really he was drowning. This often happens in swimming baths or at the seaside. And then I thought in a way it is true of life too, that a lot of people pretend out of bravery really that they are very jolly and ordinary sort of chaps but really they do not feel at all at home in the world or able to make friends easily. So then they joke a lot and laugh and people think they're quite alright and jolly nice too. But sometimes the brave pretense breaks down and then, like the poor man in this poem, they are lost.

Problems with Communication

Communication is so central to human relationships that if people have problems with it—either in expression or reception—that can lead to sadness, loneliness, and despair. As Stevie Smith observes, some people may seem to be fine on the surface but actually feel isolated and alienated. For others, these problems are more apparent.

Ken Towbin, a clinical and research psychiatrist at the National Institute of Mental Health, observes that Smith's poem speaks to a problem inherent in communication. He points out that "what we *think* we are communicating and what others *understand* can be widely divergent. When people incorrectly conclude that they understand each other, this can lead to terrible distress."

Problems with communication are present in people with a host of different emotional disorders, but may also occur in all of us in more subtle forms. Consider, for example, some of the people already mentioned in this book: Rusty, the man who had problems telling his wife he loved her; the two young men who had trouble accepting that the girls they fancied were "just not into them"; and the veterans with PTSD, who were unable to communicate properly even with their families when they returned from war. To these unfortunate souls, we can add the poor man in the present poem. Smith imagines his desperation to have extended to his life in general, like so many people. As you will see below, Smith was intimately familiar with that predicament.

One of the hardest things to do in any relationship is to listen. You may think you heard what somebody said, but were you really listening? We don't always feel like *really* listening. Often we're busy and want to get on with our day or our own thoughts. That is understandable. But in a relationship—or in life in general—it is important to listen—and look. As Smith points out, communication is not always verbal. For example, if someone is waving out at sea, it's worth wondering, "Is she or he waving or drowning?"

Early in my psychiatric training, I learned how to respond to a patient who asks, "Do you know what I mean?" Even if we *think* we know what they mean, in general it is best not to answer yes. People may be signaling to us that they are concerned that we may not have fully understood them. A better answer might be something like, "I'm not sure I do. Can you explain it again?" Although anybody can misunderstand or be misunderstood, people with communication difficulties (expressive, receptive, or both) are especially vulnerable. Such difficulties are often remediable, which may make a big difference in a person's life.

All the Lonely People

People with communication difficulties are often lonely, and vice versa. A vicious circle may develop whereby loneliness causes people to stop communicating with others, leading to more loneliness. Or communication difficulties may lead to withdrawal, an impoverished social network, and further communication difficulties.

Elsewhere in this book we have encountered solitude as a joyful, even thrilling, experience. Not so here, where loneliness is represented as painful, which it often is. So the state of being alone can be very differently experienced by different people, depending on how they look at their situation.

Mother Teresa, an expert on human suffering, observed, "The most terrible poverty is loneliness, and the feeling of being unloved." In recent years, loneliness has emerged as a factor worth studying in its own right because of its potential impact on health and well-being. For example, loneliness has been found to aggravate cardiovascular disease and depression, which can be partially improved by social support. Chronic loneliness is associated with an increased risk of death, comparable in magnitude to smoking a pack of cigarettes per day and greater than obesity or lack of exercise. There is evidence that the pain of loneliness or rejection may be registered in the same part of the brain as other forms of pain.

Acknowledging the importance of loneliness as a public health problem, the United Kingdom has appointed someone at the ministerial level to oversee initiatives to understand and treat the condition—a sort of minister of loneliness—and other European countries are following its example. Finally, medicine, science, and politics have caught up with the arts in recognizing the problem of loneliness.

In 1966, the Beatles wrote the haunting song "Eleanor Rigby," named for the lonely woman who picks up rice in a church where the wedding has been, and exhorting the listener to look at "all the lonely people," a touching message from this famous group. Likewise, in this poem a prominent poet, who dramatizes the death of an anonymous man, draws attention to those who lead lives of isolation and despair.

Deaths of Despair

In 2015, Princeton economists Anne Case and Angus Deaton coined the term "deaths of despair" to describe their observation that working-age men and women without four-year college degrees are dying of suicide, drug overdoses, and alcohol-related liver disease at unprecedented rates in the United States. In fact, the 2017 death rate has been described as equal to that of three fully loaded Boeing 737 MAX jets falling out of the sky every day for a year.

The researchers linked their observations to economic factors, notably earning inequalities, loss of economic opportunities, lack of a safety net for people who fall upon hard times, and a sense of, as Deaton puts it, "the fabric of life slowly coming apart." Even though their studies have focused on America, the authors have linked their findings to capitalism in general. Recent reports have replicated these findings in the United Kingdom. So just in case we needed proof, recent scientific observations bear out Smith's observation that some people are not waving but drowning.

Takeaways

✗ **Whenever possible, try to listen, especially when someone may be signaling distress.** Understanding someone—and showing it—is a gift in itself. Remember, people may communicate non-verbally as well as verbally—as in this poem.

✖ **Respond in a timely and helpful way.** Even a few kind words or a thoughtful gesture at the right time and in the right way can make a real difference in a person's life and may be long remembered.

✖ **If you spot a lonely person, consider doing or saying something nice.** Even a small compliment, like "You look good in that," can brighten someone's day.

✖ **If you are in distress, let others know.** If they are at first unresponsive, don't assume they are ignoring you willfully or out of indifference. They may just not be picking up the signal, so consider raising the volume or amplifying the gesture.

✖ **If you sense that you and your partner or friend are having a conflict or are not on the same wavelength, try to clarify (in a neutral way) whether you may be having trouble communicating.** If you agree that there may be a misunderstanding, this can offer you an opportunity to get back on track with each other.

The Poet and the Poem

Stevie Smith (1902–1971) was an English poet, novelist, short-story writer, and book reviewer. She won the Cholmondeley Award and Queen's Gold Medal for poetry. Her reputation as a poet has grown over the years ("Not Waving but Drowning" was rated as the second most favorite poem in the 1995 BBC survey), and she is currently one of the most highly anthologized women poets. A play, *Stevie*, based on her life, was adapted into a film starring Glenda Jackson.

Smith was the second daughter of Ethel Spear, described as a "frail romantic," who married the handsome Charles Ward Smith, a man "with a taste for drink and wanderlust." Smith described them as an "ill-assorted" couple. Her father was a shipping agent, whose business and marriage soon began to unravel. When Smith was four, her father left to join the merchant navy, returning only for very brief visits. Her parents never divorced. The mother and her two daughters moved to a suburb of north London, which was to be Smith's lifelong "house of female habitation." At age five, Smith developed tubercular peritonitis, a severe form of tuberculosis, for which she was sent to a sanatorium for three years. She was extremely distressed at being separated from her mother. She considered suicide, but paradoxically the idea fortified her resolve to live.

When her mother died in 1919 (Smith was sixteen at the time), she continued to share the house with her beloved aunt Margaret, her "Lion Aunt," who had moved in to take care of the girls when her mother became ill. Her father showed up at his wife's funeral, displaying uncharacteristic grief. He remarried the next year to a woman who called him "Tootles," which prompted Smith to remark, "If he can inspire someone to call him Tootles, there must be things about him I don't see." Smith never reconciled with her father, and when he died thirty years later, she found she was just "too busy" to attend his funeral. After Aunt Madge died in 1968, Smith stayed on in the house alone until her final illness.

Although very smart, Smith did not shine academically at school. After graduating, she trained to become a secretary and went on to work for distinguished people. She found secretarial work boring and unrewarding, but it left her with plenty of time to read and write.

In 1936 Smith's *Novel on Yellow Paper* was published and well received, and two other novels and several volumes of poetry followed. Her poetry was accompanied by whimsical line drawings.

In the 1960s she was a literary celebrity, a kind of cult figure among youthful radicals. Although Smith's star has waxed and waned, in recent years she has increasingly become appreciated as an important writer.

Smith was emotionally vulnerable and was depressed off and on throughout her life. She suffered significant early losses (the departure of her father at age four, long separation from her mother at age five, and her mother's death at age sixteen). Such losses have been associated with depression in later life. The title poem of her fourth poetry collection, *Harold's Leap* (1950), describes suicide, a subject about which she intermittently ruminated. In 1953, she became clinically depressed. Two months after she wrote "Not Waving but Drowning," she attempted to slash her wrists while at work. The empathy she felt for the drowning man in the poem suggests that she herself might not have been waving but drowning.

On medical advice, Smith retired from the company. She supplemented her modest pension by reviewing extensively for *The Observer* and other magazines. In retirement she made use of the time to return to writing poetry and produced several further collections, including one published posthumously.

Smith socialized widely and corresponded with other authors, including George Orwell. Love and men did not figure prominently in her life. Though she was once engaged, marriage was not for her. As she wrote, "Marriage, I think / For women / Is the best of opiates / It kills thoughts."

In 1970 Smith became ill with a brain tumor, and she died the following year.

Chapter Forty-Eight

SHOULD YOU RAGE?

DO NOT GO GENTLE INTO THAT GOOD NIGHT
by Dylan Thomas

Do not go gentle into that good night,
Old age should burn and rave at close of day;
Rage, rage against the dying of the light.

Though wise men at their end know dark is right,
Because their words had forked no lightning they
Do not go gentle into that good night.

Good men, the last wave by, crying how bright
Their frail deeds might have danced in a green bay,
Rage, rage against the dying of the light.

Wild men who caught and sang the sun in flight
And learn, too late, they grieved it on its way,
Do not go gentle into that good night.

Grave men, near death, who see with blinding sight
Blind eyes could blaze like meteors and be gay,
Rage, rage against the dying of the light.

And you, my father, there on the sad height,
Curse, bless, me now with your fierce tears, I pray.
Do not go gentle into that good night.
Rage, rage against the dying of the light.

My friend Joe was a fixture in the neighborhood. You could see him from hundreds of yards away—big-boned and hardy-handsome, as Gerard Manley Hopkins might have described him—gardening, mowing his lawn, or taking his huge English mastiff for a walk. Then sickness broke him. He developed one cancer, then another, then another. And each time he battled on. He sought my advice about meditation, which helped him come to terms with the surgeries required by the arrival of each new physical assault on his body.

During that time, I learned the measure of the man. He was a New Englander who had negotiated for unions, a task that required steely toughness. On one occasion, he told me, someone delivered dynamite to his front door in an unsuccessful attempt to intimidate him. Joe collected oriental artifacts: huge stone replicas of terracotta soldiers; gorgeous scholar stones of vibrant hues and intricate patterns, and carved artifacts, like a fenestrated wooden box in which a concubine could house a cricket so that its chirping might provide some small company for her during long, lonely nights of waiting. Once, as I was leaving his house, he said, "I'm not yet ready to say 'Do not go gentle into that good night.' I'd rather say, 'A coward dies a thousand deaths, the brave man dies but once.'"

"And when might you be ready to quote Dylan Thomas?" I asked.

"Only when the only other choice is to throw in the towel."

The opening line of this famous poem, widely considered Dylan Thomas's greatest work, and perhaps the greatest villanelle ever written, has become a figure of speech. As someone said to me when he heard I was writing this book, "I don't know much about poetry although, of course, I've heard of 'Do not go gentle into that good night,' but that's about it."

You may recall that we have encountered two other villanelles in this collection, "One Art" (chapter 1) and "The Waking" (chapter 39).

Thomas's poem is such a dazzling feat of verbal mastery that it is easy to get lost in the words and overlook their meaning. So let's examine that together.

The first stanza is clear. The poet advocates rage in the face of death.

In the next four stanzas, he lists four different kinds of men who rage for four different reasons: wise men, who know that it is time to die, yet rage because their words have had little impact on the world; good men, who wish that their "frail deeds" had made more of a splash; wild men who had partied ("caught and sang the sun in flight") without realizing that they hadn't taken into account how transient life is; and finally:

> Grave men, near death, who see with blinding sight
> Blind eyes could blaze like meteors and be gay . . .

These are men who have become aware only as they are dying of the intense joy they are capable of experiencing even as their vision fails. In this regard, he pays homage to the cultural meme of the blind poet, like Milton or Homer.

Finally, the quatrain arrives and with it a revelation, reminiscent of "One Art." It turns out that the poet is not only addressing the reader, but also his dying father.

Why does the poet want his father to curse him? I have no idea, but if you read the poet's biography, which I summarize below, you will find no shortage of possible reasons why his father might be angry at him. Many sons and daughters facing a dying parent might feel guilty at not having been a good enough child and therefore deserving to be chastised if not cursed. Or maybe the poet is projecting his own rage at losing his father, and he wants for them to rage together. (Incidentally, Thomas, who was also an accomplished voice actor, can be heard reading his poem. I recommend that you listen to this recording, and see if your eyes remain dry when he gets to the last stanza. Perhaps you will notice a shift in the tone of his voice between "curse" and "bless," from anger at the impending loss of his father to the longing of an adult child hungry for his dying parent's last blessing.)

Dying and Raging

Elisabeth Kübler-Ross, an early pioneer in the psychological stages of death and dying, regarded anger as one of the five stages. Although her model has now been largely discredited, the different stages can often be discerned, though not necessarily always in the sequence she suggested. In any event, she claimed that rage is stage two (after denial). Whether or not you accept her typology, rage can certainly occur as part of the process of dying, which is not surprising, given all that a person is losing. Seen in that light, this poem can be regarded as a son giving his father permission to be angry.

Raging like a Fire

So far I have equated raging with anger, but raging can also be viewed as passionate, as in "raging desire." You can see such raging passion in Thomas's biography. Considered in this way, it makes sense that he would want his father to keep raging—holding on to the passion for life—even as the light is dying and night is closing in on him.

Takeaways

✘ **Rage is a normal response in someone who is dying or facing death.** As such, it can be comforting to the dying person if this feeling is understood and accepted by loved ones.

✘ **That said, too much rage can be a bad thing, agitating a dying person.** If that is the case, professional help may be useful.

✘ **If someone close to you is dying and you are very angry or upset, you may benefit from discussing this with a wise friend or relative.** Such feelings may be a displacement of your grief and may distract you from more valuable ways to focus your emotional energy at this important time.

✘ **Likewise, after the death of a loved one, anger is not uncommon.** If you have some specific grievance in relation to the death, like the way a doctor or the police treated your relative, it is often wise to take some time to deal with your grief before taking steps to remediate that wrong. It will give you a chance to gain perspective, and you are more likely to be effective.

The Poet and the Poem

Thomas was born in 1914 in Swansea, Wales, to a revered schoolmaster and his wife, a homemaker. He was an undistinguished student, but showed an early interest in writing when he left school at age sixteen to work for the local evening newspaper. He soon began to write poetry, publishing his first poems before age twenty. These attracted the attention of the prominent poets T. S. Eliot and Stephen Spender, who helped him publish his first collection, *Eighteen Poems*, which was followed by a second, *Twenty-Five Poems*.

Thomas's distinction as a poet grew alongside a less distinguished reputation as an impish, scandalous figure on the London literary scene of the mid-1930s. He supplemented his meager income from writing with habitual cadging from his more affluent friends. He married Caitlin Macnamara in 1937, a strong woman who shared his passion for drinking and sex (not always with each other). He avoided both military service in World War II and work related to the war effort, writing to a friend, "I'd rather be a poet anyday and live on guile and beer."

Later Thomas became more successful financially, working for the BBC, both as scriptwriter and broadcaster, where his speech and reading style were in high demand. He supplemented this income with lucrative visits to America, where he became something of a cult figure—a great poet with a reckless lifestyle.

Thomas wrote longer poetic pieces that were received with varying degrees of enthusiasm. One great success was *Under Milk Wood*, his "play for voices" about the characters in the imaginary Welsh town of Llareggub, a name that is quite rude if read backwards. A highly successful version was read by the Welsh actor Richard Burton. Thomas himself made other recordings, for example of his observations of the United States and Americans, which were highly amusing. Despite these successes, Thomas was always short of money and chronically dependent on the kindness of friends and family for basic needs.

"Do not go gentle," with its mastery of style and substance, makes one wonder about the father who inspired such passion and determination to construct such a fitting memorial. According to Thomas's granddaughter Hannah Ellis, Thomas loved and admired his father, David John (D. J.), who was wise, erudite, and supportive of Thomas's ambitions. Their house was full of books, and Thomas was encouraged to read whatever caught his fancy. According to Ellis's grandmother (Thomas's wife, Caitlin), he had always written poetry to please not just himself but also his father. D. J. was a highly regarded English teacher, who read poetry aloud in the classroom, serving as a role model for Thomas in this regard.

D. J. was diagnosed with oral cancer in 1933 when Thomas was only nineteen. He had to travel to London for radiation therapy, his health improved, but he never fully recovered. In his last years, D. J. and Thomas enjoyed doing the London *Times* crossword together. D. J. was losing his eyesight at the time, which may have influenced the last tercet of Thomas's poem:

> Grave men, near death, who see with blinding sight
> Blind eyes could blaze like meteors and be gay . . .

As his father was dying and Thomas was working on the poem, he wrote to a friend, "The only person I can't show the poem to is, of course, my father, who doesn't know he's dying."

According to Ellis, his father's death in 1952 had a huge impact on Thomas "as it was the start of a year that included a rapid decline in his mental wellbeing." In addition to grieving, Thomas was physically ill, exhausted, concerned about the state of his marriage, struggling to write and in terrible debt. The downward spiral eventually led to Thomas's own death less than a year later.

On his last trip to America, although ill and exhausted, Thomas continued an affair he was having with the assistant of his American host. Was he too raging against the dying of the light? Indeed that last trip to America was to prove fatal. He became agitated, and the doctor who tried to settle him down with an injection of morphine might have hastened his demise. Unfortunately there were no good ways to treat alcoholism and alcohol abuse in those days (though AA had already been established earlier in the century). Besides, drinking was so much part of Thomas's persona as a devil-may-care poet, whose wife was often his drinking companion, that there is no evidence he would have wanted to stop drinking even if a cure had been available.

Chapter Forty-Nine

OR IS IT TIME TO GO GENTLY?

BECAUSE I COULD NOT STOP FOR DEATH
by Emily Dickinson

Because I could not stop for Death —
He kindly stopped for me —
The Carriage held but just Ourselves —
And Immortality.

We slowly drove — He knew no haste
And I had put away
My labor and my leisure too,
For His Civility —

We passed the School, where Children strove
At Recess — in the Ring —
We passed the Fields of Gazing Grain —
We passed the Setting Sun —

Or rather — He passed Us —
The Dews drew quivering and Chill —
For only Gossamer, my Gown —
My Tippet — only Tulle —

We paused before a House that seemed
A Swelling of the Ground —
The Roof was scarcely visible —
The Cornice — in the Ground —

(continued)

Since then — 'tis Centuries — and yet
Feels shorter than the Day
I first surmised the Horses' Heads
Were toward Eternity —

In this poem Emily Dickinson deals with one of the greatest myster-
ies of life—death. Is it a place, a state, a destiny, a permanent home,
a silent land? Call it what you like, but ultimately nobody really
knows what happens when we die. Will we be met by angels twang-
ing harps? By St. Peter or his emissaries at the Pearly Gates, judg-
ing whether or not we deserve admission? Or—heaven forbid!—fires
that, defying the laws of physics, never stop burning? Or perhaps . . .
nothing.

In this poem, we see Dickinson's vision of death. She starts off
in an ironic tone. She's too busy to die, so Death graciously accom-
modates her. "Don't worry, Miss Dickinson," I can hear Death say, "I
know how busy you are, so I'll swing by and pick you up."

And there she is in the carriage, just Emily and Death—and
Immortality. I wonder what immortality meant to her. Did she
mean it in the conventional sense of an immortal soul? Is it fan-
ciful to wonder whether she had any idea of the enduring value
of her work, immortal in a human sense? Or was it some abstract
and mysterious feeling that there is something about us that never
dies?

The carriage moves slowly. Ideally, death should be a dignified
affair. It brings relief, a final reckoning that her work is over, but
then, so is her leisure. Death is civil. He watches his manners, as
befits a chauffeur taking someone on her last ride.

En route to her final destination, Death takes her past some familiar landmarks that correspond to different phases of a person's life: childhood, the productive years, and then sunset.

In the next to last verse, the poet corrects herself. They didn't pass the setting sun; he passed them. In shifting to this passive image, the poet is setting aside the illusion that she is actively involved in this journey. Now things are happening to her. The idea of death is becoming more real in her imagination. Then she feels changes in her body, which becomes cold:

The Dews drew quivering and Chill.

She is wearing a gown of gossamer (that finely spun fabric of a spiderweb)—or a shroud. Her tippet, a long scarf or shawl that women sometimes wear, is made only of tulle, another ethereal fabric from which veils and delicate clothes are made.

They pause in front of her new home—the grave. Its roof, of course, is barely visible. Its cornice (the ornamental molding just below the ceiling) is obviously underground.

That's where the poet's journey stops. All sense of time is lost. Centuries have passed, yet it feels shorter than a day since:

I first surmised the Horses' Heads
Were toward Eternity—

The poem ends on a mysterious note, which reinforces the mystery of death. Is it the end or forever? Nobody knows.

The Mood of the Poem

What do you make of the mood of the poem or of the poet as she writes it? How does it leave you feeling?

To me the poet seems detached or, to use a more clinical word, dissociated. It feels like she is observing events as though they are happening to someone else.

Here is one of my favorite examples of dissociation in literature, from Charles Dickens' *Hard Times*:

"Are you in pain, dear mother?"

"I think there's a pain somewhere in the room," said Mrs. Gradgrind, "but I couldn't positively say that I have got it."

The poet seems to be saying to herself, "There is death happening somewhere over here, but I couldn't positively say that it is happening to me." The poem induces a sense of detachment, as though there is nothing to worry about. The coachman is dignified, and everything is proceeding according to protocol. The house in the ground is prepared. And all that awaits is Eternity, which even though it goes on for centuries, feels shorter than a day.

As noted in the last chapter, Elisabeth Kübler-Ross postulated different states of mind through which a dying person passes. The last state is acceptance, and perhaps it is this state (plus dissociation) that is responsible for the poem's soothing effect. We saw another example of disassociation in "The Sentence" by Anna Akhmatova, where the poet is trying to suppress traumatic memories in order to forget. We don't understand the neurochemical basis for dissociation too well, but some have suggested that it is related to endogenous opiate systems.

Takeaways

✘ **There are many ways to face death. Detachment and acceptance is one way to make it easier.** Through the regular practice of meditation, it is possible to cultivate the skill of detachment (or non-attachment) and have some control over when you choose to deploy it.

✘ **Although death is the end of life, it can also be an important stage of life, a multifaceted experience.** Each person should be permitted to go through whatever emotional stages they need in order to come to terms with death.

The Poet and the Poem

This is the third poem of Emily Dickinson's in this collection. Elsewhere, I have covered various aspects of the life of this brilliant reclusive poet. Here I would like to discuss some aspects of her religious background that shed light on her unconventional view of death.

Dickinson was raised in a Calvinist household and attended religious services with her family at the First Congregational Church in Amherst. Scholars are impressed with how much she knew about the Bible, which is reflected in her letters. In short, she had a strict religious upbringing.

Despite her conventional religious background, Dickinson's independent-mindedness was often in evidence, especially as she grew older. She balked at going to church on the Sabbath, writing that she might just as well spend Sabbath at home.

Her views of science, which she avidly embraced, over religion, are shown in the following verse:

"Faith" is a fine invention
For Gentlemen who *see*!
But Microscopes are prudent
In an Emergency!

Of the Bible she wrote:

The Bible is an antique Volume
Written by faded Men
At the suggestion of Holy Spectres

One famous event during Dickinson's year at Mount Holyoke College, which she attended after graduating Amherst Academy, was a clash with the headmistress, Mary Lyon. Lyon expected the girls to publicly declare their Christian faith. One morning she stood in front of the entire school and said, "All young ladies who wish to share that inestimable privilege of becoming Christian will please rise." Every girl in the school stood up except Dickinson, who remained quietly in her seat. Thereafter she was regarded as an impenitent for whose soul there was no hope.

We see in Dickinson's work evidence of silent rebellion against conventional religion, but we also notice the influence of hymns on the meter and rhyme of her poems. According to Peter Sacks, professor of English at Harvard University, "she lived in a bizarre psychic proximity to the church she rejected." Dickinson's independence of spirit and highly original verses have made her one of the greatest American poets.

⌁ DO NOT STAND AT MY GRAVE AND WEEP
by Mary Elizabeth Frye

> Do not stand at my grave and weep;
> I am not there. I do not sleep.
> I am a thousand winds that blow.
> I am the diamond glints on snow.
> I am the sunlight on ripened grain.
> I am the gentle autumn rain.
> When you awaken in the morning's hush
> I am the swift uplifting rush
> Of quiet birds in circled flight.
> I am the soft stars that shine at night.
> Do not stand at my grave and cry;
> I am not there. I did not die.

The first funeral I ever attended was when my grandfather died. I remember sitting in the service surrounded by solemn men and women, all looking at the coffin. I turned to my mother and said, "I feel so awful to think of Oupa lying there in that box."

"Don't feel badly," she said, "He's not in that box. That's just his body."

OK, I thought, so where is he?

That is the common question this poem addresses: where do we go when we die? Do we just disappear? Or are we transformed into something else? Or, more optimistically, do we die at all?

This poem supports the last idea, and as such is a favorite reading at funerals, where it has provided comfort and consolation to countless people.

All the forms in which the poet imagines the manifestation of the dead person's spirit are comforting: wind blowing, snow glinting, grain ripening, rain falling gently, the morning hush, birds circling, stars shining softly. All these the poet, as proxy for the deceased, would have us associate with the person who has "passed on." The poem is intended to soothe and all evidence suggests that it does.

The History of the Poem

In an introduction to *The Nation's Favorite Poems*, a BBC book based on the results of a survey by *The Bookworm*, comedian Griff Rhys Jones wrote:

> Outside the competition, the unexpected poetry success of the year from *The Bookworm's* point-of-view was an anonymous work which featured in a book on war poetry. "Do not Stand at my Grave and Weep" was left in an envelope for his parents by Steven, a soldier killed on active service in Northern Ireland, to be opened in the event of his death. It provoked an extraordinary response.
>
> A total of about 30,000 people wrote in for copies. Although it was claimed to be the creation of Navajo priests, the editors found no good evidence for any particular author.
>
> Enter "Dear Abby" columnist Abigail Van Buren, who set about finding the author—and succeeded. The surprising result

of her quest took her to Mary Elizabeth Frye, a Baltimore home-maker, who had written the poem shortly before the second World War when she and her husband were housing a young German Jewish girl. Their houseguest was worried about her ailing mother in Germany, but was advised against returning, given the rising anti-Semitism she would likely encounter. When her mother died, the daughter grieved that she never had a chance to "stand by my mother's grave and shed a tear."

Frye said that the words of comfort about what she felt about life and death just came to her, and she jotted them down on a brown paper shopping bag. Because people liked the poem, Frye made many cop-ies and circulated them privately. The poem had a curiously soothing quality and became popular in different countries and for people of different races, religions, and social status. It remains wildly popular.

Sentiments such as those in this poem have been expressed before and elsewhere. One example can be found in a famous let-ter written by Captain Sullivan Ballou, an officer in the Union Army in the Civil War, to his wife, Sarah. His regiment took part in the First Battle of Bull Run, in which he was a senior officer. While on horseback to direct his men, he was hit by a cannonball and died as a result of his wound. He was thirty-two; Sarah was twenty-four. She probably never received the letter during his lifetime, as it was found with his effects. Here are a few excerpts:

I have, I know, but few and small claims upon Divine Providence, but something whispers to me—perhaps it is the wafted prayer of my little Edgar—that I shall return to my loved ones unharmed. If I do not, my dear Sarah, never forget how much I love you, and when my last breath escapes me on the battlefield, it will whisper your name.

Ballou expresses hopes that he will live and return to her and his children, but goes on to comfort her should he not return alive:

> But, O Sarah! If the dead can come back to this earth and flit unseen around those they loved, I shall always be near you; in the brightest day and in the darkest night—amidst your happiest scenes and gloomiest hours—always, always; and if there be a soft breeze upon your cheek, it shall be my breath; or the cool air fans your throbbing temple, it shall be my spirit passing by.
>
> Sarah, do not mourn me dead; think I am gone and wait for thee, for we shall meet again.

Perhaps Frye's poem and Ballou's letter are both effective for the same reason: they were written with an earnest attempt to comfort. Frye's poem has had that effect thousands of times over. One can only hope that Ballou's letter provided similar comfort to his grieving widow.

Takeaways

✖ **The idea that the dead live on within us can be a great source of comfort.** We can remember them for their special attributes—their words, gestures, kindness, and humor. We can remember them in response to any cue that reminds us of them, including, as this poem suggests, many aspects of nature.

✖ **In a certain sense, therefore, the dead are still alive.**

✖ **Although it may be a comfort to visit the grave of a loved one or to light a candle on an anniversary of a death, it is also a comfort to feel their presence in relation to the myriad stimuli of our daily lives.**

On Poetry and Death

In this section, we have considered poetry that looks at aging and dying from many angles.

Berry depicts the slow process of aging and how to embrace it gently or at least adjust to it.

Yeats, writing as an Irish airman, foresees his death, but accepts it as the price to pay for "this lonely impulse of delight." Perhaps John Gillespie Magee feels likewise about death as compared to the thrill of high flight.

In Auden's poem, Icarus, young and exuberant, forgets the danger of flying too high and falls to his death as all around him go about their daily lives unnoticing or unmoved.

In Smith's poem, a drowning man is mistaken for someone waving at the people on the shore. She goes on to explain that some people are drowning all their lives. Dylan Thomas counsels his dying father to rage against the dying light, while Dickinson presents a gentle journey from her home to the crypt in a state that feels as though she is part dead, yet still part living.

"Do not stand at my grave and weep" reprises an idea that runs through several poems in this collection that, in one way or another, suggest there may be life after death in remembering our loved ones.

A FEW LAST THOUGHTS

As I think about the poems in this book, what I have learned from them, and how they might help people, certain images come to mind.

At times the poems have seemed to me like precious stones, refracting the ambient light and filling the room with color. At other times, they have been like lamps, illuminating the dark caverns of the mind, revealing new ways to understand old mysteries.

Beyond these images of delight, however, the poems have felt like medicine or balm, and their poets like healers speaking to us across the ages.

It has been an honor to interpret these great works through the lens of one who has spent my career trying to understand and heal the troubled mind and to help people reach the outer bounds of their potential.

I believe that these poems have the power to heal, transform, and enliven. Perhaps some of them have done so to you. If not, I hope they have at least offered a brief reprieve from an all-too-often troubled world.

SOURCE MATERIALS
AND FURTHER READING

For the biographies of the poets, I have used mostly web-based data sources, cross-referenced with one another to increase confidence in accuracy. Sources used include Poetry Foundation, Wikipedia, Poets.org, Academy of American Poets, Britannica, Encyclopedia .com, and Oxford Dictionary of National Biography (especially good on British poets; certain specific instances are mentioned below to reference specific quotes). These sources have been supplemented by published materials, as listed below.

I have also included recordings of poets reading and discussing their own poems, and other noteworthy recordings.

GENERAL READING AND RESOURCES

Penn Sounds is a web-based resource where many poets have recorded
their poems, some of which are included in this collection.

Favorite Poem Project: https://www.favoritepoem.org.

The Nation's Favourite Poems. Foreword by Griff Rhys Jones. London: BBC Books, 1996.

Sieghart, William, ed. *The Poetry Pharmacy: Tried-and-true Prescriptions for the Heart, Mind, and Soul.* Great Britain: Particular Books, 2017.

SOURCE MATERIALS FOR CHAPTERS

Introduction

Wassiliwizky E. et al. "The emotional power of poetry: neural circuitry, psychophysiology and compositional principles." *Social Cognitive and Affective Neuroscience*, 2017 Aug; 12(8); 1229–1240.

Chapter 1

Toíbín, Colm. *On Elizabeth Bishop.* Princeton: Princeton University Press, 2015.

Pierpont, Claudia Roth. "Elizabeth Bishop's Art of Losing." In *The New Yorker*, February 27, 2017.

Pennebaker, James W., and Joshua M. Smyth. *Opening Up by Writing It Down.* New York: Guilford Press, 2016.

Chapter 2

Chapman, Gary. *The Five Love Languages.* Chicago: Northfield, 2001.

Chapter 3

Epstein, Daniel Mark. *What Lips My Lips Have Kissed: The Loves and Love Poems of Edna St. Vincent Millay.* New York: Henry Holt, 2001.

Millay, Edna St. Vincent. "Pity me not because the light of day." Audio recording. YouTube (website), accessed Dec. 9, 2020: https://www.youtube.com/watch?v=zns1Tt0LlNs

Chapter 4

Mendelson, Edward. "W. H. Auden." In *The Oxford Dictionary of National Biography.* Oxford: Oxford University Press, 2011.

Chapter 5

Gilbert, Jack. "The Art of Poetry." In *The Paris Review* 175 (fall-winter 2001).

Chapter 7

Gibran, Khalil. *The Prophet*. New York: Knopf, 1923.

Hiddleston, Tom. "Love after Love." Audio recording. YouTube (website), accessed Dec. 9, 2020: https://www.youtube.com/watch?v=2hTvGy fA5WY.

Chapters 8–10

Bryson, Bill. *Shakespeare: The World as Stage*. New York: Harper Collins, 2007.

Delahoyde, Michael. "Shake-speare's Sonnets," Washington State University (website), accessed Dec. 8, 2020: https://public.wsu .edu/~delahoyd/shakespeare/sonnets.html.

Rolfe, W. J., ed. "Are Shakespeare's Sonnets Autobiographical?" From *Shakespeare's Sonnets*. New York: American Book Company, 1905. Shakespeare Online (website), Aug. 20, 2009: http://www .shakespeare-online.com/sonnets/sonnetsautobio.html.

Vendler, Helen. *The Art of Shakespeare's Sonnets*. Cambridge: Harvard University Press, 1997.

West, David. *Shakespeare's Sonnets*. London: Duckworth Overlook, 2007.

Chapter 11

Auden, W. H. *Tell Me the Truth about Love: Ten Poems*. New York: Vintage, 1994.

Chapter 12

Jamison, Kay Redfield. *An Unquiet Mind: A Memoir of Moods and Madness*. New York: Knopf, 1995.

Chapters 15 and 17

Gill, Stephen. "William Wordsworth." In The *Oxford Dictionary of National Biography*.

James, William. *The Varieties of Religious Experience*. New York: Longmans, Green, & Co., 1902.

Lao-Tzu. *Tao Te Ching*. Translated by Jonathan Star. New York: Tarcher Cornerstone, 2008.

Mill, John Stuart. *Autobiography*. Oxford: Oxford University Press, 2015 (1873).

Pearson, Craig. *The Supreme Awakening*. Fairfield, Iowa: Maharishi University of Management Press, 2013.

Rosenthal, Norman E. *Super Mind*. New York: Tarcher Perigree, 2016.

———. *Transcendence*. New York: Tarcher Perigree, 2011.

Chapter 18

Dickinson, Emily. *Selected Poems of Emily Dickinson*. New York: Modern Library, 1996.

Johnson, Thomas H., ed. *The Complete Poems of Emily Dickinson*. Boston: Little, Brown, 1890.

Chapter 19 and 20

Jamison, Kay Redfield. *Touched with Fire: Manic-Depressive Illness and the Artistic Temperament*. New York: Free Press, 1993.

Chapter 23

Smith, Constance Babington. *John Masefield: A Life*. Oxford: Oxford University Press, 1978.

Chapter 24

Millgate, Michael. "Thomas Hardy." In *The Oxford Dictionary of National Biography*. Oxford: Oxford University Press, 2006.

O'Connor, Kate Suzanne. "The Warfare of Our Higher and Lower Selves." BA thesis, University of British Columbia, 2009: https://open .library.ubc.ca/cIRcle/collections/ubctheses/24/items/1.0105192.

Chapters 26 and 27

Ali, Rozina. "The Erasure of Islam from the Poetry of Rumi." In *The New Yorker*, January 5, 2017: 1–8.

Barks, Coleman. *The Essential Rumi*. San Francisco: HarperOne, 1995.

Chapter 34

Akhmatova, Anna. *The Complete Poems of Anna Akhmatova*. Translated by Judith Hemschemeyer. Boston: Zephyr Press, 2014.

——. "The Sentence." Read by Nancy Nersessian. Audio recording. The Favorite Poem Project (website), accessed Dec. 8, 2020: http://www.favoritepoem.org/poem_TheSentence.html.

Powers, Kevin. "What Kept Me from Killing Myself." In *The New York Times*, June 16, 2018: https://www.nytimes.com/2018/06/16/ opinion/sunday/books-saved-me-from-suicide.html.

Yellin, Jerry, and Sarina Grosswald. *The Resilient Warrior*. Friendswood, Texas: TotalRecall Publications, 2011.

Chapter 37

Bhagavad-Gita. Translated by Maharishi Mahesh Yogi. London: Penguin Arkana, 1969.

Chapter 39

Damasio, Antonio. *Descartes' Error: Emotion, Reason, and the Human Brain*. New York: Putnam, 1994.

Chapter 40 and 41

Cavafy, Constantine. *Complete Poems*. Translated by Daniel Mendel-
sohn. New York, Knopf, 2014.

———. *Complete Poems of Cavafy*. Translated by Rae Dalven, New York:
Harcourt Brace, 1976.

Chapter 42

Betts, Dwayne. *A Question of Freedom: A Memoir of Learning, Survival,
and Coming of Age in Prison*. New York: Avery, 2010.

Randall, Dudley, ed. *The Black Poets*. New York: Bantam, 1985.

Reddy, Sumantha. "A Prescription of Poetry to Help Patients Speak
Their Minds." In *The Wall Street Journal*, Dec. 1, 2019: https://www
.wsj.com/articles/a-prescription-of-poetry-to-help-patients-
speak-their-minds-11575196200.

Chapter 44

Mendelson, Edward. "The Secret Auden." In *The New York Review
of Books*, March 20, 2014: https://www.nybooks.com/articles/
2014/03/20/secret-auden/.

Chapter 45

Freeman, Morgan, and Gwendolyn Brooks. "We Real Cool." Audio
recording. Natural Beauty behind Words (website), June 8, 2015:
https://naturalbeautybehindwords.wordpress.com/2015/06/08/
morgan-freeman-and-gwendolyn-brooks-reading-we-real
-cool/.

Chapter 47

Cacciopo, John T., and William Patrick. *Loneliness: Human Nature and
the Need for Social Connection*. New York: Norton, 2008.

Gawande, Atul. "Why Americans Are Dying of Despair." In *The New Yorker*, March 16, 2020: https://www.newyorker.com/magazine 2020/03/23/why-americans-are-dying-from-despair.

Goodwin, Matthew. "'Deaths of Despair' Aren't Just a U.S. Problem." Bloomberg Opinion (website), Jan. 22, 2020: https://www.bloomberg.com/opinion/articles/2020-01-22/-deaths-of-despair-is-a-u-k-problem-too.

Stevie Smith. "Not Waving but Drowning." Audio recording, accessed Dec. 9, 2020: https://www.youtube.com/watch?v=UZN vQXNJAcU.

Chapter 48

Ellis, Hannah. "D. J. Thomas: The Man That Introduced Dylan Thomas to Poetry." Dylan Thomas (website), accessed Dec. 9, 2020: https://www.discoverdylanthomas.com/d-j-thomas-man-introduced-dylan-thomas-poetry.

Kübler-Ross, Elisabeth. *On Death and Dying*. New York: Scribner, 1997 (1969).

Thomas, Dylan. "Do not go gentle into that good night." Audio recording, accessed Dec. 9, 2020: https://www.youtube.com/watch?v=1mRec3VbH3w.

Chapter 49

Ulrich, F. Lanius, Sandra L. Paulsen, and Frank M. Corrigan, eds. *Neurobiology and Treatment of Traumatic Dissociation: Toward an Embodied Self*, chapter 5: "Dissociation and Endogenous Opioids: A Foundational Role." Springer Publishing Company Connect (website), accessed Dec. 9, 2020: https://connect.springerpub.com/content/book/978-0-8261-0632-2/part/part01/chapter/ch05.

PERMISSIONS

ACKNOWLEDGMENTS

I have many to thank for helping me produce this book. Peter Sacks encouraged me from the beginning and guided me through the entire creative process. Mitch Horowitz connected me with G & D Media, where Gilles Dana, Evan Litzenblatt, and Ellen Goldberg were unfailingly supportive. Thanks for superb editorial help to Richard Smoley and a group of unofficial editors, who helped me in countless ways, including Bob Roth, Simon Shapiro, Patrick Bernuth, Richard Ross, Colleen McDermott, Sherah Bloor, Wendy Lachman, and Gertrude Eaton. Some brought me helpful poems, notably Ruth Goldman, Dan Kracov, Brian Lavin, and Barbara Parry. Others granted me interviews: Ben Berman, Reginald Dwayne Betts, Judy Booth, Richard A. Friedman, Jay Giedd, CT Gordon, Ilaria Nardini-Gray, Adora Lee, David Medalie, Nancy Nersessian, Kevin Powers, Elizabeth Prelinger, Kenneth Towbin, John Ulrich, and Tom and Liz Wehr. Special thanks to Mark Allen, Susan Lieberthal, John Schlapobersky, Fredda Plesser, John Pfordresher, John Purkiss, Jacq Burns, Jo Watts and Helena.org for their kind assistance. I could not have accomplished this project without Dan McQuaid, the glue and ink who helped put everything together. Finally, Leora and Josh, always my muses, thank you.

INDEX

Index   347

comparisons with other works,
155–156, 159, 164, 165
poet and the poem, 157–158
takeaways, 157
Dartmouth College, 146
Darwin, Charles, 50
David (King), 195–198
"Dead, The" (Joyce), 93–94
death and dying
acceptance of, 81, 320
anger and, 310–314
of children of poets and writers,
152–153, 242, 248
comfort for the living and, 94–
95, 96, 287, 323–326
communicating about, 301–303,
306–307
deaths of despair, 306
dying too soon, 289–295
funerals and, 77–81, 82, 323–324
hope and, 167
Icarus myth and, 36, 37, 205,
208, 283–287, 302, 327
immortality and, 317–321
as inevitable, 81, 195–198
keepsakes and, 94–95, 96
loss of a loved one, 77–81
love after death, 17–18, 91–96
of parents, 79, 92, 94–95, 169–
170
of parents of poets and writers,
13, 20, 106, 146, 152–153,
254, 267, 308, 309, 310–313,
315–316
peaceful sense of, 150
"Psalm 23" (Psalm of David)
and, 195–198

psychological stages of, 313,
320, 321
risk-taking behavior and. *see*
risk-taking behavior
stopping the clock and, 77–81,
186–187
suicide and. *see* suicide/suicidal
thoughts
vision of death, 317–321
Deaton, Angus, 306
decision making
choices in, 142–146
prefrontal cortex and, 251
dementia patients, 112
depression
accepting, 171–172
attachment theory and, 11
clinical, 63–66, 67, 173–174, 309
cognitive distortion and, 12
death of loved one and, 169–170
deaths of despair, 306
loneliness and, 305
manic depression, 83–85
poetry in healing, 105, 106,
137–138, 169–170, 265–266
of poets and writers, 67–68, 69,
96–97, 105, 134, 147, 158, 309
in post-traumatic stress
disorder. *see* post-traumatic
stress disorder (PTSD)
in seasonal affective disorder
(SAD), 119–122, 201–202
self-criticism and, 65–67,
68–69
suicide and. *see* suicide/suicidal
thoughts
Descartes, René, 251

ABOUT THE AUTHOR

Norman E. Rosenthal is a psychiatrist, researcher and writer with a lifelong interest in poetry. As a psychiatrist he is best known for first describing seasonal affective disorder (SAD) during his twenty year tenure at the National Institute of Mental Health, and pioneering its treatment with light therapy. He has authored or co-authored hundreds of scholarly papers and ten books including the *New York Times* bestseller *Transcendence* and the National bestsellers *The Gift of Adversity* and *Super Mind*.

In *Poetry Rx*, Rosenthal draws upon his encyclopedic knowledge of psychiatry and psychotherapy to illustrate how great poems can help us in our most profound human circumstances and predicaments, such as loving and losing; responses to nature; the search for meaning; aging and dying; and other aspects of the human condition.

Rosenthal currently maintains a clinical and coaching practice in suburban Maryland and continues his research and writing. He is a clinical professor of psychiatry at Georgetown University School of Medicine.

CPSIA information can be obtained
at www.ICGtesting.com
Printed in the USA
JSHW031426180421
13637JS00001B/1